PEOPLE AS AN AGENT OF ENVIRONMENTAL CHANGE

Symposia of the Association for Environmental Archaeology No. 16

Edited by R. A. Nicholson and T. P. O'Connor

Oxbow Books
2000

Published by
Oxbow Books, Park End Place, Oxford OX1 1HN

ISBN 1 84217 002 3

This book is available direct from
Oxbow Books, Park End Place, Oxford OX1 1HN
(Phone: 01865–241249; Fax: 01865–794449)

and

The David Brown Book Company
PO Box 511, Oakville, CT 06779, USA
(Phone: 860–945–9329; Fax: 860–945–9468)

and

via our website
www.oxbowbooks.com

Printed in Great Britain at
The Short Run Press
Exeter

Contents

List of Contributors

MARGARET A. ATHERDEN
University College of Ripon and York St John
York YO3 7EX

C. J. CASELDINE
Department of Geography
University of Exeter
Exeter EX4 4RJ

F. M. CHAMBERS
Centre for Environmental Change and Quaternary Research
Cheltenham and Gloucester College of Higher Education
Francis Close Hall
Cheltenham GL50 4AZ

RICHARD C. CHIVERRELL
Institute for Manx Studies
6 Kingswood Grove
Douglas
Isle of Man JM1 3LX

B. J. COLES
Department of History and Archaeology
University of Exeter
Exeter EX4 4QE

A. DUNN
Centre for Byzantine Studies,
School of Historical Studies
University of Birmingham
Edgbaston
Birmingham B15 2TT

GEORGINA H. ENDFIELD
School of Geography
The University of Nottingham
Nottingham NG7 2RD

CLIVE GAMBLE
Department of Archaeology
University of Southampton
Southampton SO17 1BJ

F. M. GRIFFITH
Environment Department
Devon County Council
Devon

J. A. HALL
University College of Ripon and York St John
York YO3 7EX

J. M. HATTON
Department of Geography
University of Exeter
Exeter EX4 4RJ

RUPERT HOUSLEY
Department of Archaeology
University of Glasgow
Glasgow G12 8QQ

J. M. LANTING
Department of Archaeology
University of Groningen
Postraat 6, 9712ER Groningen
The Netherlands

SARAH E. METCALFE
Department of Geography
The University of Edinburgh
Edinburgh EH8 9XP

T. M. MIGHALL
School of Natural and Environmental Sciences
Coventry University
Coventry CV1 5FB

REBECCA NICHOLSON
Department of Archaeological Sciences
University of Bradford
Bradford BD7 1DP

W. F. O'BRIEN
Department of Archaeology
University College Galway
Republic of Ireland

TERRY O'CONNOR
Department of Archaeology
University of York
York YO1 7EP

SARAH O'HARA
School of Geography
The University of Nottingham
Nottingham NG7 2RD

MARK PATTON
Department of Archaeology
Trinity College
Carmarthen SA31 3EP

JAAP SCHELVIS
Alkumaheerd
Wirdumerweg 1
9917 PA Wirdum
The Netherlands

TIM SLUCKIN
Department of Mathematics
University of Southampton
Southampton SO17 1BJ

DAVID SMITH
Department of Ancient History and Archaeology
University of Birmingham
Birmingham B15 2TT

JAMES STEELE
Department of Archaeology
University of Southampton
Southampton SO17 1BJ

RICHARD TIPPING
Department of Environmental Science
University of Stirling
Stirling FK9 4LA

R. ESMÉE WEBB
Yamaji Language Centre
PO Box 433
Geraldton, WA 6531

PEOPLE AS AN AGENT
OF ENVIRONMENTAL CHANGE

An Introduction

The papers in this volume revisit one of the concerns which dominated environmental archaeology through the 1960s and 1970s, namely the timing, nature, and extent of human impact on the environment. This concern can be seen as allied to anxieties in western society at that time about the destructive nature of human technological 'progress' and the prospect of human populations booming beyond terrestrial carrying capacity. Against that background, the premise that humans have been environmentally destructive throughout prehistory, though most particularly since the adoption of settled agriculture, had an obvious resonance. Detrimental consequences of human activity were seen in such instances as Dimbleby's classic study of the devlopment of heathland habitats in Britain (Dimbleby 1962), and the ready acceptance of an 'overkill' model of Pleistocene extinctions (Martin & Wright 1967), a subject to which Patton returns in this volume.

During the intervening couple of decades, our view of global ecosystems has changed, and attitudes to human impact on those ecosystems has changed. On the one hand, it has become increasingly clear that terrestrial environments are in a constant state of change. Older concepts of systems remaining in a stable climax state until troublesome humans came meddling have been replaced by models which stress the dynamic nature of ecosystems, and which question whether stability is ever more than superficially apparent (e.g. see Putman 1994, 138–40). From this point of view, humans become just one agent of change in a dynamic world. On the other hand, ozone depletion and the gradual submergence of small Pacific states (and East Yorkshire) have made it only too clear that human activity has the potential to alter environments on a truly global scale, and a largely man-made 'haze' rendered the atmosphere over large parts of island southeast Asia barely breathable. As our ability to monitor global systems in detail has developed, so has the realisation that human impact is apparent virtually everywhere. With this has come a welcome paradigm shift from regarding 'nature' as something 'other', to be feared, exploited or protected according to one's view, to seeing

humans as a part of 'nature', having responsibility for it, and perhaps seeking to mitigate the worst aspects of our impact, but an integral part of the biosphere none the less. This view, and the consequences which flow from it, has been eloquently explored by Tickell (1997), who reminds us that extinctions are an integral part of terrestrial life processes, an observation which can be both reassuring (mammoths had it coming) and threatening (so have we).

What has all of this to do with the present volume? Given that attitudes to global environments have undergone a change over the last generation, the intention was to see whether the concerns which were previously so apparent in environmental archaeology could still be seen, or whether our interpretation of the palaeoenvironmental record now reflects prevailing social and political attitudes. It was also an opportunity to draw together a series of studies in environmental archaeology which are connected not by period or geographical constraints, nor by their principal data source, but by a theme which links them quite explicitly to human activity and thus to archaeology in its broadest sense.

Another element in the rationale for this volume is exactly that connection with archaeology. Over recent years, environmental archaeology has come in for some fairly virulent criticism (Thomas 1990), some of which has stuck, despite a spirited response (O'Connor 1991; Wilson 1995). In private, as it were, the discipline has ruminated about its purpose and meaning, and its relationship with archaeology, geography, and palaeontology, amongst other things (Boyd 1990; Reitz *et al* 1996). In short, there have been signs of a mid-life crisis assailing environmental archaeology. By setting the terms of reference of this volume squarely in the realm of human activity, the editors intend to underline the point that environmental archaeology *is* archaeology, because archaeology is about people, not artefacts, and people are, inescapably, an integral part of terrestrial environments. We cannot legitimately study one without the other. Social scientists and geographers are steadily developing the field of human ecology, moving it away from the drab determinism of

Julian Steward and the 1960s to something more 'holistic' which incorporates ideational and social factors. This view is set out in various papers in Crumley (1994), and most elegantly expressed by Ian Simmons (1997).

We start this volume with sediments, deliberately placing the abiotic environment up front, with Richard Tipping's critique of the difficulties of establishing sufficiently precise chronologies to allow the geomorphic effects of human activity to be adduced. A clutch (or whatever the group noun should be) of pollen papers follows, ranging from a regional study in Greece, to a study of the impact of prehistoric extractive industry in Ireland, to regional studies in Orkney and Yorkshire, and a case study in the use of fungal spores and other palynomorphs. The pursuit of 'anthropogenic indicators' has a long history in environmental archaeology, and we believe that this group of papers shows a valuable diversity of approaches to the question of sorting out human impacts in pollen profiles.

Humans have an impact on arthropods, and *vice versa*, in numerous ways. Two very different papers explore this theme. Jaap Schelvis gives an overview of the use of mites as indicators of environmental change in coastal areas, and David Smith investigates the use of a particular group of water beetles as a means of monitoring past fluvial environments. The remaining papers are regional studies of various sorts, ranging from the use of anthropological and ethnohistorical data in Western Australia, through the highlands of Central Mexico, to a surprisingly 'unknown' area of mid-Devon. Finally, we return to the 'big' questions of human impact, with Patton's discussion of island extinctions in the Mediterranean, and Steele *et al* review of the latest evidence for the rate of human expansion through South America.

To return to our starting point, although questions of human impact on the environment were topical thirty years ago, it is doubtful that anything like the diversity of approaches and ideas which has been assembled here could have been put together in the 1960s or 1970s. That is not to criticise the development of ideas or methodology at that time, but points out, we believe, that environmental archaeology has moved on. In particular, our understanding of the place of people in ecosystems is now more subtle, and our preparedness to look for data in unexpected ways and places is greater. It is to be hoped that in another generation, another volume of papers will look back on this one, and reflect how much further archaeology has moved on.

We end on a sad note. At a late stage of preparing this volume, we were saddened to hear of the death of Camilla Dickson, one of the contributors to this volume, and a valued friend and colleague to many in environmental archaeology. We will miss her quiet erudition and amiable company. As Rupert Housley explains below, Camilla was a link with the pioneering days of Sir Harry Godwin and his Cambridge colleagues, and it is apt, therefore, that we dedicate this volume to her memory.

Acknowledgements

The editors are grateful to all of those who were involved in the 1995 AEA Conference, notably John McIlwaine, Susan Ward, and Brian Connell. Most of all, though, we are grateful to the contributors to that conference and to this volume for their forbearance through what has been an unexpectedly long gestation, as external events made a nonsense of well-lain plans.

Boyd, W.E. (1990). Towards a framework for environmental archaeology: environmental archaeology as a key to past geographies. *Circaea* **7**(2), 63–79.

Crumley, C.L. (ed. 1994) *Historical Ecology: Cultural Knowledge and Changing Landscapes*. Santa Fe: School of American Research Press.

Dimbleby, G.W. (1962). *The Development of British Heathlands and their Soils*. Oxford: OUP.

Martin, P.S. and Wright, H.E. 1967. *Pleistocene Extinctions: the Search for a Cause*. New Haven: Yale University Press.

O'Connor, T.P. (1991). Science, evidential archaeology, and the new scholasticism. *Scottish Archaeological Review* 8, 1–7.

Putman, R.J. 1994. *Community Ecology*. London: Chapman & Hall.

Reitz, E.J., Newsom, L.A., and Scudder, S.J. (1996). *Case Studies in Environmental Archaeology*. New York: Plenum Press.

Simmons, I.G. (1997) *Humanity and Environment. A Cultural Ecology*. Harlow: Addison Wesley Longman.

Wilson, B. 1995. On the curious distortions behind the charge of scientism against environmental archaeology. *Scottish Archaeological Review* **9/10**, 67–70

*This volume of papers is dedicated to the memory
of Camilla Dickson, a friend and colleague fondly remembered*

Obituary: Camilla Ada Dickson 1932–98

Born and bred in the Cambridgeshire village of Histon, Camilla Dickson, née Lambert, became one of the leading scientists in the comparatively new field of archaeobotany, the interplay of botany and archaeology. Her scientific career began in Cambridge University when she became the technician in the Sub-department of Quaternary Research of the Botany School and worked under Professor Sir Harry Godwin F.R.S., the foremost pioneer of the plant ecology of the glacial and interglacial periods in Britain. In the 1950s when such work was at its greatest peak in Cambridge, she learned a highly critical approach to the identification of pollen grains and macroscopic fossils, notably seeds. Many of Sir Harry's later papers on Quaternary palaeoecology depended totally on the practical skills of Camilla Lambert who in 1964 married James H. Dickson, then one of Sir Harry's last research students and now Professor of Archaeobotany and Plant Systematics at Glasgow University. In the early 1960s Camilla and Jim had collaborated in the botanical investigation of the Ashgrove Bronze Age cist in Fife and produced results which became famous because the pollen analyses can be interpreted as indicating either a flower bouquet or honey/mead.

In the mid 1970s, when her children, Peter and Kate, were of sufficient age, Camilla Dickson took up again her scientific work, concentrating to great effect almost exclusively on archaeobotany of Scotland. Her first major success concerned the investigation of the silted up east annexe ditch of the Bearsden Roman fort. Working with her husband, she proved that the ditch had a substantial component of sewage, rich in the food plants consumed by the Roman troops. Much of the organic material was bran from the imported cereals the troops had eaten and expelled. Part of the proof was a heroic little experiment, conducted unknown to Professor Dickson; she ate for some days only whole meal bread, sieved her excreta and examined it down the microscope. The product so very closely resembled the Roman bran that when her husband was to comment he said "Why are you looking at the Bearsden material again?" But it was not Bearsden c. AD145 but Milngavie 1978! Camilla Dickson's work on the Bearsden plant remains has since become very well known not least for her pioneering work on the recognition microscopically minute scraps of cereal pericarps but also the likes of Dill, Lentil, Coriander and Broad Bean.

Her work expanded to cover all periods of Scottish history, most recently on the plant remains from silts deposited in the mid 15th century drains under Paisley Abbey. Greater Celandine was recognised for the first time in Scottish archaeology, Monk's Rhubarb in British archaeology and Mace in world archaeology; the latter must have been gathered in what is now Indonesia and traded all the way to Scotland probably via the Low Countries. There have been several publications on prehistoric and later Orkney and Shetland. She has finished a highly detailed study of the middens of Skara Brae, Orkney, the celebrated Neolithic village; one of the most remarkable findings was the identification of no less than four types of drift wood, likely to have crossed the Atlantic from North America.

In 1990 she delivered the Goodfellow Lecture to the Glasgow Natural History Society. The title was a very apt one, Memoirs of a Midden Mavis - The Study of Ancient Diets and Environments from Roman Plant Remains. The expression midden mavis is a Scottish one. Mavis means song thrush and midden mavis applies to a woman who earns her living raking over rubbish tips. See *The Glasgow Naturalist* 22, pages 65–76.

Camilla Dickson had no formal scientific qualifications whatever – not even an A level – but she possessed abundantly those attributes that really matter: great observational skill and perseverance. She was always pleased to pass on her skills in pollen and macroscopic fossil analyses to beginners. There have been many messages of gratitude sent to her husband by now distinguished scientists in Britain and Europe. That over 160 people attended her memorial service in Glasgow University Chapel is another measure of the respect in which she was held by friends and fellow scientists.

She died after a long, brave fight against lung cancer and only two days after returning from a curtailed botanical and archaeological holiday in Crete with her husband. Only after her illness was diagnosed did she begin to write a book which will be the summation of her scientific career. The provisional title is *People, Plants and Diet in Ancient Scotland*. The book is very largely complete and will be finished by her husband.

This is an expanded version of the obituary published in *The Herald* on May 23rd 1998.

1. Accelerated Geomorphic Activity and Human Causation: Problems in Proving the Links in Proxy Records

Richard Tipping

The Holocene record of geomorphological activity derived from fluvial deposits is increasingly being used to test the significance of the two most likely causal agents, climate change and human impact. One simple test is to assess the synchroneity of geomorphic events between catchments. However, the dating controls currently employed on British river systems are argued to be so imprecise that any application of this test is premature.

Keywords: Holocene, rivers, alluviation, anthropogenic impact, dating.

INTRODUCTION

Geomorphic activities in temperate areas in the Holocene are known to be episodic. Phases of stability tend to be separated by periods of instability (Bell & Walker 1992). The evidence derives from a number of sources, from soils inwashed across peats (Edwards, Hirons & Newell 1991; Tipping 1995) to valley floor sediment sinks in colluvial fills (Bell 1982; 1983) and lake basins (Pennington 1981; Dearing 1986). An increasingly exciting source of evidence is the fluvial record (Gregory 1983; Gregory, Thornes & Starkel 1991; Needham & Macklin 1992), which has the potential to integrate the sediment erosion record over archaeologically relevant landscape-scales. These systems, perhaps more than lacustrine and slope records, have emphasised the pulsed or episodic record of sediment transfer. Weaknesses in their application include the observation that a number of within-channel changes do not leave records of change that persist, and the likelihood that some changes in depositional environment are autogenic responses to internal, not externally driven, variables (Schumm 1977; Burrin 1985). Nevertheless, the records left by river systems, principally ones of sediment accumulation (aggradation) and down-cutting (channel-trenching or incision) have added considerably to the understanding of Holocene environmental change (Burrin & Scaife 1988; Macklin & Lewin 1994). It is this record that will be examined in this contribution, and in particular the records from British river systems.

What triggers these periods of often quite profound sediment erosion and re-distribution is clearly of great interest to archaeologists and palaeo-environmental scientists. Two features of the Holocene environment have been identified as being important in precipitating increased soil and sediment movement. These are climate and land use. The arguments are complex. For example, much might depend on what is meant by climatic impact. Climatic fluctuations are widely recognised in the Holocene (Lamb 1977; 1995; Bell & Walker 1992), and periods of increasing effective precipitation (Barber 1982; Barber *et al.* 1994; Harrison & Digerfeldt 1993) may be expected to result in greater sediment yields (Langbein & Schumm 1958). But the seasonal distribution of rainfall is critical, and from this can be inferred that vegetation cover is a significant moderating factor in temperate latitudes (Knox 1972; Thornes 1988; 1990). Although climate change is increasingly seen as rapid, if not abrupt, and therefore more effective as a destabilising agent, we must also recognise that extreme singular events within any dominant climatic regime can be very important in generating sediment (Rumsby & Macklin 1994).

The important role of vegetation cover in ameliorating erosion naturally leads to consideration of anthropogenic mechanisms of vegetation removal. These include deforestation or woodland clearance, and its relative scale or intensity, but also critical is the relative importance of arable agriculture and ploughing to break the formerly continuous sod cover (Boardman *et al.* 1990).

These two factors of climate and land-use are not mutually exclusive. The interactions between these can be seen in Macklin & Needham's (1992, 16) suggestion that river alluviation is *"climatically driven but culturally blurred"*, with the inference that although primarily climatic in derivation, sediment re-mobilisation on valley floors can be induced by changes in the intensity or character of prehistoric and historic land uses. Nevertheless, the assumption that climate has supremacy is open to debate (Bell & Walker 1992; Goudie 1995).

CORRELATION

Bell and Walker (1992) have recently reviewed the issue of dominant control, and whilst arriving at no decisive conclusion, suggest that *"Ultimately the debate . . . may be partly resolved by the extent to which alluvial discontinuities prove to be coeval from one area to another"* (p. 201). One test, therefore, is to assess whether periods of accelerated geomorphic activity can be correlated between widely separated catchments, the implication being that widespread synchroneity is most likely to have a climatic control.

Such inter-catchment comparisons have indeed been attempted. Burrin and Scaife (1988) compiled data from a select number of ten inland catchments (e.g., unaffected by sea-level change), predominantly from southern England. They concluded that *"the onset of alluviation is seemingly asynchronous, varying between sites from one valley to the next. Hence, the alluvial record for the most recent period of earth history is variable in both space and time"* (p. 214). Macklin and Lewin (1994) took a larger data-set of twenty-five inland catchments. They smoothed the data from individual catchments by assigning dated alluvial units to contiguous 400–year blocks, and concluded that there was *"widespread synchrony of Holocene fluvial episodes in Britain, particularly over the last 5000 years"* (p. 119).

These two reviews arrived at diametrically opposing conclusions as to the degree of synchroneity in fluvial deposition. In part this may have arisen from different treatments of the data, and in this regard Macklin and Lewin's smoothing and grouping of the data, though reasonable, would tend to result in enhanced temporal patterning. Spatial variability within catchments in the types

of geomorphic change – the complex response to change of river systems (Schumm 1977; Brown 1990; 1991) – is a more pronounced interpretative difficulty, such that careful analysis is required to establish catchment-wide significance in river behaviour.

Clearly, what is also being tested in these comparisons is the quality of the temporal correlations. That ostensibly the same data-set can be interpreted in such radically different ways may indicate that the data used are incapable of interrogation at the high level required. This is the theme to be examined in this paper. There will be no re-examination in this contribution of the temporal patterns themselves, and the reader is referred to the reviews of Burrin and Scaife (1988) and Macklin and Lewin (1994) for these.

DATING CONTROLS ON BRITISH FLUVIAL RECORDS

The means by which fluvial records are dated vary. Macklin and Lewin (1994) identify four approaches: (a) by radiocarbon dating of wood or peat beneath, within or overlying alluvial deposits; (b) by the occurrence of archaeological remains (whether artefactual or constructional) in some stratigraphic relation to alluvial units; (c) by bio-stratigraphic controls, usually through pollen analysis of alluvial sediments; and (d) by soil-stratigraphic controls. To these might be added the advances made in applying luminescence dating (TL and its variants, e.g., OSL) to minerogenic sediments (Bailiff 1992; Macklin, Passmore & Rumsby 1992).

It is not possible here to review the quality of dating controls at all the sites for which fluvial chronologies have been constructed. But some discussion of the application of these different approaches is necessary, using selected examples.

Alluvial deposits in southern Britain tend to accumulate as stacked fills, vertically accreted 'layer-cake' stratigraphies of minerogenic channel-overbank sediments (e.g. Burrin & Scaife 1984). These are nearly always lacking in organic matter for radiocarbon dating, and much effort has been invested in establishing the chronology of these discrete fills through pollen analysis, through correlation with dated sequences from more organic-rich deposits. Such correlations are the basis of the southern English chrono-sequences assessed by Burrin and Scaife (1988). Alluvial sediments are not ideal sources of pollen, because preservation can be poor and because the processes of pollen incorporation are complicated. Scaife and Burrin (1992) illustrate some of the complexities in their model of pollen recruitment to riverine sediments. Nevertheless, it is possible that their model under-estimates some significant inputs. If mineral inwash bands within lake basins are taken as analogues of alluvial deposits on valley floors, then major phases of sediment erosion / re-distribution contain pollen assemblages that by no means represent contemporaneous plant communities. Hirons (1988) suggested that up to 85% of the pollen carried in eroding sediment can be non-contemporaneous, reworked from sediments being eroded. The alluvial deposits analysed by Burrin and Scaife are products of major erosional events, and it is not clear that the resultant pollen stratigraphies can be used chrono-stratigraphically by comparison with sequences from more securely stratified deposits.

Soil-stratigraphic approaches have been pursued most notably by Robertson-Rintoul (1986) on the minerogenic terrace sequences of the River Feshie in north-central Scotland. This chrono-sequence of soils developed on inorganic sand-and-gravel terrace deposits have an added significance in having been adopted in long-term slope-stability models (e.g. Brooks, Richards & Anderson 1993). These terrace-surface soils are podsols, and Robertson-Rintoul developed a number of quantitative measures to determine the relative stages of maturity. The sequence becomes more mature with age, as anticipated, and using two assumed 'fixed' dated points and assuming constant rates of podsolisation, Robertson-Rintoul was able tentatively to suggest ages for the five terrace fills capped by the soils. This chronology relies, of course, on both these 'fixed' points and on the assumption of uniform rates of pedogenesis.

The earliest 'fixed' point is an age of *ca.* 13000 BP on the highest and oldest terrace, fluvioglacial in origin, in the reach. This age is derived not by direct dating but by assuming this to be a reasonable age for deglaciation from the Dimlington Stadial ice-sheet. This cannot satisfactorily be defended (Price 1983) because deglaciation could have occurred at any time between, say, *ca.* 16000 and 13000 BP. The second 'fixed' point, a single ^{14}C date (HAR-4535) of *ca.* 1950 cal. BC (Stuiver & Pearson 1993) on charcoal from a buried soil sealed by alluvial sediments, is derived from a tributary of the Feshie terraces, and can only be placed within the Feshie sequence by assuming comparable rates of pedogenesis; this is close to a circular argument. In addition, uncertainties over the veracity of dates obtained from soil-derived charcoal are well-known. Neither of these are secure age-controls. Bain *et al.* (1993) obtained an additional ^{14}C date of around 4350 cal. BC (Stuiver & Pearson 1993) for a tributary terrace, but the fact that aggrading terrace surfaces of this age were not identified from Robertson-Rintoul's initial work tends to emphasise the limitations of the dating controls in the Feshie.

It is also very unlikely that Robertson-Rintoul's second assumption, of a constant rate of podsolisation, holds true. Chelation processes are dependent on organic matter accumulation, which is not constant (Ugolini 1968), and being a predominantly biochemical process it can be expected that podsolisation is temperature-dependent (Birkeland 1984). Yet the oldest soil-stratigraphic unit in the Feshie sequence is older than, and separated in time from other units by, the glacial phase of the Loch Lomond

Stadial (Sissons 1976), which would retard podolisation rates. It may indeed be that Lateglacial Interstadial soils were destroyed during the Loch Lomond Stadial (Pennington 1977; Lowe & Walker 1984), such that the oldest soil is itself of early Holocene age, making unclear the value of the 'fixed' point of 13500 cal. BC (above).

The dating controls for the Feshie sequence are very poor. This has significance for the sophisticated models of Brooks, Richards and Anderson (1993), but more importantly in the present context is that this sequence is used, seemingly without critical assessment, by Macklin and Lewin (1994) in their synthesis.

Archaeological finds (cf. Needham & Macklin 1992) and radiocarbon dates both have the same problems of contextual association. In other words, the chronological significance of such dating controls depends very much on the stratigraphic context. In geomorphically active areas such as aggrading floodplains organic matter accumulation can be rare, and seemingly non-existent in southern England (above). Where organic deposits are found there is the temptation to sample and date. But often the derivation of the organic materials, and arguments as to their *in situ* nature, are inadequately discussed. These elements are clearly critical, however. Brown and Keough (1992) usefully described the concept of the 'geomorphic potential' of a radiocarbon or other date, and implicit in this is the notion that some dates are geomorphically insensitive, neither defining the critical phases of terrace construction or incision. Macklin and Lewin (1994) acknowledge that these types of dating control have weaknesses, and that phases of alluviation are more poorly dated than their chronological controls might indicate. This is because often these controls only establish the ages of deposits / events pre- or post-dating the alluvial phase, and not the phase of fluvial change itself. Thus the 'envelope' in which a fluvial event is bracketed is frequently very imprecise. Combined with this weakness is the recognition that the majority of individual alluvial units / events are dated by reference to only single radiocarbon assays (Macklin & Lewin 1994).

There is in any assessment of dating controls the need to review critically the validity and 'potential' of individual dates (e.g., King 1984; Tipping 1987). Macklin and Lewin (1994) argued that they had selected sites in which the chronologies were "fixed with some certainty" (p. 110). Beyond this statement there is no further discussion of individual sites. The first catchment in their data-set (e.g., the most northerly catchment) is here reviewed as an example.

The soil-stratigraphic data in Glen Feshie of Robertson-Rintoul (1986) have been questioned (above), but Macklin and Lewin (1994) also incorporated data on debris-cone evolution in Glen Feshie by Brazier and Ballantyne (1989). One phase of debris-flows is dated to after *ca.* 10 cal. AD from two radiocarbon dates on soil organic matter. Despite there being interpretative problems of mean residence time in such materials (Matthews 1993), acknowledged by

Brazier and Ballantyne, they argued that these were unimportant through the relative immaturity of the soil. This soil overlies an older debris-flow deposit, and it is possible that this deposit could not have formed much before 2000 BP if the soil had no time to accumulate 'old' carbon. If correct, then the geomorphic significance of the radiocarbon dates is lessened because they are seen to be sandwiched within, and not at the beginning, of a phase of debris-cone accumulation. The initiation of this late prehistoric phase remains undated, and so is of limited correlative value. Such an interpretation is not made either by Brazier and Ballantyne (1989) or Macklin and Lewin (1994), but appears legitimate from the data presented. Dating controls in other catchments might fruitfully be re-examined.

There are thus profound weaknesses in the construction of fluvial chronologies, and so the resultant phases of accelerated activity are very poorly temporally defined. The smoothing of the data-set in Macklin and Lewin's study can be regarded as a necessary step in coping with such imprecise information, but then to accept that arguments concerning synchroneity or diachroneity have to be considered at temporal resolutions approaching half a millennium are not grounds for confidence in the technique. It is suggested here that the different catchment- or reach-derived chronologies are presently too poorly constructed to allow us to employ Bell and Walker's (1992) testing of coevality or synchroneity.

IMPROVING TEMPORAL RESOLUTION

The possibilities for improving the temporal resolution of analyses are, perhaps, not encouraging. Of the new developments in radiocarbon dating, 'wiggle-matching' probably offers most potential in temporal precision (Pilcher 1991), but in alluvial environments it is difficult to see whether organic matter accumulation can satisfy the condition of constant accumulation rate necessary for its application (van Geel & Mook 1987). Our other potentially high-precision method of correlation, tephra-chronology (Dugmore 1989; Dugmore, Larsen & Newton 1995), has very limited potential given the predominantly minerogenic composition of both sediments and silica tephra particles – a case of 'needles in haystacks'. TL and OSL dating (Bailiff 1992) clearly allow the possibility of dating hitherto undateable mineral sediments, but at present the laboratory errors around mean ages are in the order of 10%, generally greater than for radiocarbon dating in the late Holocene. The precision of these assays will need to improve markedly if we are to use direct sediment-dating as a precise correlative tool.

There is a second factor in correlation that should be reviewed here. Whilst being concerned with the limitations of constructing chronologies from alluvial environments, the overriding concern is with establishing causal links with proxy records for both climate change and land use

in prehistory and history. It should not be forgotten that these proxy records can also be rather imprecisely dated. Many of these records derive from organic materials such as peats, as for example the climatic indices constructed for raised mosses by Barber (1981), or palynological indicators of land use (Behre 1986), and these are at least potentially capable of improved temporal resolution from the application of the techniques discussed above.

There is a second problem with these proxy records, however, which is that they are frequently difficult to interpret. Successful correlation between cause and geomorphic effect requires not only a high level of temporal resolution, but also that the cause is readily discerned. In the prehistoric period the diverse proxy records available (Bradley 1985) are not unambiguous in interpretation (Bell & Walker 1992).

CONCLUSIONS

The demonstration of synchroneity in fluvial events is a valid test of primary cause, climatic or anthropogenic. Recent reviews (Burrin & Scaife 1988; Macklin & Lewin 1994) have produced no consensus on this problem. This paper has argued that the existing data-set for catchments in the British Isles provides an inadequate resource for such sophisticated correlative tests. Perhaps more than other proxy records of geomorphic change, river systems and sediments are very poorly dated. Current 'state-of-the-art' dating approaches seem ill-equipped for fluvial deposits, and this lack of precision in dating these sediments may persist. It is argued, therefore, that any attempt at assessing synchroneity between catchments is currently, at best, premature.

REFERENCES

Bailiff, I.K. (1992). Luminescence dating of alluvial deposits, pp. 27–36 in Needham, S. and Macklin, M.G. (eds.) *Alluvial Archaeology in Britain*. Oxford: Oxbow Books.

Bain, D.C., Mellor, A., Robertson-Rintoul, M.S.E. and Buckland, S.T. (1993). Variations in weathering processes and rates with time in a chronosequence of soils from Glen Feshie, Scotland. *Geoderma* **57**, 275–293.

Barber, K.E. (1981). *Peat Stratigraphy and Climate Change*. Rotterdam: Balkema.

Barber, K.E. (1982). Peat-bog stratigraphy as a proxy climate record, pp. 103–113 in Harding, A.F. *Climatic Change in Later Prehistory*. Edinburgh: Edinburgh University Press.

Barber, K.E., Chambers, F.M., Maddy, D., Stoneman, R. and Brew, J.S. (1994). A sensitive high-resolution record of late-Holocene climatic change from a raised bog in northern England. *The Holocene* **4**, 198–205.

Behre, K-E. (1986). *Anthropogenic Indicators in Pollen Diagrams*. Rotterdam: Balkema.

Bell, M.G. (1982). The effects of land-use and climate on valley sedimentation, pp. 127–142 in Harding, A.F. *Climatic Change in Later Prehistory*. Edinburgh: Edinburgh University Press.

Bell, M.G. (1983). Valley sediments as evidence of prehistoric land-use on the South Downs. *Proceedings of the Prehistoric Society* **49**, 119–150.

Bell, M. and Walker, M.J.C. (1992). *Late Quaternary Environmental Change. Physical and Human Perspectives*. Harlow: Longman.

Birkeland, P.W. (1984). *Soils and Geomorphology*. Oxford: Oxford University Press.

Boardman, J., Foster, I.D.L. and Dearing, J.A. (1992). *Soil Erosion on Agricultural Land*. Chichester: Wiley.

Bradley, R.S. (1985). *Quaternary Paleoclimatology*. London: Allen and Unwin.

Brooks, S.M., Richards, K.S. and Anderson, M.G. (1993). Shallow failure mechanisms during the Holocene: utilisation of a coupled slope hydrology-slope stability model., pp. 149–176 in Thomas, D.S.G. and Allison, R.J. (eds.) *Landscape Sensitivity*. Chichester: Wiley.

Brown, A.G. (1990). Holocene floodplain diachrony and inherited downstream variations in fluvial processes: a study of the River Perry, Shropshire. *Journal of Quaternary Science* **5**, 39–51.

Brown, A.G. (1991). Hydrogeomorphology and palaeoecology of the Severn basin during the last 15,000 years: orders of change in a maritime catchment, pp. 147–169 in Gregory, K.J., Starkel, L. and Thornes, J.B. (eds.) *Fluvial Processes in the Temperate Zone During the Last 15,000 Years*. Chichester: Wiley.

Brown, A.G. and Keough, M. (1992). Palaeochannels, palaeo-land surfaces and the three-dimensional reconstruction of floodplain environmental change, pp. 185–202 in Carling, P.A. and Petts, G.E (eds.) *Lowland Floodplain Rivers: Geomorphological Perspectives*. Chichester: Wiley.

Burrin, P.J. (1985). Holocene alluviation in southeast England and some implications for palaeohydrological studies. *Earth Surface Processes and Landforms* **10**, 257–271.

Burrin, P.J. and Scaife, R.G. (1984). Aspects of Hoocene valley sedimentation and floodplain development in southern England. *Proceedings of the Geological Association* **95**, 81–96.

Burrin, P.J. and Scaife, R.G. (1988). Environmental thresholds, catastrophe theory and landscape sensitivity: their relevance to the impact of man on valley alluviation, pp. 211–232 in Bintliff, J.L., Davidson, D.A. and Grant, E.H (eds.) *Conceptual Issues in Environmental Archaeology*. Edinburgh University Press.

Dugmore, A.J. (1989). Icelandic volcanic ash in Scotland. *Scottish Geographical Magazine* **105**, 168–172.

Dugmore, A.J, Larsen, G. and Newton, A.J. (1995). Seven tephra isochrones in Scotland. *The Holocene* **5**, 257–66.

Edwards, K.J, Hirons, K.R and Newell, P.J (1991). The palaeo-ecological and prehistoric context of minerogenic layers in blanket peat: a study from Loch Dee, southwest Scotland. *The Holocene* **1**, 29–39.

van Geel, B. and Mook, W.G. (1987). High-resolution of ^{14}C dating of organic deposits using natural atmospheric ^{14}C variations. *Radiocarbon* **31**, 151–155.

Goudie, A. (1995). *The Changing Earth. Rates of Geomorphological Processes*. Oxford: Blackwell.

Gregory, K.J. (1983). *Background to Palaeohydrology*. Wiley.

Gregory, K.J., Lewin, J. and Thornes, J.B. (1987). *Palaeohydrology in Practice*. Chichester: Wiley.

Harrison, D.P. and Digerfeldt, G. (1993). European lakes as palaeohydological and palaeoclimatic indicators. *Quaternary Science Reviews* **12**, 233–248.

Hirons, K.R. (1988). Recruitment of cpr² pollen to lake sediments: an example from Co. Tyrone, Northern Ireland. *Review of Palaeobotany and Palynology* **54**, 43–54.

King, G.A. (1985). A standard method for evaluating radiocarbon dates of local deglaciation: application to the deglaciation history of Southern Labrador and adjacent Quebec. *Geographie Physique et Quaternaire* **39**, 163–182.

Knox, J.C. (1972). Valley alluviation in southwestern Wisconsin. *Annals of the Assoc. of American Geographers* **62**, 401–410.

Lamb, H.H. (1977). *Climate: Present, Past and Future*. Methuen.

Lamb, H.H. (1995). *Climate, History and the Modern World* (2nd. Ed). London: Routledge.

Langbein, W.B. and Schumm, S.A. (1958). Yield of sediment in relation to mean annual precipitation. *Transactions of the American Geophysical Union* **39**, 1076–1084.

Lowe, J.J. and Walker, M.J.C (1984). *Reconstructing Quaternary Environments*. Harlow: Longman.

Macklin, M.G. and Lewin, J. (1994). Holocene alluviation in Britain. *Zeitschrift für Geomorphologie Supplement* **88**, 109–122. Macklin, M.G. and Needham, S. (1992). Studies in British alluvial archaeology: potential and prospect, pp. 9–25 in Needham, S. and Macklin, M.G. (eds.) *Alluvial Archaeology in Britain*. Oxford: Oxbow.

Macklin, M.G., Passmore, D.G. and Rumsby, B.T. (1992). Climatic and cultural signals in Holocene alluvial sequences: the Tyne basin, northern England, pp. 123–140 in Needham, S. and Macklin, M.G. (eds.) *Alluvial Archaeology in Britain*. Oxbow.

Needham, S. and Macklin, M.G. (1992). *Alluvial Archaeology in Britain*. Oxford: Oxbow.

Pennington, W. (1977). The Late Devensian flora and vegetation of Britain. *Philosophical Transactions of the Royal Society of London* **B280**, 247–271.

Pennington, W. (1981). Records of a lake's life in time: the sediments. *Hydrobiologia* **79**, 197–219.

Pilcher, J.R. (1991). Radiocarbon dating for the Quaternary scientist, pp. 27–34 in Lowe, J.J. (ed.) *Radiocarbon Dating: Recent Applications and Future Potential*. Cambridge: Quaternary Research Association.

Price, R.J. (1983). *Scotland's Environment during the Last 30,000 Years*, Edinburgh: Scottish Academic Press.

Robertson-Rintoul, M.E.S. (1986). A quantitative soil-stratigraphic approach to the correlation and dating of post-glacial river terraces in Glen Feshie, western Cairngorms. *Earth Surface Processes and Landforms* **11**, 605–17.

Rumsby, B.T. and Macklin, M.G. (1994). Channel and floodplain response to recent abrupt climate change: the Tyne basin, northern England. *Earth Surface Processes and Landforms* **19**, 499–515.

Scaife, R.G. and Burrin, P.J. (1992). Archaeological inferences from alluvial sediments: some findings from southern England, pp. 75–92 in Needham, S. and Macklin, M.G. (eds.) *Alluvial Archaeology in Britain*. Oxford: Oxbow.

Schumm, S.A. (1977). *The Fluvial System*. New York: Wiley-Interscience.

Sissons, J.B. (1976). *The Geomorphology of the British Isles: Scotland*. London: Methuen.

Stuiver, M. and Pearson, G.W. (1993). High precision biodecal calibration of the radiocarbon time scale AD 1950 – 500 BC and 2500 – 6000 BC. *Radiocarbon* **35 (1)**, 1–23.

Thornes, J.B. (1988). Erosional equilibria under grazing, pp. 193–219 in Bintliff, J.L., Davidson, D.A. and Grant, E.H. (eds.) *Conceptual Issues in Environmental Archaeology*. Edinburgh: Edinburgh University Press.

Thornes, J.B. (1990). *Vegetation and Erosion*. Chichester: Wiley.

Tipping, R. (1987). The prospects for establishing synchroneity in the early postglacial pollen peak of *Juniperus* in the British Isles. *Boreas* **16**, 155–163.

Tipping, R. (1995). Holocene landscape change at Carn Dubh Dubh, near Pitlochry, Perthshire. *Journal of Quaternary Science* **10**, 59–75

Ugolini, F.C. (1966). Soils, pp. 29–58 in Mirsky, A. (ed.) *Soil Development and Ecological Succession on a Deglaciated area of Muir Inlet, Southwest Alaska*. Columbus: Ohio State University Institute of Polar Studies Report No. 20.

2. Palynological Evidence from the Strymon Delta, Macedonia, Greece

M. A. Atherden, J. A. Hall and A. Dunn

Palynological evidence is presented from three cores from the Strymon Delta in eastern Greek Macedonia. The research forms part of a multi-disciplinary project on the Holocene palaeogeography and archaeology of the delta. Archaeological work has mapped the settlement history of the delta since Bronze Age times and has sought to establish the location and periodicity of the major ports. Eion, Amphipolis and Khrysoupolis succeeded one another as major loci of settlement and trade, and the reasons for their changing fortunes relate partly to changes in the palaeogeography of the delta at three specific periods, ie. early Holocene, Classical (*ca.* 500 BC) and Byzantine (*ca.* AD 350). The palynological research has broadly confirmed these conclusions and has thrown further light on the probable locations of the harbours of Eion and Khrysoupolis. The pollen diagrams also enable a reconstruction of the vegetation history of the delta, which is related to the known history of the wider Macedonia region.

Keywords: Palynology, Strymon Delta, archaeology, Greek Macedonia.

INTRODUCTION

The delta of the River Strymon opens on to the Gulf of Orphani (or Strymonic Gulf), just east of the Chalkidiki Peninsula (23.8 degrees east, 40.8 degrees north) (Figure 2.1). The work reported here forms part of the Strymon Delta Project, co-directed by A. Dunn (Birmingham), R. Catling (Oxford), Kh. Koukouli-Khrysanthaki (Greek Archaeological Service) and Kh.Tziavos and Kh. Anagnostou (Greek National Centre for Marine Research). It is a multi-disciplinary palaeogeographical and archaeological study, focussed on the changing loci and relative importance of ports and settlements on the delta of the Strymon river. The time span covered by the archaeological work is the Late Bronze Age (*ca.* 1200 BC) to the Late Ottoman period (nineteenth century) but the palaeogeography of the delta has been reconstructed for the whole of the Holocene from stratigraphic borings and palynological studies.

Greek Macedonia is underlain by Mesozoic limestones and older crystalline rocks (eg schists), uplifted in the Tertiary to form the 'Rhodope Ridge', which includes the mountain massifs of Pangaion to the north and Holomon to the west of the delta. In the lowlands, these Mesozoic rocks lie buried beneath deep Tertiary sediments eroded from the mountains and younger Quaternary deposits. Recent alluvium covers wide areas in the Strymon valley and the Plain of Drama, both of which held large lakes in historic times.

The climate of this part of eastern Greek Macedonia is temperate, with mean monthly temperatures ranging from 6 to 25°C and precipitation totalling *ca.* 550mm pa. The vegetation history of the area has been studied by several authors, including van der Hammen *et al.* (1965), Wijmstra (1969), Greig & Turner (1974), Turner & Greig (1975) and Bottema (1982). From their work it is evident that mixed deciduous woodland dominated by oaks (*Quercus*

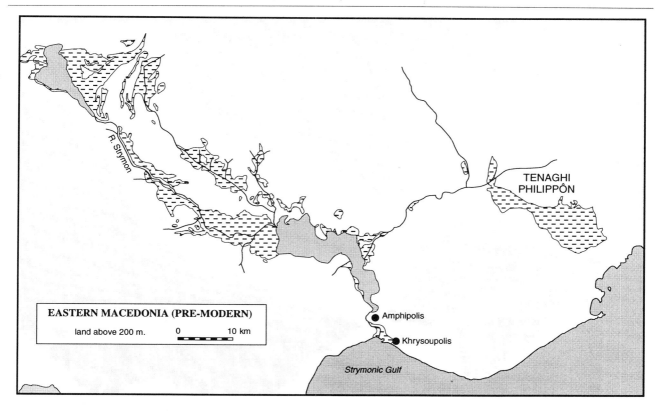

Figure 2.1: Map to show the location of the Strymon Delta within Greek Macedonia.

spp.) was established in the Early Holocene over practically all the lower ground, with woods of Greek fir (*Abies cephalonica*) above *ca.* 800 metres. Beech (*Fagus*) spread into the area from *ca.* 2600 BC onwards and formed a co-dominant with fir on the higher ground. Sweet chestnut (*Castanea sativa*) was an important constituent of the deciduous woods from Bronze Age times onwards; other trees included elm (*Ulmus*), lime (*Tilia*), hornbeam (*Carpinus*), hop hornbeam (*Ostrya*), ash (*Fraxinus excelsior*), manna ash (*Fraxinus ornus*) and hazel (*Corylus avellana*). Human impact from prehistoric times onwards gradually reduced the extent of this woodland cover and converted much of the lowland landscape to a patchwork of cultivated crops, pasture and semi-natural vegetation. However, considerable areas of woodland survived, especially on the higher ground, until the last few centuries.

The present vegetation contains substantial remnants of woodland cover in the mountains and foothills (Polunin 1980). Below *ca.* 800 metres the woods are dominated by deciduous and evergreen oaks, with abundant sweet chestnut and a very rich ground flora. Above that altitude woods of Greek fir and beech dominate, whilst coastal areas in the Chalkidiki Peninsula have extensive woods of Aleppo pine (*Pinus halepensis*). On the foothills, felling and grazing pressure over the years have led to the replacement of the woodlands with maquis or scrub (*shiblyak*), consisting of trees and shrubs in a permanently sub-climax state

(Bellier *et al.* 1986; Ogilvie 1920). Greater grazing pressure produces either garrigue (*phrygana*), dominated by undershrubs and aromatic herbs which cannot form taller vegetation, or steppe grassland. The plains are rich agricultural land where wheat, tobacco, tomatoes, melons and vegetables are grown. Olive groves and vineyards cover parts of the plains and foothills, interspersed with fruit orchards.

THE ARCHAEOLOGICAL SURVEY

Sites of all periods from Late Bronze Age onwards have been mapped from surface sherding and/or excavated finds (Figure 2.2). The aim of the archaeological study was to establish the chronology of the major settlements in the delta and explore their functions. The three most important centres were Eion, Amphipolis and Khrysoupolis. A central hypothesis was that each of them was at one time the locus of the delta's centre of maritime traffic. The location of Amphipolis has been known since the nineteenth century to be in the north of the delta (number 11 on Figure 2.2). Khrysoupolis is now conclusively identified with the site known as 'Kaledes' in the central part of the delta (number 1) (Dunn 1990). The acropolis of Eion was almost certainly on the hill of Profitis Ilias in the south-eastern part (number 2) but the location of the harbour associated with this

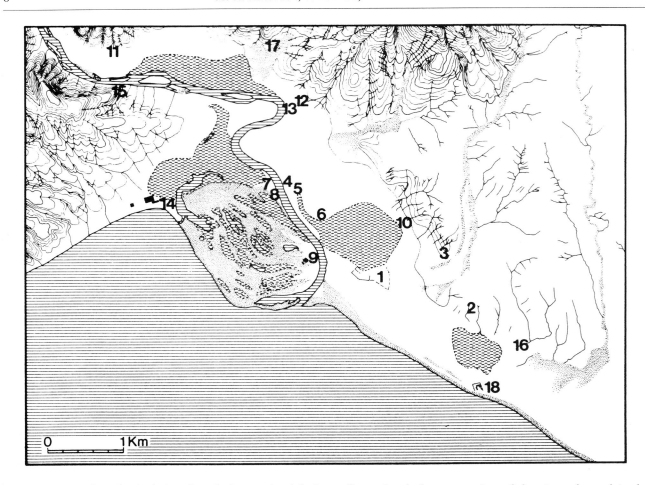

Figure 2.2: Archaeological sites in relation to the delta's configuration before re-cutting of the river channel in the 1930's. Known settlements: 1 = Khrysoupolis (Middle Byzantine – Early Ottoman); 2 = Eion (Late Bronze Age – Classical); 9 = Make Han (Ottoman); 11 = Amphipolis (Classical – Late Byzantine); 14 = Chai Agzi (Ottoman); 18 = Tuzlar Chiftlik (Ottoman). Other sites marked represent finds from various periods: 3,4,15,17 = Hellenistic; 4,10,12,17 = Roman; 3,4,5,6,7,8,12,17 = Byzantine; 12,13,16 = Ottoman.

settlement is a matter for dispute. Most archaeologists have maintained that it was under the site of Khrysoupolis, and a priority of the field survey and excavation work was to test this and alternative theories. In the later Ottoman period (nineteenth century) two customs depots are recorded as operating in the delta and the locations of these were also recorded (numbers 9 and 14).

The survey, together with trial trenches at Eion and Khrysoupolis, has enabled the sequence of primary centres before and after Amphipolis, and their periodicity, to be established. Eion was the earliest of the three main settlements. Pottery suggests that it was occupied from the Late Bronze Age through the Classical period, when the acropolis was destroyed by the Athenians in 354 BC. However, excavations and geomorphological studies failed to find any evidence to support the theory that the harbour associated with Eion lay under the site of Khrysoupolis. It is possible that the harbour is buried under part of the alluvial fan on which Khrysoupolis stands, but more likely it is located further to the north-east of Khrysoupolis, where

a resistivity survey found large manmade anomalies at a depth of two metres (Tziavos *et al.* 1988; Catling *et al.* in press).

The next centre to gain ascendancy was Amphipolis, which was the main settlement from Classical to Early Byzantine times (*ca.* 500 BC to AD 600). The chronology of its final abandonment is still unclear (Bakirtzis 1988). In Late Byzantine times a smaller rural settlement was established on the site, but for this project the question is why Amphipolis never re-emerged as a city. Could it have become inaccessible to ships as the delta developed towards the sea (prograded) (see Figure 2.3)? Could the delta have prograded significantly between the sixth and the tenth centuries, by which time Khrysoupolis had been built in its littoral and alluvial setting?

From Middle Byzantine to Early Ottoman times, Khrysoupolis was the main port of the delta. Located in the eastern-central part of the delta, it could only have functioned as a port if the river flowed then through the old eastern channel which may be seen from pre-1930

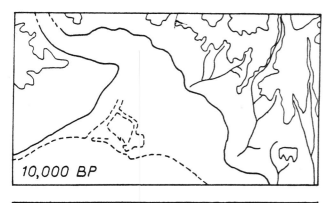

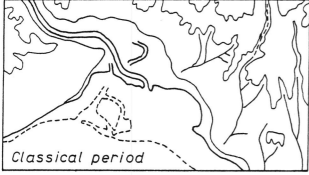

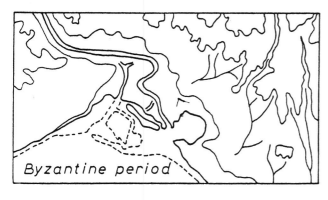

Figure 2.3: Hypothetical evolution of the Strymon Delta system during the Holocene. Top = 10,000 BP, middle = Classical period (c. 500 BC), bottom = Byzantine period. Dashed line indicates the present coastline. After Tziavos, Pavlakis and Anagnostou, 1988.

maps of the area. Khrysoupolis is first recorded in AD 984 but could have been founded in the ninth century. One of the questions to be answered here is whether the large central lagoon in the delta could have been the harbour for Khrysoupolis, whose north wall respects the curve of the lagoon. The town was still a port in AD 1502, having been absorbed into the Ottoman state in the late fourteenth century. Numerous maritime records attest its importance for shipping until the early sixteenth century but by AD 1546 it had been abandoned. It was recorded in that year that ships entered the rivermouth and sailed 'one league' upstream to Marmara, on the north-western side

of the delta. If so, it was probably the western inlet (the one re-cut as the riverbed in the 1930s) which the ships were using while the eastern channel which had brought Khrysoupolis its trading status was becoming unnavigable. There are Italian, Greek and Ottoman documentary references which show that only small craft could enter the rivermouth at Khrysoupolis by the sixteenth century, so the loci of trade and shipping would have moved (Dunn in press).

The two customs depots mentioned in nineteenth century records have been identified with the sites of Make Han (number 9 on Figure 2.2) and Chai Agzi (number 14), but there is no evidence of settlements developing there. An Ottoman saltern is known to have been operating in the south-eastern part of the area at Tuzlar Chiftlik (number 18), perhaps the site of recorded Byzantine salterns, and the site of one of the probable anchorages of ancient Eion (see below). These salterns did involve some residential as well as industrial activity, but there was no town in the delta. The survey also established that all the delta's older habitation sites were abandoned by Early Ottoman times (Catling *et al.* in press). So, although this was obviously an important locus for exports and imports, being the only reasonable access point along the coast of Macedonia east of Thessaloniki until the railway was constructed, the delta ceased to be the site of either towns or of villages like site number 12. We do not seek an environmental explanation for this almost total desertion, but we do seek through the conjunction of texts, archaeology, palynology and sedimentology to explore further the economic functions of Eion, Amphipolis and Khrysoupolis, within the long-term framework of the delta's evolution.

THE CORING PROGRAMME

From the archaeological and sedimentological work it is clear that the changing palaeogeography of the river and its delta holds clues to an understanding of the settlement and land use history of the delta. Today the seaward part of the delta consists of sand dunes and shingle ridges backed by brackish-water lagoons (Figure 2.4). There are extensive wetland areas in the north and centre of the delta and in the isolated area of the Tuzla Marsh in the south-east. The river flows to the sea through a channel in the western part of the delta cut in the 1930s. The upper part of the river channel is lined with managed reedswamps (*Phragmites australis*). Adjacent areas of land above flood level support olives, fruit orchards and some table vines. Before 1930 the river was flowing in a more easterly course, past Khrysoupolis, as shown by British Army maps from the First World War. In order to elucidate the former courses of the river, a series of 16 vibro-cores was taken by the Greek oceanographers from various parts of the delta (Figure 2.5). Analysis of the stratigraphy revealed that the position of both the coastline and the river had

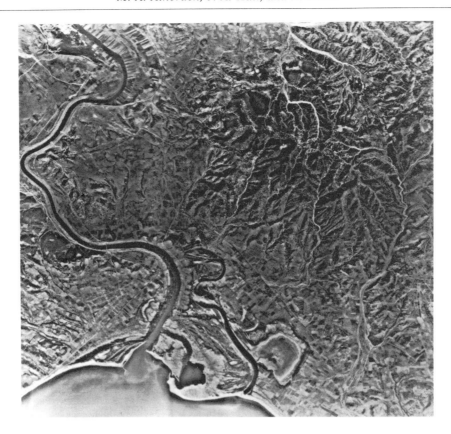

Figure 2.4: Aerial photograph of the Strymon Delta after re-cutting of the river channel in the 1930's.

altered substantially during the last three millennia of the Holocene.

Reconstructions have been made for three periods, the Early Holocene, the Classical period (*ca.* 500 BC) and the Byzantine period (*ca.* AD 350) (Figure 2.3). From these it can be seen that there was a large embayment of the sea in the Early Holocene, which the river entered from a wide estuary. By Classical times, the river was flowing through a course in the western part of the delta but its mouth was being diverted progressively eastwards by the progradation of sand or shingle bars from the west. These changes to the rivermouth may have led to changes in the flow of the upper course of the river, such as the development of sand banks and shoals, impeding navigation to Amphipolis.

By Byzantine times, the westerly course had been abandoned and the upper course flowed further east before turning southwards to reach the sea in the eastern part of the delta. The large lagoon just east of the mouth of the delta was still open to the sea. Throughout Late Byzantine and Ottoman times, ie the period of supremacy of Khrysoupolis as a port, the river flowed in this easterly course. The locations of other archaeological sites from the period support this interpretation (numbers 4 ,5, 7 and 8). The present coastline is shown for comparison. It will be apparent that a considerable amount of material has accumulated in the delta since Byzantine times. This

accumulation of sediment must have caused major changes in navigation and hence port activity in the delta area during the last few centuries, leading to the abandonment of Khrysoupolis as a port.

Pollen analysis was used to provide further details of the changing palaeogeography of the delta and to try to answer some of the archaeological questions (Atherden & Hall 1994). Samples for palynological analysis were taken from the vibro-cores and sent back to England for research at the University College of Ripon and York St John. Three cores were analysed, Deep Strymon I (DSI), Strymon 1 (S1) and Strymon 3 (S3), shown on Figure 2.5 as numbers I, 1 and 3.

The site of DSI is a marshy area in the north of the deltaic plain, just north of the present upper river course. The core was 21.7m. long; the stratigraphy is shown on Table 2.1. The pollen content was very variable; the main part of the core with good pollen preservation was between 9.0 and 13.5m., with a smaller part above 2m. Radiocarbon dates were obtained from the University of Arizona AMS Facility, which was able to cope with the small quantities of carbon in the samples (Table 2.2). A date from near the base of the core shows that the sediments began to accumulate near the beginning of the Holocene. The section with good pollen preservation in the central part of the core appears to span the Late Mesolithic and Early

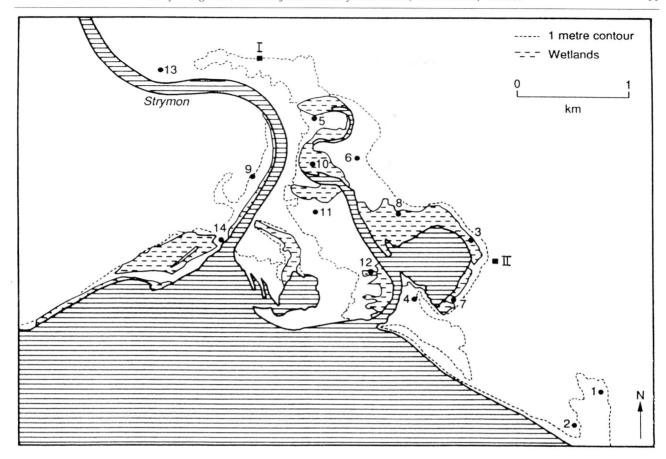

Figure 2.5: Vibrocoring sites in the Strymon Delta. I – Deep Strymon I, 1 = Strymon 1, 3 = Strymon 3. Other numbers refer to sites of vibrocores not discussed in this paper but used in the reconstruction of the palaeogeography of the delta.

Neolithic periods. There is then a gap until the Roman period, which corresponds to the upper part of the core. The existence of pebbles in the section between the two pollen-rich parts suggests that the river may have flooded into the site at this stage, possibly preventing pollen from accumulating in the sediments. By Roman times, a stable depositional environment had been re-created, perhaps because of obstructions in the river channel. This may have been part of the process of change which led to the decline of the port of Amphipolis by Early Byzantine times.

Core S1 was taken from the Tuzla Marsh in the south-eastern part of the delta. This area was open sea in the Early Holocene but the marsh began to form in Late Holocene times as progradation of alluvial fans and littoral drift combined to cut off the area from the open sea. The core was 3.1m. long; the stratigraphy is shown on Table 2.3. There are two sections of the core with good pollen preservation, 3.1–2.7m. and 2.1–0.9m. Radiocarbon dates for the lower zone cannot be separated statistically but indicate a Late Bronze Age or Early Iron Age date. The upper pollen-rich zone spans the period from the Classical or Hellenistic period to the Early Byzantine.

The site of Eion's acropolis lies just north of this site but the location of the harbour is unknown. As the period of settlement at Eion corresponds with the gap in the pollen record from S1, it is at least a possibility that a breach in the seaward barriers, either natural or manmade, allowed the site to serve as a harbour for Eion. After Eion was destroyed in Late Classical times, the harbour may have silted up and quiet deposition may have been re-established, with suitable conditions for pollen preservation.

The third core, S3, was taken from the north-east side of the lagoon area in the centre of the delta. From the maps of the projected palaeogeography of the delta in Early Holocene and Classical times (Figure 2.3), it is clear that deposition at this site could not have commenced until sometime in the Byzantine period. The core was 2.7m. deep; the stratigraphy is shown on Table 2.4. The lower section, from 2.7 to 2.0m., has good pollen preservation but the upper part of the core has a discontinuous pollen record. This site is quite close to the location of Khrysoupolis, so it was hoped that the palynological work would throw light on the question of whether or not the lagoon had served as the harbour for the town in Middle Byzantine to Ottoman times.

Table 2.1: Outline stratigraphy of the DSI core, based on field notes by the geomorphologists.

0 – 120 cm	Not Sampled
120 – 200 cm	Mixed clays and sands, with organic remains and occasional shell fragments
200 – 680 cm	Coarse sands and clays with pebbles
680 – 1565 cm	Alternating layers of sandy clays and clayey sands
1565 – 1620 cm	Sandy clay with lenses of dark greenish-grey clay
1620 – 1850 cm	Grey, coarse-grained sand and pebbles with shell fragments
1850 – 1910 cm	Sedimentary clay
1910 – 1960 cm	Grey-olive clayey sand and pebbles
1960 – 1990 cm	Sandy clay with pebbles and shell fragments
1990 – 2080 cm	Grey-olive clayey sand with occasional shell fragments
2080 – 2170 cm	Fine-grained sand with some clay

Table 2.2: Radiocarbon dates obtained from the University of Arizona AMS Facility, Tucson, Arizona. Calibrations are for one standard deviation and follow Pearson, G.W. and Stuiver, M. (1993), Radiocarbon 35, 25–33, and Kromer, B. and Becker, B. (1993). Radiocarbon 35, 125–135.

Lab. No.	Site and sample depth	C–14 years BP	Calibrated range
AA 16471	DSI 130 – 132 cm	1725 +/- 55	AD 248 – 407
AA 16470	DSI 908 – 910 cm	7055 +/- 80	5970 – 5797 BC
AA 16469	DSI 1354 – 1356 cm	7700 +/- 70	6550 – 6427 BC
AA 15798	DSI 2088 – 2090 cm	9695 +/- 90	9037 – 8671 BC
AA 16465	S1 90 – 100 cm	1520 +/- 50	AD 534 – 611
AA 16464	S1 200 – 210 cm	2265 +/- 50	391 – 206 BC
AA 16463	S1 260 – 270 cm	2870 +/- 55	1119 – 929 BC*
AA 16462	S1 300 – 310 cm	2830 +/- 55	1030 – 908 BC*
AA 16468	S3 70 – 80 cm	2670 +/- 60	844 – 799 BC**
AA 16467	S3 160 – 170 cm	1300 +/- 70	AD 662 – 786**
AA 16466	S3 200 – 210 cm	560 +/- 60	AD 1315 – 1431
AA 15799	S3 260 – 270 cm	754 +/- 50	AD 1246 – 1292

* These two dates can not be statistically separated.
** These two dates are considered to be unreliable (see text).

The radiocarbon dates for this site pose some problems of interpretation (Table 2.2). The basal two dates are in sequence and both within the Late Byzantine period, which fits well with other evidence for the beginning of deposition at the site. However, the upper two dates are older than the lower ones, the top one, in particular, yielding an inconceivable Early Iron Age date! Two points should be noted concerning the dating of this core. Firstly, the amount of carbon in the top sample in particular was very low (0.3%), which renders determination of the age very difficult. Secondly, the lagoon is defined on this side by an active alluvial fan fed by a seasonal gully (*remma*), which cuts through the archaeological deposits of ancient Eion and which is slowly burying the eastern side of Khrysoupolis. The possibility of contamination from material washed on to the site via the *remma* cannot be discounted. Bearing in mind these points, it is proposed to accept the lower two dates and reject the upper two dates for this core. If this is done, it may be inferred that deposition probably began in the thirteenth century AD. This suggests that the area may still have been open water during the early period of settlement at Khrysoupolis and the lagoon may therefore have acted as the harbour. Deposition of silt leading to saltmarsh formation would proceed most rapidly at the northern end of the lagoon, so perhaps the harbour started to silt up from Late Byzantine

Table 2.3: Outline stratigraphy of the S1 core, based on field notes by the geomorphologists.

0 – 90 cm	Yellowish sandy clay
90 – 300 cm	Grey marine clay with shell fragments

Table 2.4: Outline stratigraphy of the S3 core, based on field notes by the geomorphologists.

0 – 160 cm	Yellow-grey clay with occasional organic fragments, quartz grains and some iron
160 – 220 cm	Grey clay with occasional organic fragments
220 – 260 cm	Dark grey clay with abundant organic remains
260 – 270 cm	Organic material

times onwards, to the point where by the mid sixteenth century the harbour could no longer be used and Khrysoupolis was abandoned.

THE POLLEN DIAGRAMS

The palynological samples sent for analysis consisted of contiguous 10cm blocks for S1 and S3 and 2cm samples taken at 8cm intervals for DS1. Standard laboratory techniques were used (Faegri & Iversen 1989) and a minimum of 200 pollen grains was counted from each level. Pollen grains and spores were identified with the use of standard keys and pollen reference material. The TILIA and TILIA-GRAPH programmes were used to draw the pollen diagrams (Grimm 1991). The pollen diagrams provide information about both the local delta vegetation and that of the wider region. The three cores form a time sequence and will be discussed in chronological order.

i) Deep Strymon (Figure 2.6)

The main pollen zone on this diagram spans the Mesolithic-Neolithic transition. Although this is of little relevance to the history of settlement in the delta, it is of interest in relation to other diagrams published from eastern Macedonia. The zone is dominated by arboreal pollen (AP), particularly *Pinus* and *Quercus* spp, with notable records for *Alnus* and *Corylus*. Other trees whose pollen is present in sufficient quantity to indicate a presence in the local region are *Abies* (probably in the mountains), *Betula*, *Ulmus*, *Tilia*, *Carpinus* and *Ostrya*. Others represented only by occasional single grains, such as *Fraxinus ornus* and *Juglans*, are probably to be attributed to long distance transport. The non-arboreal pollen (NAP) amounts are low

and probably many of the taxa represented were local, especially the aquatics.

Occasional cereal-type grains may be interpreted as coming from wild grasses and the few records for *Olea* probably come from wild trees growing in the rich coastal maquis of Macedonia. There is no real sign of change in the vegetation during the Mesolithic-Neolithic transition on this diagram, except for a very slight increase in *Pinus* and decrease in *Quercus* and *Corylus*. This confirms the evidence from other diagrams in the region (eg. Wijmstra 1969; Greig & Turner 1974) for these early cultures having no noticeable effects on the regional woodland cover. Willis and Bennett (1994) discuss the possible reasons for this lack of impact with the advent of the first farming cultures. It may be that population numbers were too low to produce effects of sufficient magnitude to be recorded in the regional pollen rain. Another possibility is that cultivation was not a very important part of the early farming enterprise, playing a subordinate role to hunting and/or pastoralism.

The top zone on this diagram represents part of the Roman period. Figures for AP are lower except for *Pinus*, which may have been spreading on to coastal areas at this time. The range of trees and shrubs is slightly smaller, for instance there is no *Carpinus* this time, which may indicate a reduction in woodland within the catchment. There is a large increase in grasses (Poaceae) and other NAP types, including a few cereal records (shown as Poaceae >40 microns), suggesting agricultural activity in the area of Amphipolis but it is interesting that the records for *Olea* are no greater than in the earlier period, so olive groves were presumably not a feature of the delta at this time. The rise in Chenopodiaceae at the top of the diagram probably reflects the spread of local saltmarsh conditions.

ii) Strymon 1 (Figure 2.7)

The lower zone on this diagram has been shown to correspond to the Late Bronze Age or Early Iron Age period, although the statistical overlap between the dates for the top and bottom of the zone makes it impossible to judge how long a time period it represents. Trees and shrubs make up 60–80% of total pollen. There are significant records for *Quercus* and *Pinus* and lower values recorded for *Alnus* and *Corylus*. A wide range of other tree types is recorded at low frequencies, including *Abies*, *Betula*, *Ulmus*, *Tilia*, *Fraxinus excelsior*, *Fagus*, *Carpinus* and *Ostrya*. *Castanea*, *Juglans* and *Platanus* are all recorded in small amounts and are usually considered to have been cultivated from the Bronze Age onwards (Bottema 1982; Bottema & Woldring 1990).

The major feature of interest in the zone is the very high values for *Olea*, reaching over 30% of total pollen at their maximum. This must represent olive cultivation on the delta itself, probably quite close to the Tuzla marsh site. It is significant that the only archaeological site in the area to yield material from this period is Eion, which lay

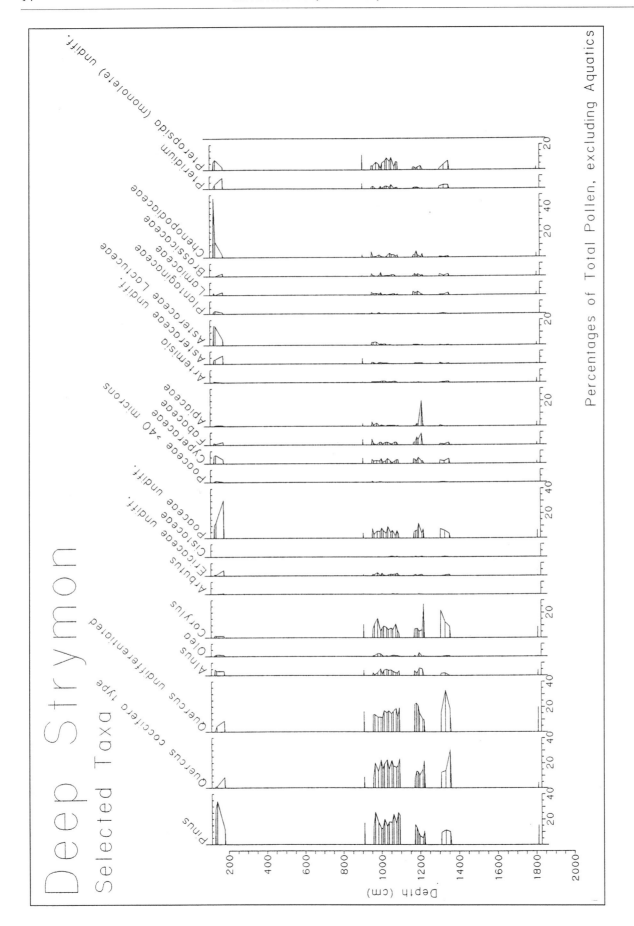

Figure 2.6: Pollen diagram from Deep Strymon I.

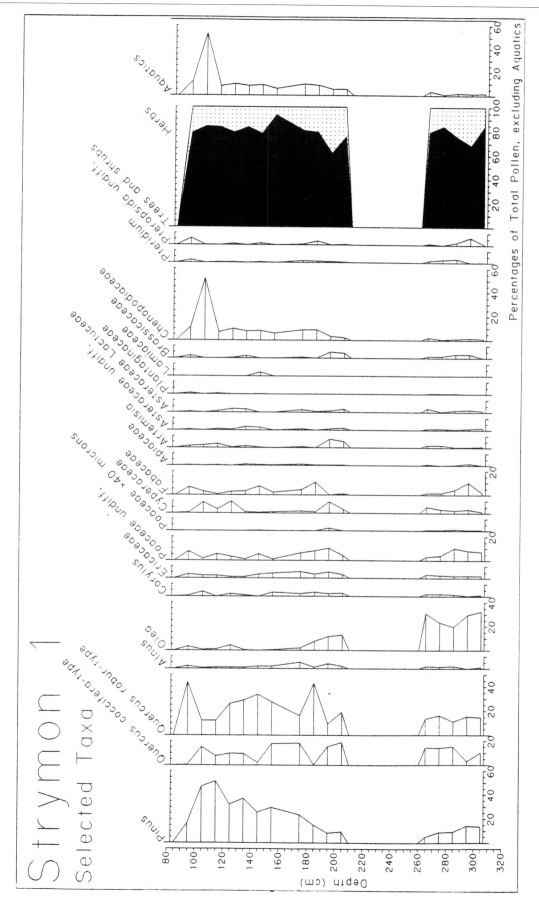

Figure 2.7: Pollen diagram from Strymon 1.

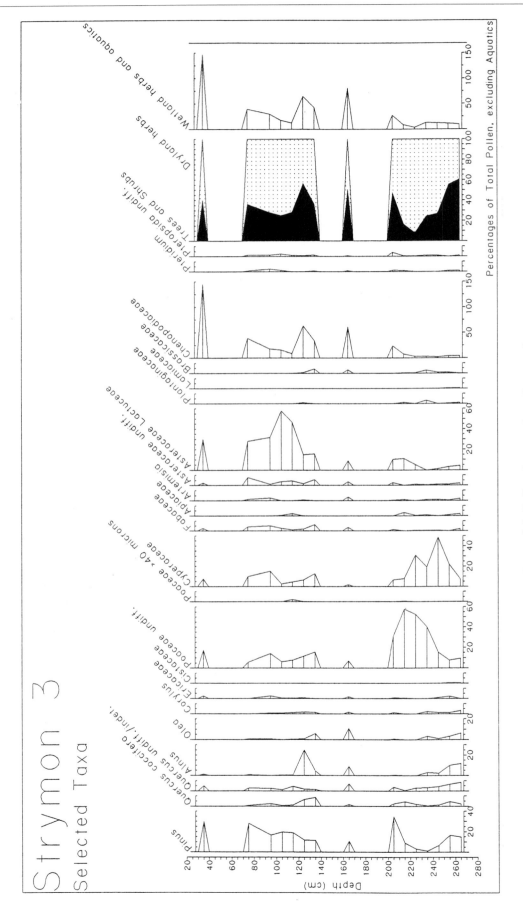

Figure 2.8: Pollen diagram from Strymon 3.

a period of olive cultivation during the Iron Age at Tenaghi Philippon, so it may have been a regional expansion. There are consistent records for cereals but values for Poaceae are low throughout this diagram. The range of weed taxa includes Fabaceae, Brassicaceae and others but Plantaginaceae are low and pasture indicators are scarce. This zone has the appearance of a major agricultural period, which suggests the settlement of Eion may have been an important one for the cultivation of olives and cereals.

The upper pollen-rich zone represents the period from Classical or Hellenistic times to Early Byzantine. There are more trees recorded, especially *Pinus* but also *Quercus* (particularly deciduous oaks), and the range of small pollen records for other trees is similar to that found in the lower zone. However, the *Olea* curve is much smaller, falling from almost 15% at the base of the zone to a few percent higher up. The peak at the base corresponds with a peak for cereals and several weed taxa. The picture is one of less intense agricultural activity than in the Iron Age, allowing a regeneration of trees. This would fit well with the archaeological evidence for a lack of settlement at Eion during this period. Those agricultural indicators which are recorded may have come from further away from the site. Aquatics are more important in this zone, in which Chenopodiaceae rise to a peak of *ca.* 50% of total pollen at 104cm. This represents the spread of local saltmarsh vegetation, which led eventually to the marsh becoming a terrestrial habitat which did not preserve pollen well after the Early Byzantine period (90cm depth).

iii) Strymon 3 (Figure 2.8)

The lowest pollen-rich zone on this diagram corresponds with the Late Byzantine period. It is dominated by Poaceae and Cyperaceae pollen, with a range of open ground taxa, especially Asteraceae Lactuceae. Most of these pollen types may have come from local site vegetation but the high Poaceae values could suggest grazing. There are a few signs of agricultural activity, with *Olea* (though considerably less than in the lower zone on S1), cereals and *Vitis* – the typical 'Mediterranean triad'. The range of AP is wide but quantities are lower than at S1. This could reflect a lower amount of woodland in the region by this time or a more local catchment for this particular site. Its position in the central part of the delta is further away from potentially cultivable land than that of the other two sites.

The upper part of this diagram is problematic because of the dating and the interruptions to pollen preservation. The isolated sample at 160–170cm shows slightly more *Olea*, less *Pinus* and more Chenopodiaceae than the lower part of the diagram. The zone from 140–70cm has significant Chenopodiaceae records with a double peak, possibly suggesting an interrupted succession to saltmarsh, as a result of a very dynamic geomorphological environment. The very high records for Asteraceae Lactuceae presumably refer to a weed growing on the marsh. There are plenty of other weed taxa recorded, eg *Artemisia*, *Hypericum*, Caryophyllaceae, Brassicaceae, Dipsacaceae, but no definite indicators of cultivation as opposed to waste ground. Amongst the tree pollen, *Pinus* increases, *Juglans* is recorded and there is a peak of *Alnus* at the base of the zone, but the range of taxa recorded is reduced, with no *Ostrya*, *Castanea* or Cupressaceae. A peak of *Alnus* was also seen on the Gravouna diagram (Greig & Turner 1975) at a level post-dating the Late Byzantine period, so it is possible that this was a regional phenomenon. The sample from 35cm is dominated by a massive peak for Chenopodiaceae (140% total pollen), indicating an advanced succession of saltmarsh. It is interesting to note that, although values are low, several maquis taxa, eg *Phillyrea*, *Pistacia*, are recorded on this diagram, indicating the greater prevalence of this vegetation type by this time period. The lower slopes of Mount Pangaion have dense maquis and scrub woodland today, in which both these genera are common.

CONCLUSIONS

The three pollen diagrams between them span a considerable period of time and range of cultural periods, albeit with some gaps in the record. They have increased our knowledge of land-use in the delta and have provided tentative answers to some of the archaeological questions. On the whole, they seem to tell a local story, with very few records for vegetation types which do not occur in the immediate vicinity of the delta, such as maquis and garrigue, although these types are notoriously under-recorded on pollen diagrams from Greece and elsewhere.

The Strymon Delta Project has illustrated some of the benefits of a multi-disciplinary approach to solving archaeological problems. Although there is clearly much more to be learned, it is hoped that this study contributes to our understanding of the economic functions of ancient and medieval settlements on the Strymon Delta.

Acknowledgements

The authors should like to thank the following colleagues for their contributions to this work:- R. Catling (University of Oxford), Kh. Koukouli-Khrysanthaki (Keeper of Prehistoric and Classical Antiquities, Eastern Macedonia), Kh. Tziavos and Kh. Anagnostou (Greek National Centre for Marine Research). Cartographic assistance with some of the figures was given by H. Buglass, School of Antiquity, University of Birmingham.

REFERENCES

Atherden, M.A. and Hall, J.A. (1994). Holocene pollen diagrams from Greece. *Historical Biology* **9**, 117–130.

Bakirtzis, Kh. (1988–1991). Anaskaphi Khristianikis Amphipoleos, *Praktika tis Arkhaiologikis Etaireias 1988,* 135–142; 1989, 216–221; 1991, 212–219.

Bellier, P., Bondoux, R.C., Cheynet, J.C., Geyer, B., Grelois, J.P. and Kravari, V. (1986). *Paysages de Macedoine.* Paris.

Bottema, S. (1982). Palynological invest-igations in Greece with special reference to pollen as an indicator of human activity. *Palaeohistoria* **24**, 257–289.

Bottema, S. and Woldring, H. (1990). Anthropogenic indicators in the pollen record of the Eastern Mediterranean, pp. 231–265 in Bottema, S., Entjes-Nieborg, G. and van Zeist, W. (eds.), *Man's Role in the Shaping of the Eastern Mediterranean Landscape.* Rotterdam: Balkema.

Catling, R., Dunn, A. and Koukouli-Khrysanthaki, Kh. (in press). The Strymon Delta survey: a preliminary report. *Arkhaiologikon Deltion.*

Dunn, A. (1990). The Byzantine topography of southeastern Macedonia: a contribution. *Récherches franco-helleniques* **1**, 307–332.

Dunn, A. (in press). Loci of maritime traffic in the Strymon Delta (IV–XVIIIcc): commercial, fiscal, manorial. *Oi Serres Kai i periokhi tous.*

Fægri, K. and Iversen, J. (1989). *Textbook of Pollen Analysis,* IV, edit. by Fægri, K., Kaland, P.E. and Krzywinski, K. Chichester: John Wiley and Sons.

Greig, J.R.A. and Turner, J. (1974). Some pollen diagrams from Greece and their archaeological significance. *Journal of Archaeological Science* **1**, 177–194.

Grimm, E.C. (1991). *TILIA and TILIA-GRAPH.* Springfield: Illinois State Museum.

Hammen, T. van der, Wijmstra, T.A. and Molen, van der (1965). Palynological study of a very thick peat section in Greece and the Würm glacial vegetation in the Mediterranean region. *Geologie and Mijnbouw* **44**, 37–39.

Ogilvie, A. (1920). A contribution to the geography of Macedonia. *The Geographical Journal* **55**, 1–34.

Polunin, O. (1980). *Flowers of Greece and the Balkans.* Oxford: Oxford University Press.

Turner, J. and Greig, J.R.A. (1975). Some Holocene pollen diagrams from Greece. *Review of Palaeobotany and Palynology* **20**, 171–204.

Tziavos, C., Pavlakis, P. and Anagnostou, C. (1988). The search for archaeological sites in the Strymon Delta using geological and geophysical methods, pp. 7–1 in Jones, R. and Catling, H (eds.), *New Aspects of Archaeological Science in Greece,* British School at Athens.

Wijmstra, T.A. (1969). Palynology of the first 30 metres of a 120 metre deep section in northern Greece. *Acta Botanica Neerlandica* **18**, 511–527.

Willis, K.J. and Bennett, K.D. (1994). The Neolithic transition – fact or fiction? Palaeoecological evidence from the Balkans. *The Holocene* **4**, 326–330.

3. Prehistoric Copper Mining and its Impact on Vegetation: Palaeological Evidence from Mount Gabriel, Co. Cork, South-West Ireland

T. M. Mighall, F. M. Chambers, J. M. Lanting and W. F. O'Brien

Excavations at Copa Hill, Cwmystwyth, mid-Wales and at Mount Gabriel, Co. Cork, south-west Ireland have provided evidence that they are two of a growing number of known early mining sites in the British Isles that date back to the Bronze Age. Charcoal fragments, pieces of wood and features characteristic of firesetting make up part of the archaeological evidence that suggests mining activities required prodigious amounts of wood-fuel to mine the ore.

Palaeoecological analyses of peat samples taken from sites close to the area of mining activity at Copa Hill and Mount Gabriel indicate that, although large amounts of wood may have been consumed by mining operations, the effect on the landscape, in particular woodlands, was not as devastating as first presumed. Factors such as the duration of mining, the selectivity and availability of wood, and woodland management possibly reduced the loss of woodland cover in the vicinity of the mines.

Keywords: Bronze Age, copper mining, vegetational history, pollen analysis, Mount Gabriel.

INTRODUCTION

The excavation in Wales and Ireland of a series of Bronze Age copper mines, namely Copa Hill, Cwmystwyth (Timberlake & Switsur 1988; Timberlake 1990a; Timberlake & Mighall 1992), Parys Mountain and Nantyreira (Timberlake 1990b), Great Orme (Dutton & Fasham 1994), Mount Gabriel, Co. Cork (O'Brien 1994a) and Ross Island, Killarney (O'Brien 1994b), has increased our understanding of the prehistoric mining process. A significant proportion of the material recovered from mine spoil heaps, mine gallery floors and infill deposits includes charcoal and wood pieces. Combined with evidence for firesetting, these finds have provided an insight into the exploitation of the environment surrounding the mines, most notably woodlands as a source for wood fuel. Either by quantifying the amount of wood fuel needed for mining operations, based on the amount of debris left in mine spoil tips, or through reasoning or speculation, some

archaeologists have suggested that the amount of wood exploited for mining in prehistory could have been substantial (Cernych 1978) and this demand could have resulted in the demise of local woodlands (Stos-Gale *et al.* 1988; O'Brien 1990).

A logical progression of this interest in environmental change during the tenancy of mines is to investigate the impact of these industrial activities on the landscape using palaeoecological techniques. Mighall and Chambers (1993a; 1993b) have demonstrated that the impact of early mining on woodlands at Copa Hill, Cwmystwyth was probably not as severe as first presumed. The duration and scale of mining, allied with possible woodland management or a low demand for wood, seem to have reduced the level of woodland clearance during the known tenancy of these sites. A preliminary investigation of a peat deposit located above the Bronze Age copper mines close to the summit of Mount Gabriel resulted in similar findings. Small declines

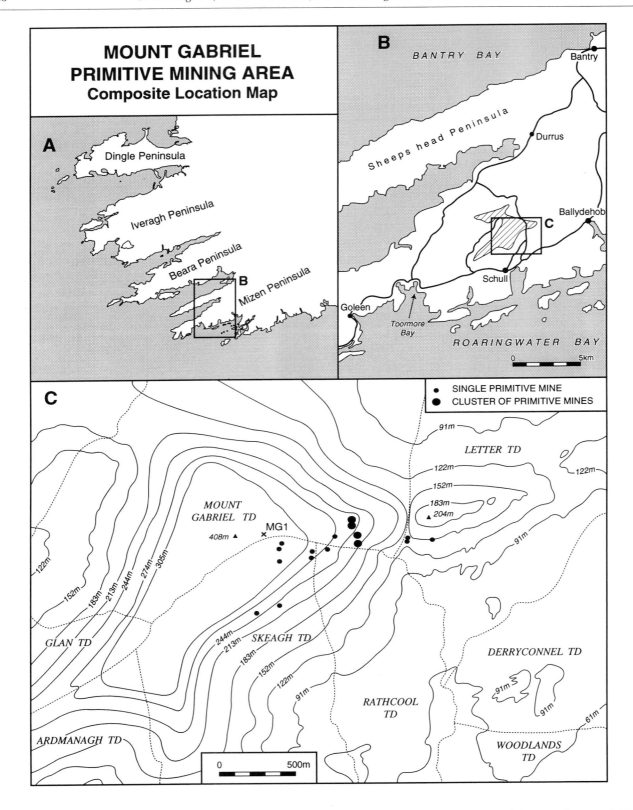

Figure 3.1: (a and b) Location of Mount Gabriel, Co. Cork, south-west Ireland. (c) Location of the sampling site MG1. Adapted from O'Brien (1994a).

in arboreal pollen taxa suggest that the impact of mining did not have a detrimental effect on local woodland. However, the absence of radiocarbon age determinations on the part of the peat core thought to provide a record of vegetational change during the Bronze Age means that those results must be treated with caution (Mighall & Chambers 1994).

Mount Gabriel is located on the Mizen Peninsula, several kilometres to the north of the village of Schull, Co. Cork (Figure 3.1). The Mount Gabriel-type mines are spread over the south and east slopes of Mount Gabriel, at an altitude between 60 and 335m. Recent interest in this site was initiated by Jackson (1968; 1980), who obtained a radiocarbon date of 3450±120 BP for charcoal sampled from one of the prehistoric mine dumps, providing evidence that mining activity took place during the Bronze Age. The subsequent discovery of 31 mines produced abundant evidence normally associated with early mining sites discovered elsewhere in the British Isles, including large quantities of charcoal, evidence for firesetting and stone hammers (O'Brien 1990). More importantly, a programme of radiocarbon dating of charcoal and wood finds at Mount Gabriel has firmly established that mining occurred between approximately 1700 and 1500 cal. BC. More detailed reviews of all aspects of this work are presented in Jackson (1968; 1980) and O'Brien (1987; 1990; 1994a).

This paper presents additional pollen and charcoal data and a series of radiocarbon dates permitting a re-evaluation of the findings presented by Mighall & Chambers (1994). The data are part of a continuing study that aims to investigate the extent to which human activity has influenced the regional environment of the Mizen Peninsula, Co. Cork, south-west Ireland. Particular emphasis in this paper has been given to establishing whether Bronze Age copper mining has influenced the processes of vegetational change as recorded within a mountain basin peat deposit located above the mines, close to the summit of Mount Gabriel. The pattern of arboreal pollen is also considered in relation to tree-ring analyses conducted on wood removed from the mines during archaeological excavations.

METHODS

Field and laboratory work

This study is based on the pollen and charcoal record derived from a peat core (MG1), extracted in July 1990, from a mountain peat basin situated just east of the Mount Gabriel summit, at an altitude of 366m. The core was extracted using a Russian corer (Jowsey 1966) and sub-samples of 5mm thickness and 2g wet weight were prepared for pollen analysis after Barber (1976). *Lycopodium clavatum* tablets were added to each sub-sample (Stockmarr 1971) in order to calculate pollen and charcoal con-

centrations. Generally, 500 land pollen grains were counted for each sample, except for sub-samples containing only a sparse amount of pollen, when the total land pollen count was restricted to 300. Charcoal was analysed using the point-count estimation method described by Clark (1982). Sub-samples of peat cut from the MG1 core were sent for radiocarbon dating to the Centre of Isotopic Research at Groningen University.

Pollen diagram

A pollen percentage diagram from the site, labelled MG1, is presented in Figure 3.2. The pollen diagram was drawn using the programme TILIA version 1.08 and TILIA.GRAPH, version 1.08, designed by Grimm (1991). All pollen data are expressed as a percentage of total land pollen (TLP), excluding spores and aquatics. Spores and aquatic pollen taxa are expressed as percentages of total land pollen. A cross denotes a taxon represented by less than 1% TLP. Plant nomenclature follows Stace (1991) and Bennett *et al.* (1994), except for the Pteropsida which is labelled as *Filicales*. To aid description the pollen diagram is divided into local pollen assemblage zones (LPAZ), identified statistically using the programme CONISS (Grimm 1991).

Construction of the LPAZs is based on statistical results from the full pollen sequence and they are coded accordingly in order to be consistent with any subsequent publication of the pollen data from the sampling site MG1. The characteristics of each LPAZ are summarised in Table 3.1. Radiocarbon dates are presented in Table 3.2. Calibrated ages were determined using the computer program Calib 3.0 (Stuiver & Reimer 1993) but they are expressed in uncalibrated years BP in the text.

RESULTS

Radiocarbon dates

The radiocarbon dates provide a range of ages to place the pollen record shown in Table 3.1 during the mid- to late Holocene, *ca.* 4500 to 2000 BP. In order to correlate the period of known Bronze Age mining with the vegetational history of site MG1, an age/depth curve was constructed (Figure 3.3). Radiocarbon dates obtained from samples recovered during archaeological excavation generally fall between 3000 and 3500 BP. A radiocarbon date of 3000±30 BP from a basal sample of peat infilling one of the mines suggests that mining activity ceased sometime before this date. The remainder of the radiocarbon dates taken from either primary spoil, charcoal and wood pieces recovered from mining sediments fall within the age range of 3450±120 BP and 3130±80 BP suggesting that copper was being mined during this period (O'Brien 1994a). This corresponds to a peat depth of approximately 370cm and

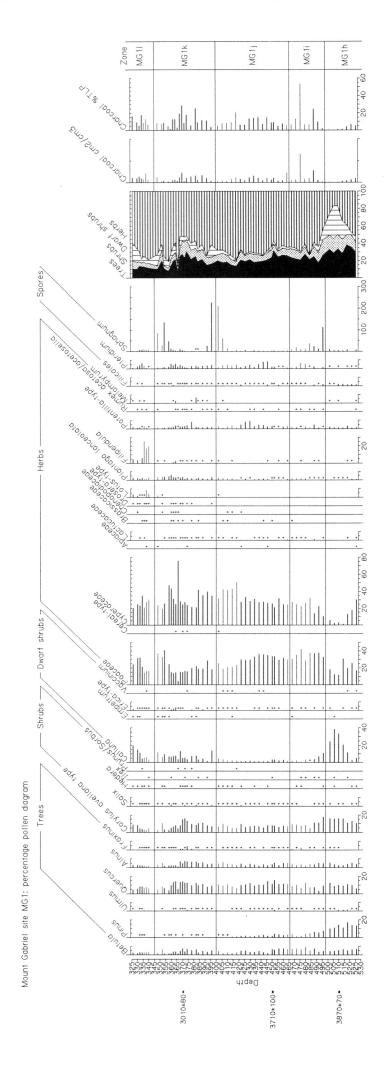

Figure 3.2: Pollen percentage diagram for sampling site MG1 between 325 and 525 cm.

Table 3.1: Characteristics of local pollen assemblage zones (LPAZ) in the pollen diagram from sampling site MG1.

LPAZ	CHARACTERISTICS
MG1l	Lower AP values, except *Corylus*. High Poaceae, Cyperaceae and *Calluna*.
MG1k	Low AP. High Poaceae and Cyperaceae. Rising *Calluna* and *Plantago lanceolata*.
MG1j	Low AP, dominated by *Quercus*. High Poaceae and Cyperaceae.
MG1I	Falling *Pinus* and *Corylus* values. High Poaceae, rising Cyperaceae. Lower *Calluna*, increasing *Plantago lanceolata*.
MG1h	AP averages 30% TLP, characterised by *Pinus, Corylus* and *Quercus*. Rising *Calluna*. Lower Cyperaceae and Poaceae values in the latter part of the LPAZ.

Table 3.2: Radiocarbon dates from Mount Gabriel, sampling site MG1. The calibrated maximum age ranges (cal AD or cal BC) are expressed to one standard deviation.

Site	Depth (cm)	Code no.	Radiocarbon date (BP)	Calibrated Age Range (cal. BC/AD) to one sigma
MG1	370 – 371	GrN – 21472	3010 ± 80	1387 – 1120 cal. BC
	450 – 451	GrN – 21473	3710 ± 100	2272 – 1943 cal. BC
	510 – 511	GrN – 21474	3870 ± 70	2459 – 2200 cal. BC

425cm at site MG1, lower down the peat core than originally suggested by Mighall & Chambers (1994).

Pollen source areas and pollen recruitment

The apparent dominance of herbaceous taxa, especially Poaceae and Cyperaceae, throughout the period shown in the pollen diagram (Figure 3.2) might be misleading. Mighall & Chambers (1994) argued that the pollen record could represent a more local vegetational community than a regional one. The mire from which the peat core was extracted is relatively small, with a maximum diameter of 100m. Results from models of the pollen catchment area for a site of this size suggest that the bulk of the pollen falling onto the mire surface is primarily derived from plants of local or extra-local origin, with the regional pollen component accounting for approximately 10% of the total amount of pollen (Jacobson & Bradshaw 1981). Less attention has been given to the proportion of the pollen rain attributable to more distant sources. Given the location of the sampling site close to the summit of the mountain, it is possible that this relatively exposed site at high altitude received a greater contribution of its pollen from long-range sources than at a site situated at a lower altitude. It is possible, therefore, that either or both of these two factors might mask any changes in the vegetational landscape on the lower slopes and this may affect the interpretation of the pollen data presented in this paper. Alternatively, recruitment of a higher regional proportion of pollen (above that predicted by Jacobson and Bradshaw's model) onto the mire surface might result from upward transport of pollen, especially from the slopes of Mount Gabriel, by wind. Markgraf (1980) and Price & Moore (1984) postulate that pollen can be moved to mires located at higher altitudes by updraughts. This could be beneficial when trying to detect the impact of mining as the majority of the mines are located on the mid- to lower slopes of Mount Gabriel. In order to overcome the problem of pollen source areas and recruitment, further palaeoecological work is now being conducted at other sites, located on the mid-slopes of Mount Gabriel and in the surrounding lowlands.

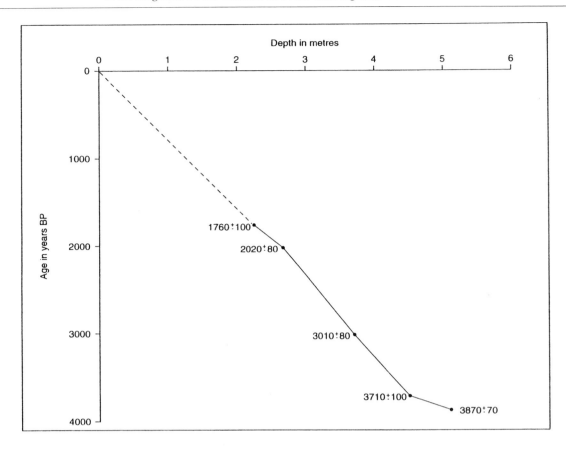

Figure 3.3: Plot of radiocarbon dates against sediment depth for sampling site MG1.

Vegetational landscape ca. 4000–1500 BP

Before the onset of mining, the vegetational landscape surrounding Mount Gabriel appears to have been dominated by herbaceous taxa, characterised by mainly grasses and sedges. This is reflected in the total pollen sum where the herbaceous pollen component is in excess of 50% during LPAZs MG1i, MG1j and MG1k. Pollen percentages of Poaceae and Cyperaceae generally exceed 20% TLP respectively except for a series of lower values between 525 and 500cm that coincide with a shortlived peak in *Calluna* frequencies. This rise in *Calluna* pollen suggests an expansion of heathers on either drier parts of the mire surface or possibly colonising organic acid soils on the surrounding slopes of Mount Gabriel, along with *Potentilla, Empetrum* and *Erica*-type species, which are also recorded in the pollen diagram. Although *Calluna* pollen values never regain such values, it remains a noticeable component along with Poaceae and Cyperaceae throughout the remainder of the mid- and late Holocene pollen spectra at this site. Occasional high values of *Sphagnum* spores accompany the presence of mire pollen taxa such as *Narthecium, Filipendula, Lotus*-type and *Drosera*-type indicating the existence of damper areas, possibly on the mire surface itself.

Despite the potential problems in determining the source of the pollen record, woodland appears to have been present in the pollen catchment area throughout the mid- to late Holocene period. LPAZ MG1i is characterised by consistent values of *Betula, Alnus* and *Quercus*, and a decline in the percentages of *Pinus* and *Corylus* suggesting that the role of pine and hazel as major woodland components is diminishing. By the time mining is thought to have commenced during LPAZ MG1j (*ca.* 425cm), it appears that the vegetational landscape of Mount Gabriel comprised an oak-hazel-dominated woodland set in a relatively open landscape. The arboreal pollen sum averages between 20 and 40% TLP with *Quercus* values accounting for approximately 8 to 12% TLP and *Corylus* values generally rising from approximately 5% TLP to 13% TLP close to the end of the known period of mining midway through LPAZ MG1k (*ca.* 375cm). *Betula* and *Alnus* values fluctuate between 2 and 7%, whilst *Pinus, Salix* and *Fraxinus* regularly occur with values of less than 2% TLP. *Ilex* and *Prunus/Sorbus*-type pollen are recorded occasionally, with values below 1% TLP. Then, midway through LPAZ MG1k values for *Corylus* and *Quercus, Alnus* and *Betula* drop sharply from 375 to 364cm. Thereafter, *Quercus* and *Alnus* pollen percentages generally remain between 5 and 10% TLP.

DISCUSSION

Previous studies have discussed the potential impact of prehistoric mining activities on the landscape. Mighall (1992), and Mighall & Chambers (1993a; 1993b; 1994) have suggested that the effect of mining on woodlands was not as severe as first presumed. It was suggested from pollen data gained from Copa Hill, Cwmystwyth, mid-Wales and from preliminary palynological investigations at Mount Gabriel, that factors such as the duration and scale of mining, the possible use of woodland management techniques and the selectivity of wood fuel from natural stands of woodland all contributed to minimising the impact of mining. This section considers whether the pollen data presented in this paper support the views expressed in earlier papers and, in particular, the extent to which the pollen and tree-ring data are in accordance.

The presence of the principal arboreal taxa in the pollen record is consistent with the wood and charcoal remains recovered from the Mount Gabriel mines. Tree-ring analysis of the wood recovered from mine 3 on Mount Gabriel suggests that the charred wood assemblage was dominated by *Quercus* and *Salix,* whilst the waterlogged wood assemblage mainly consisted of *Quercus* and *Corylus* (McKeown 1994). A further six species: *Alnus, Betula, Corylus, Ilex, Fraxinus* and *Pinus* were identified from the charcoal assemblage found in mine 3 and all of the species listed were also present in the waterlogged assemblage apart from *Pinus* (McKeown 1994). The relative proportion of the wood and charcoal remains appears to be quite consistent with the pollen data. Oak and hazel feature prominently whilst the other taxa form the minor components of both datasets. *Salix* is the only major exception, with a high amount of willow being present in the charcoal recovered from mine 3, suggesting that it was widely used during firesetting. This implies that a reasonable amount of willow must have been present in the Mount Gabriel area for the miners to exploit. However, the taxon does not feature prominently in the pollen record, occurring throughout the inferred period of mining with values below 2% TLP. Mighall & Chambers (1994) explained this apparent discrepancy between the pollen and archaeological charred and waterlogged wood datasets by suggesting that more concentrated areas of particular arboreal taxa may lie outside the pollen source area of site MG1, therefore the removal and use of a certain arboreal taxon may have gone undetected in the pollen record. Alternatively *Salix* is insect-pollinated and is relatively under-represented in the pollen record. Due to their preference for wet substrates, willow trees are more likely to be found in valley bottoms, therefore pollen data collected from sites located on the lower slopes of Mount Gabriel should account for this discrepancy.

Fraxinus, Alnus, Pinus, Corylus, Betula and *Ilex* were also selected for firesetting but their low percentage representation in the charcoal assemblage suggests that they were of minor importance (McKeown 1994) and,

furthermore, it reflects their limited occurrence in the Mount Gabriel area. Quite simply, it could be argued that the miners exploited the woodland that was both available and accessible.

Recent studies suggest that total wood consumption in the Mount Gabriel mines may have been in the order of 1500 to 2000 tonnes over a putative mining period of approximately 200 years (O'Brien 1994a). This high demand is not reflected in part of the pollen diagram presently under consideration. There is no evidence for the large-scale removal of woodland, and the total arboreal pollen sum generally fluctuates between 25 and 35% TLP. A shortlived and small reduction in *Betula, Pinus* and *Quercus* occurs between 426cm and 406cm. *Betula* and *Quercus* recover to their original values by 400cm and continue to rise in value to around 375cm. This is reflected in the total arboreal pollen sum where the tree and shrub component increases to approximately 40% TLP. This pattern of increasing arboreal pollen taxa is inconsistent with the hypothesis that prehistoric mining activities destroyed woodland. Throughout the majority of the proposed area of Bronze Age copper mining at Mount Gabriel, there appears to have been relatively little impact on woodland. Only *Pinus* values fail to recover, and they remain below 1% TLP for the remainder of the late Holocene. *Pinus* is known to have been used in the mines, usually in the form of charred splints thought to have been used in underground lighting (O'Brien 1994a). The limited use of pine appears to have been controlled to some extent by its availability.

One interpretation of the pattern of arboreal pollen data might be that the dominant tree types used for mining were deliberately managed. Tree-ring analysis of wood recovered from the mines indicates a preference for young stems of limited diameter but there was a variation in the age and size of the material recovered for individual tree taxa (McKeown 1994). This variation makes it difficult to establish if wood was managed in some way. Ash wood recovered from the mine 3/4 site was young and small in size, suggesting that it may have been coppiced. This would explain why there is no noticeable change in the pollen values for *Fraxinus*, except for some minor peaks at around 375cm. McKeown (1994), however, casts some doubt on whether ash would have been coppiced. Ash only forms a minor component of the waterlogged and charcoal assemblages and its low availability for mining purposes is also reflected in the pollen record where it never exceeds 1% TLP until the latter stages of the proposed period of mining. Taxa such as *Fraxinus* and *Ilex* are also likely to be under-represented palynologically.

The tree-ring results for other tree taxa showed no age or size clustering and therefore they were unlikely to have been coppiced. An absence of any firm evidence for coppicing does not mean that the timber exploited by miners was not inadvertently or deliberately managed. McKeown (1994) suggests that exploitation of recently established trees colonising abandoned clearings, the use of adventitious coppicing techniques (cutting the same areas of natural woodland on a number of occasions would produce coppice-like material) or draw-felling of stems (deliberate selection of wood on the basis of size) could lead to a diversity in the age/size structure of the wood assemblages recovered from the Mount Gabriel mines. A form of adventitious management might have been the most favoured method during the Bronze Age given that *Quercus*, *Corylus*, and to a lesser extent, *Alnus* and *Betula* are recorded with values between 5 and 15% TLP and imply that natural stands of woodland were readily available for exploitation. The pattern of arboreal pollen from site MG1 provides some supporting evidence that some form of woodland management occurred during the mining period. There is no major decline in arboreal pollen percentages, which would be expected if the estimated figures of wood consumption for mining are correct.

Any form of management would prevent woodland in the Mount Gabriel area from being permanently destroyed. This might explain why a pattern of rising arboreal pollen values occurs at Mount Gabriel during the mid- to late Holocene when compared with the progressive reduction in woodland cover at other sites in the region. Elsewhere in south-west Ireland, pollen analytical studies have shown that the mid- to late Holocene, especially between 4500 and 2000 BP, is characterised by progressive declines in woodland representation with, in some localities, sporadic regeneration (cf. Lynch 1981; Barnosky 1988; Dodson 1990). Thus, a major feature of many of the pollen diagrams produced for the south-west region of Ireland is a period of permanent woodland removal during the Bronze Age. Throughout this period, the presence of non-arboreal taxa, including cereal-type pollen and *Plantago lanceolata* and an expansion of Poaceae pollen, suggest that human activity was responsible for the demise of woodlands, presumably to open up the landscape for agriculture. In contrast, the need for wood fuel as part of the mining process at Mount Gabriel might have encouraged, miners to preserve woodland, via a management strategy, rather than destroy it permanently.

Furthermore, Mighall & Chambers (1993a, 1993b) proposed that the duration of mining might have had an important influence on the impact of mining on woodlands. Although the exact time period for mining cannot be determined, the suite of radiocarbon dates suggests that the main period of mining took place over two hundred years, between 3260 ± 30 BP and 3430 ± 30 BP. Thus, the wood fuel requirements on an annual basis would have been approximately 7.5 to 10 tonnes assuming the estimates of the total amount of wood fuel consumed are roughly correct. If these figures represent a fair estimation, the annual demand for wood fuel used in the Mount Gabriel mines might have been too low to register a severe change in the amount or composition of woodland in the area surrounding the mines. Alternatively, as previously mentioned, the pollen record derived from site MG1 might not have recorded any major changes in the arboreal pollen

sum as a result of mining and we must await results from lower altitude sampling sites.

One characteristic feature of the prehistoric mines excavated in the British Isles is the abundance of charcoal. High amounts of charcoal incorporated into mine gallery floor sediments have been attributed to the use of firesetting during ore procurement. Firesetting is a technique employed by miners that involves the burning of branchwood placed against the rockface containing the metal ore to induce rock fracturing (Pickin & Timberlake 1988). One consequence of firesetting would be the production of high amounts of airborne charcoal. In theory this charcoal could be dispersed, deposited and subsequently incorporated into surrounding peat and soils, and therefore it would be detectable through microscopic charcoal analysis. Charcoal curves calculated using the method suggested by Clark (1982) and as a percentage of total land pollen are shown in Figure 2 and they show a very similar pattern. Notwithstanding the problems of distinguishing natural and anthropogenically induced fires from microscopic charcoal records (Chambers 1993), the higher charcoal values during the first half of LPAZ MG1k lends some support to the hypothesis that increased charcoal contained within the peat core is a result of firesetting. However, the charcoal pattern recorded at sampling site MG1 is not wholly consistent with the idea that firesetting produced the bulk of the charcoal. During the early stages of the known mining period (between 425 and 396cm), charcoal values remain low. This might be due to differential wind dispersal preventing charcoal from being carried up to the mire or, alternatively, the intensity of firesetting was greater during the later stages of the mining period.

A number of alternative explanations could be posited in order to explain the charcoal records. Charcoal could be produced as a result of natural fires occurring on the slopes of Mount Gabriel or on the mire surface itself. Higher *Calluna* values are recorded during LPAZ MG1k, and other taxa, known to have an affinity to recently burnt ground, such as *Potentilla*-type and *Melampyrum*, are also well represented. However, values for *Pteridium* and *Potentilla*-type do not increase when compared to earlier phases of high charcoal values suggesting that their occurrence during the mining period is not in response to increased burning. Moreover, there is no major change in the proportion of arboreal pollen suggesting that fire has not been used to clear areas of woodland for agriculture.

It is interesting to note that a permanent decline of woodland at Mount Gabriel takes place during the late Holocene, coinciding with the late Bronze Age period. A marked change in the arboreal pollen spectrum occurs between 376cm and 358cm during LPAZ MG1k, where the dominant tree and shrub taxa fall in value. *Corylus* declines from 16 to 4% between 376cm and 366cm, *Quercus* from 14 to 4% between 370cm and 358cm, *Betula* from 7% to 1.4% between 370cm and 366cm, and *Alnus* from 7 to 1% between 370cm and 366cm. A radiocarbon date of 3010 ± 80 BP was obtained from a sub-sample taken from the MG1 peat core between 370 and 371cm. Therefore, the decline in arboreal pollen occurs sometime before this date and it might correlate with the later stages of the mining period. Arboreal pollen values do not recover indicating the permanent removal of woodland. Thus, by the time mining is known to have ceased – *ca.* 3200 to 3100 BP (O'Brien 1994a) – the amount of woodland cover had been dramatically reduced. The total arboreal pollen sum from 368cm is below 20% TLP. Tree taxa do not recover from this decline and generally remain below 15% TLP for the remainder of the late Holocene except for the occasional shortlived peak. The pattern of permanent woodland clearance, as suggested by the Mount Gabriel pollen data, is also consistent with the major decline of woodland taxa further to the north-west at Cashelkeelty (Lynch 1981), indicating that in pockets of Co. Cork, the late Bronze Age represents one of the most intense periods of woodland clearance.

Besides mining, agriculture may have played some part in lowering the amount of woodland within the Mount Gabriel district, especially the reduction in woodland cover from 375cm to 368cm. There is evidence in the pollen diagram to suggest that both pastoral and arable agriculture were practised throughout the later stages of LPAZ, MG1j and the first half of LPAZ MG1k, both of which correlate with the mining period. High percentages of Poaceae and *Plantago lanceolata* and *Pteridium* are present during LPAZ MG1j and MG1k. All three taxa are thought to indicate either pastoral agriculture or the colonisation of abandoned areas of land or openings created by woodland clearance (Edwards 1985).

Evidence for arable activity is less forthcoming. Cereal-type pollen is, however, recorded at 402cm and during the decline of arboreal pollen percentages between 375cm and 368cm. Associated with cereal-type pollen are high values of Poaceae pollen and the presence (albeit sporadic) of a suite of non-arboreal pollen taxa normally affiliated with arable farming in Ireland (cautiously suggested by Edwards 1985) including Apiaceae, Brassicaceae, Chenopodiaceae and *Rumex* spp. Thus, there is circumstantial evidence within the pollen record to suggest that humans were present in the Mount Gabriel region, practising agriculture as well as mining. It is difficult, however, to establish whether agriculture or mining was the more influential in contributing to the permanent removal of woodland at Mount Gabriel during LPAZ MG1k because the exact timespan of mining during the Bronze Age is unknown. This decline of woodland might have occurred during the final stages of metal ore procurement, which would suggest that the miners might have abandoned any form of woodland management. Alternatively, mining might have ceased by this time and this disturbance phase represents an expansion of agricultural activity in the Mount Gabriel area. It is relevant to note that there are a number of small stone circle complex monuments around Mount Gabriel which indicate middle to late Bronze Age settlement activity. The boulder burial site of Cooradarrigan, where one of the monuments is dated to 3080 ± 35 BP, is a good example (O'Brien 1992).

One other feature shown in the pollen record that merits some comment is the rise of *Calluna* pollen values concomitant with the decrease in arboreal pollen taxa midway through LPAZ MG1k. *Calluna* pollen values continue to increase steadily from LPAZ MG1k onwards suggesting that expansion of blanket peat occurred during the Bronze Age in the vicinity of the sampling site. There has been some discussion with regard to the inception and expansion of blanket peats in Ireland during the Holocene. It is generally believed that the timing of blanket peat initiation is variable throughout Ireland but an increase in the spread of blanket peat, probably as a result of human activity and/or climate, occurred during the mid- to late Holocene correlating with the Bronze Age (Edwards 1985; O'Connell 1990; Monk 1993). At sites in south-west Ireland the permanent decline of arboreal pollen has generally coincided with an expansion of *Calluna* pollen and *Sphagnum* spores (Monk 1993). The gradual rise in *Calluna* pollen values, combined with more sporadic peaks in *Sphagnum* spore values, suggests that some expansion of blanket peat was also taking place during the mining period at Mount Gabriel. *Calluna* pollen values continue to rise after the main episode of woodland clearance from 370cm onwards suggesting that conditions were still favourable for blanket peat growth and soil acidification. Furthermore, a radiocarbon date of 3000 ± 30 BP obtained from a peat sample infilling one of the mining adits (O'Brien 1994a) provides additional evidence that environmental conditions were conducive to peat initiation and growth during the late Bronze Age. Therefore, it is conceivable that mining activities, along with agricultural activities, might have indirectly played some part in promoting blanket peat growth in the Mount Gabriel area.

CONCLUSIONS

During the main period of known mining activity the total arboreal pollen percentage generally increases in value suggesting that woodlands were not destroyed as a result of metal ore procurement. Only a small decline in the curves for certain arboreal pollen taxa is observed at the beginning of mining period and, with the exception of pine, these taxa recover to their pre-mining values. Increasing arboreal pollen values appear to be a dominant pattern in the pollen spectra, suggesting an expansion of woodland during the mining period. Factors such as woodland management, the scale and duration of mining and availability of wood fuel from natural stands of woodland possibly played a role in maintaining woodland cover at Mount Gabriel.

Moreover, there is good similarity between the pollen and charred and waterlogged wood assemblages recovered from the mines. Oak and hazel were the dominant woodland constituents during the mining period, whilst other arboreal taxa, namely alder, birch, ash, holly and pine formed minor woodland components. This pattern is clearly reflected in the charred and waterlogged wood assemblages recovered from the mines. The only exception is willow which appears to have been only a minor woodland constituent but features strongly in the charred wood assemblages. The results of palynological work conducted at sites situated at the base of Mount Gabriel and in the surrounding region may resolve this discrepancy.

A multi-disciplinary approach will also overcome any potential problems created by the indeterminate pollen catchment area of MG1. If the duration of mining and woodland clearance is shortlived or small in scale, it is possible that the impact may not be detected at MG1. If so, other sampling sites may record any changes undetected at MG1. Furthermore, fine resolution pollen analysis of sediments deposited during the known mining period will also provide a more detailed record of vegetation changes during the Bronze Age.

There are also some patterns in the Mount Gabriel pollen diagram that are consistent with sites elsewhere in south-west Ireland. Permanent woodland clearance appears to have taken place during the late Bronze Age at Mount Gabriel but some ambiguity still exists over the role of mining in that process. The expansion of blanket peat also coincides both with the mining period and the first recording of cereal-type pollen, suggesting that human disturbance, either agriculture or mining, played some part in promoting peat growth.

Acknowledgements

Thanks are due to L. Elliott and S. Turnbull for field assistance, and the Palaeoecology laboratory and Geography Department at the University of Keele for use of facilities. The cartographic unit in the Geography Division at Coventry University helped in the production of Figures 1 and 3. The Royal Irish Academy and Coventry University provided some funding for fieldwork and travel. Comments from a referee also helped to improve this paper.

REFERENCES

Barber, K.E. (1976). History of vegetation, pp. 5–83 in Chapman, S.B. (ed.) *Methods in Plant Ecology*. Oxford: Blackwell.

Barnosky, C. (1988). A late-glacial and post-glacial pollen record from the Dingle Peninsula, County Kerry. *Proceedings of the Royal Irish Academy* **88B(2)**, 23–37.

Bennett, K.D., Whittington, G. and Edwards, K.J. (1994). Recent plant nomenclatural changes and pollen morphology in the British Isles. *Quaternary Newsletter* **73**, 1–6.

Cernych, E.N. (1978). Aibunar – A Balkan copper mine of the fourth millennium BC (investigations of the years 1971, 1972 and 1974). *Proceedings of the Prehistoric Society* **44**, 203–217.

Chambers, F.M. (1993). Late-Quaternary climatic change and human impact: commentary and conclusions, pp. 247–250 in Chambers, F.M. (ed.) *Climate change and human impact on the landscape*. London: Chapman and Hall.

Clark, R.L. (1982). Point count estimation of charcoal in pollen preparations and thin sections of sediments. *Pollen et Spores* **24**, 523–535.

Dodson, J.R. (1990). The Holocene vegetation of a prehistorically inhabited valley, Dingle Peninsula, Co. Kerry. *Proceedings of the Royal Irish Academy* **90B**, 151–174.

Dutton, A. and Fasham, P. (1994). Prehistoric copper mining on the Great Orme, Llandudno, Gwynedd. *Proceedings of the Prehistoric Society* **60**, 245–286.

Edwards, K.J. (1985). The anthropogenic factor in vegetational history, pp. 187–220 in Edwards, K.J. and Warren, W.P. (eds.) *The Quaternary History of Ireland*. London: Academic Press.

Grimm, E. (1991). *TILIA and TILIA.GRAPH*. Illinois: Illinois State Museum.

Jackson, J.S. (1968). Bronze Age copper mine on Mount Gabriel, west Country Cork, Ireland. *Archaeologia Austriaca* **43**, 92–103.

Jackson, J.S. (1980). Bronze Age copper mining in counties Cork and Kerry, pp. 9–29 in Craddock, P.T. (ed.) *Scientific Studies in Early Mining and Extractive Metallurgy*. British Museum Occasional paper no **20**, London: British Museum.

Jacobson, G.L. and Bradshaw, R.H.W. (1981). The selection of sites for paleovegetational studies. *Quaternary Research* **16**, 80–96.

Jowsey, P.C. (1966). An improved peat sampler. *New Phytologist* **65**, 245–248.

Lynch, A. (1981). *Man and the Environment in South-West Ireland*. Oxford, British Archaeological Reports British Series 85.

McKeown, S.A. (1994). The analysis of wood remains from mine 3, Mount Gabriel, pp. 265–280 in O'Brien, W.F. (ed.) *Mount Gabriel: Bronze Age Copper Mining in Ireland*. Galway: Galway University Press.

Markgraf, V. (1980). Pollen dispersal in a mountain area. *Grana* **9**, 127–146.

Mighall, T.M. (1992). *Palaeoecological aspects of early mining and metalworking in upland Wales*. Unpublished Ph.D. thesis, University of Keele.

Mighall, T.M. and Chambers, F.M. (1993a). The environmental impact of prehistoric mining at Copa Hill, Cwmystwyth, Wales. *The Holocene* **3(3)**, 260–264.

Mighall, T.M. and Chambers, F.M. (1993b). Early mining and metalworking: its impact on the environment. *Historical Metallurgy* **27(2)**, 71–83.

Mighall, T.M. and Chambers, F.M. (1994). Vegetation history and Bronze Age mining on Mount Gabriel: preliminary results, pp. 289–298 in O'Brien, W.F. (ed.) *Mount Gabriel: Bronze Age Copper Mining in Ireland*. Galway: Galway University Press.

Monk, M.A. (1993). People and environment: in search of the farmers, pp. 35–52 in E. Shee Twohig, E. and Ronayne, M. (eds.) *Past Perceptions: the Prehistoric Archaeology of South-West Ireland*. Cork: Cork University Press.

O'Brien, W.F. (1987). The dating of the Mount Gabriel-type copper mines of west Cork. *Journal of the Cork Historical and Archaeological Society* **92**, 50–70.

O'Brien, W.F. (1990). Prehistoric copper mining in south-west Ireland: the Mount Gabriel-type mines. *Proceedings of the Prehistoric Society* **56**, 269–290.

O'Brien, W.F. (1992). Boulder-burials: a later Bronze Age megalith tradition in south-west Ireland. *Journal of the Cork Historical and Archaeological Society* **97**, 11–35.

O'Brien, W.F. (ed.) (1994a). *Mount Gabriel: Bronze Age Copper Mining in Ireland*. Galway: Galway University Press.

O'Brien, W.F. (1994b). Ross Island: the beginning. *Archaeology Ireland* **9**, 24–27.

O'Connell, M. (1990). Origins of Irish lowland blanket bog, pp. 49–71 in Doyle, G. (ed.) *Ecology and Conservation of Irish peatlands*. Dublin.

Pickin, J. and Timberlake, S. (1988). Stone hammers and firesetting: A preliminary experiment at Cymystwyth mine, Dyfed. *Bulletin Peak District Mines Historical Society* **10**, 165–167.

Price, M.D.R. and Moore, P.D. (1984). Pollen dispersion in the hills of Wales: a pollen shed hypothesis. *Pollen et Spores* **26**, 127–36.

Stace, J. (1988). *New Flora of the British Isles*. Cambridge: Cambridge University Press.

Stockmarr, J. (1971). Tablets with spores used in absolute pollen analysis. *Pollen et Spores* **13**, 615–621.

Stos-Gale, Z., Gale, N. and Papastamataki, A. (1988). An early Bronze Age copper smelting site on the Aegean island of Kythnos II: Scientific evidence, pp. 11–22 in Ellis-Jones, J. (ed.) *Aspects of Ancient Mining and Metallurgy*. Bangor, 1986. Bangor: University College Press.

Stuiver, M. and Reimer, P.J. (1993). Extended ^{14}C data base and revised CALIB 3.0 ^{14}C age calibration programme. *Radiocarbon* **35**, 215–223.

Timberlake, S. (1990a).Excavations and fieldwork on Copa Hill, Cwmystwyth, pp. 22–29 in Crew, P. and Crew, S. (eds.) *Early Mining in the British Isles*. Plas Tan y Bwlch Occasional Paper No. 1 Ffestiniog: Snowdonia Press.

Timberlake, S. (1990b) Excavations at Parys Mountain and Nant-yreira, pp. 15–21 in Crew, P. and Crew, S. (eds.) *Early Mining in the British Isles*. Plas Tan y Bwlch Occasional Paper No. 1 Ffestiniog: Snowdonia Press.

Timberlake, S. and Mighall, T.M. (1992). Historic and prehistoric mining on Copa Hill, Cwmystwyth. *Archaeology in Wales* **32**, 38–44.

Timberlake, S. and Switsur, R. (1988). An archaeological investigation of early mineworkings on Copa Hill: new evidence for prehistoric mining. *Proceedings of the Prehistoric Society* **54**, 329–333.

4. A Preliminary Investigation into the Use of Fungal Spores as Anthropogenic Indicators on Shetland

Andrew Hoaen and Geraint Coles

Several genera of fungi have potential for indicating the presence of herbivore dung, and so inferred grazing, in palaeoecological sequences. A pilot study undertaken in Shetland, close to an area of prehistoric settlement, shows a degree of coincidence between the pollen evidence and inference from fungal spores. Although only a preliminary investigation, this result should encourage further research into fungal spores.

Keywords: Fungal spores, pollen, palynofacies, Shetland, herbivore dung.

INTRODUCTION

The use of the pollen record to identify the impact of human populations on vegetation, either directly, or through their management of livestock, is widely seen as providing a means of identifying changes in landuse. Many plants loosely termed indicator taxa actually have very broad environmental tolerences (Van Geel 1978) and consequently interpretations of landuse from pollen data can be ambiguous. This problem is especially acute when attempting to establish whether changes in vegetation are due to herbivore grazing and trampling pressure (Spence 1979). To that end this paper examines a method for the identification of landuse change based on the presence of certain groups of fungal spores.

Fungal spores are preserved and recovered in palynological preparations, but their potential contribution to palaeoecology has only begun to be assessed in the past twenty years (see papers by Van Geel 1978 onwards). Because of the large number of fungal spores, algal cysts and other *incertae cedis* fossils found in palynological preparations (over a thousand have so far been identified), some studies will require a total analysis of the recovered palynological assemblage – a palynofacies approach,

(Traverse 1988) while others may benefit from studying specific groups of microfossils such as cyanobacteria or fungal spores.

The paper will describe five spore types that have potential as indicators of herbivore activity in palaeoecology. This may prove of particular value in island locations where large herbivores are thought to have been absent before their introduction by Neolithic populations.

DISPERSED FUNGAL SPORES AS ENVIRONMENTAL INDICATORS

Fungi, broadly speaking, are a large and diverse kingdom with over a 100,000 described species. Their chief characteristic is an inability to photosynthesize, so to obtain nutrients they must exist as saprophytes on dead organic matter or as parasites of living organisms. Fundamentally, most fungi consist of two main components: a system of tubes (or hyphae) used for feeding, which make up the mycelium, and specialized reproductive structures that can range in size from the microscopic to the toadstool.

There are several genera of fungi that are obligate (that

Figure 4.1: Delitschia type. Ellongate, ellipsoidal, monoseptate inaperturate spore with smoot to faintly scabrate surface. Septum transverse, median, 1–5 µm thick, no septal plate visible. Spore outline constricted about median septum. Poles tapering to sharp apices. Single wall <1 µm thick. 28–47 x 9–15 µm (Clark 1994 type MOI008).

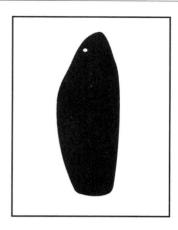

Figure 4.3: Cercophora type. Ascospores 15–18 x 6–8 µm, truncate at the basal side and tapering at the apical end. One apical sub-pore ca. 0.7 µm in diameter occasionally with one septum (van Geel 1982 T.112).

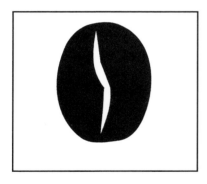

Figure 4.2: Sporomiella type. Small ca. 10 µm diameter spores, dark brown, smooth with a distinctive sigmoid germinal aperture. Possibly found in groups of up to eight (From Davis 1987).

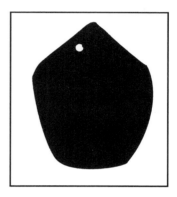

Figure 4.4: Tripterospora type. Ellipsoidal brown ascospores, with a truncated base, ca. 20 x 15 µm with a 1–2 µm diameter pore near the apex (van Geel 1983 T.169).

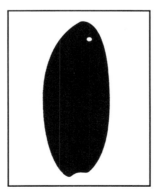

Figure 4.5: Podospora type. One celled, ellipsoidal, smooth brown ascospores with a bluntly conical basal end ca. 39–44 x 16–23 µm, with an annulate pore 2 µm in diameter below the apex (after van Geel 1981 T.368).

is specialized) on dung and also several genera that are facultative (that is not specialized) but preferring dung (Hawksworth *et al.* 1983). These genera have been used by several authors (Clarke 1994; Davis 1987; Van Geel *et al.* 1983b) to infer the presence of grazing herbivores within archaeological and peat sediments and in the catchments of lake basins, presumably through grazing and use of the water source (Clarke 1994; Davis 1987; Van Geel *et al.* 1981; Van Geel *et al.* 1983a).

The following genera of fungal spores have been identified as obligate fungal spores of dung and have been found in archaeological and palaeoecological sediments. All are members of the Ascosmycetes and are from these genera *Delitschia* (Figure 4.1) (Ellis & Ellis 1988), and *Sporomiella* (Figure 4.2) (Ahmed & Cain 1972), they are readily identified and are obligate genera which grow on a wide variety of animal dung but are noted especially from herbivore dung (Clarke 1994; Davis 1987).

Three genera of the Sordariaceae have also been used as dung indicators in palaeoecology: *Cercophora* (Figure 4.3), *Tripterospora* (Figure 4.4), and *Podospora* (Figure 4.5). Though predominately fimicolous, species of both *Cercophora* and *Podospora* are known from a range of vegetative material, wood, straw and leaves (Lundqvist 1972). These genera are not therefore by themselves always good indicators of herbivore dung in palaeo-ecology.

Morphological studies of fossil fungal spores are in their infancy and for this reason it is often better to refer to spores as of a particular type e.g. *Podospora* type. Distinction of these types is made on the basis of a sub apical pore, a flattened apice and on the overall shape and symmetry of the spore head.

The use of different fungal spores as indicators of herbivore activity has been attempted in both the Old and New World. Davis noted that the concentration of fossil *Sporomiella* rose in six basins of the western states of the U.S. This he found was coincident with overgrazing during the historic period in these areas e.g. at Pecks Lake where *Sporomiella* spores rise to 3% of the pollen sum in this period. Spores of *Sporomiella* did not always accompany overgrazing for reasons that are as yet unclear. They are common in modern surface samples however "only where grazing herbivores are locally present" (Davis 1987, 290).

A Dutch group at the Hugo de Vries University has been using the presence of: *Podospora*, *Tripterospora* and *Cercophora* type to infer the presence of grazing animals. In some cases this can be correlated with the presence of a dated archaeological site within the area of the sampling location, e.g. at DeBorchet in Holland, where in zone F large numbers of *Cercophora* type and *Podospora* type are interpreted as being due to frequent visits by grazing herbivores (Van Geel *et al.* 1981, 406).

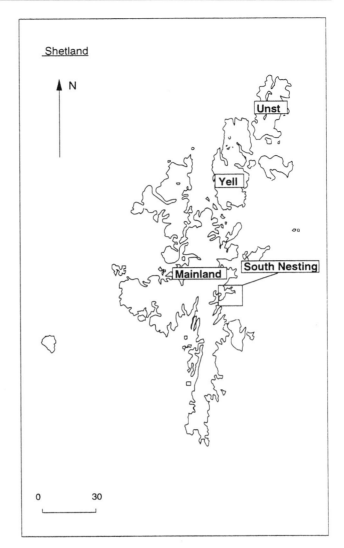

Figure 4.6: Shetland, showing the location of the study area (after Dockrill 1992).

THE STUDY SITE

The South Nesting peninsula of Shetland (Figure 4.6) is situated on the east side of Mainland approximately 10 km north of Lerwick. The geology of the area is of Precambrian age and comprises part of the Whiteness division with flaggy psammites interleaved with limestones. The under-lying geology to some degree governs the land use of the area with areas of enclosed farmland closely following the belts of limestone. The available farmland allows a mixture of arable and pastoral activity within the catchments of the site. The soils of the area are a mixture of peaty podsols and brown soils.

Archaeology

Recent field survey of the South Nesting area has located over 260 monuments of all types. Within the catchment of

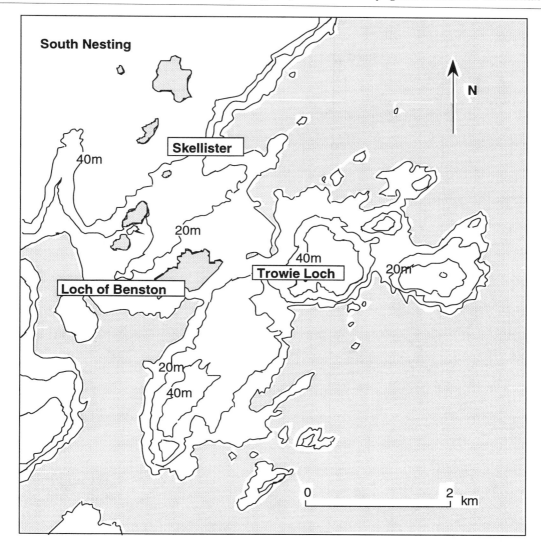

Figure 4.7: The South Nesting area.

Trowie Loch excavations have recently been completed of a house site and kerb cairn, and several other prehistoric and later sites have been located (Dockrill 1992). A peat sequence close to the archaeological excavations was recovered from the infilled portion of the Trowie Loch basin to provide a suitable sequence for palynofacies analysis, and to answer questions relating to the vegetation history and human impact in the area.

Physical description

The site at Trowie Loch is situated on the South Nesting peninsula (Figure 4.7) of Mainland, Shetland. Trowie Loch is a small irregularly shaped brackish loch, sitting in a small basin. The loch is fed by a small stream that drains the Loch of Benston to the South East, and is drained via a tidal inlet into the Vadill of Garth. The sampling location sits on the edge of enclosed land within the infilled basin.

After exploratory work in the basin, a sampling site was chosen which was as close as possible to the area of archaeological interest and which would also provide the best possible sequence.

Two overlapping cores were taken using a 5cm diameter Russian corer, and from a site 50cm away samples were recovered using a 15cm diameter Russian corer for subsequent radiocarbon dating.

Approximately 2.5m of sediment were recovered. 0–27cm was a dark brown peat, 27–180cm comprised sedge peat, 180–250cm was comprised of lake muds. The sequence included a change in regime from a lake environment to a marsh.

Pollen was identified using the key in Moore, Webb & Collinson (1991) and a reference collection at the Dept. of Archaeology in Edinburgh. Fungal spores were identified using published material and with the aid of type materia kept at the Hugo de Vries Institute in Amsterdam.

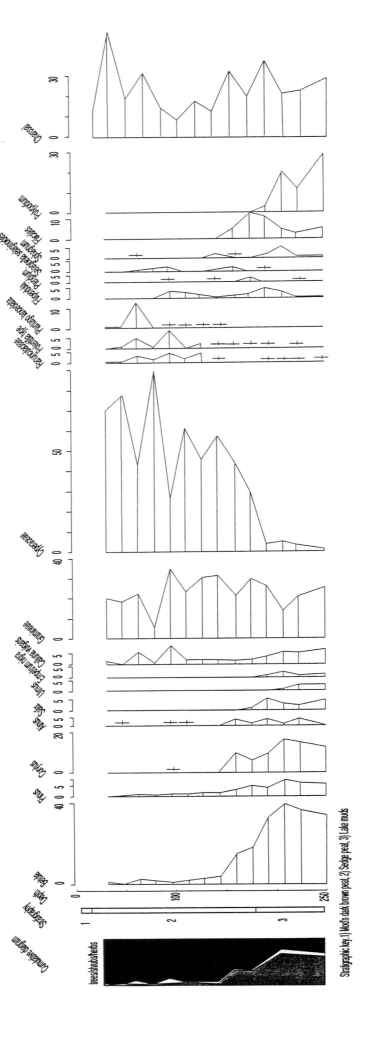

Figure 4.8: Selected pollen taxa from Trowie Loch.

Samples were processed using the method in Moore, Webb and Collinson (1991) except where samples were minerogenic when Bromoform separation was used to separate the mineral fraction from the organic fraction. Plant nomenclature follows Clapham *et al.* (1987). Fungal spores were counted within a pollen sum of 300. A number of different fungal spore types were logged at each level. Data on these will be presented separately. The pollen sum was calculated as percentages of Total land pollen, fungal spores are calculated as percentages of Total land pollen + fungal spores.

The pollen sequence has similarities to other diagrams from the Shetland Islands and only a brief summary of the pollen analysis and selected spore taxa will be presented here.

POLLEN ANALYSIS

The diagram (Figure 4.8) has been zoned on the basis of observed changes in the main taxa. The main stratigraphic change is hydrological from deposition in a lake to a marsh. This leads to the domination of the spectra by Cyperaceae after 180cm. The following zonation is based on total land pollen (excluding spores and aquatics).

The diagram falls neatly into three main zones. A basal zone dominated by *Betula, Corylus, Polypodium* and Gramineae from 250–190cm (TL1). Within the second zone (TL2) 190–160cm a change from lacustrine sediments to terrestrial peats occurs, the pollen record is still dominated by *Betula* and *Corylus* but with a marked increase in Cyperaceae from 176cm (TL2). This zone ends abruptly with a dramatic reduction in tree and shrub pollen after 160cm. From 144cm to the surface the diagram is dominated by Cyperaceae, and there is the continuous presence of *Plantago lanceolata* and increasing amounts of *Ranunculus* and *Potentilla* type (TL3). There is a record of a cereal pollen grain (anlD>8 microns) at 128cm.

The curve of *Sporomiella* type spores begins at 160cm and is continuous to the top of the column (Figure 4.9). Fluctuations are apparent in the curve. Other fungal types are present in low quantities from this point though not continuously.

DISCUSSION

The lowest zone would appear to begin at some point in the middle Holocene. Total tree pollen is in excess of 50% throughout the zone. *Betula* and *Corylus* are well established indicating areas of open woodland, within the catchment. This is supported by the high values of Gramineae pollen, and levels of *Polypodium* and Filicales undiff. suggesting a mosaic of woodland with some tall herb vegetation as indicated by the *Filipendula* curve. Low values for *Calluna vulgaris* indicate the presence of

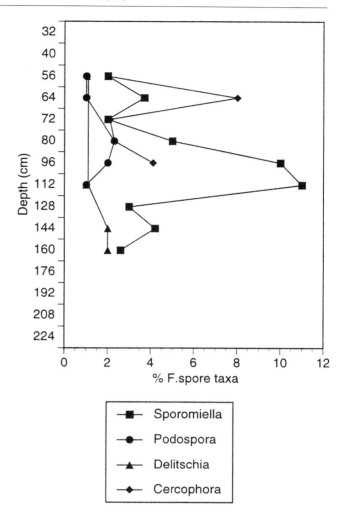

Figure 4.9: Spore taxa from Trowie Loch.

limited heathland. The basal zone appears to postdate the early Holocene and tree and shrub vegetation appear to be firmly established. Given the high values of tree pollen it would appear that this zone is similar to that of Johansens zone M3 at Murraster (Johansen 1975) and zone SBS-2b from Scord of Brouster (Keith-Lucas 1986). The high values of tree taxa e.g. Betula values in excess of 30% differentiate this site from the nearby undated site at Grunna water (Edwards *et al.* 1993). Several different types of fungal spores were logged during this phase but none of the five types indicative of dung or human activity were identified in the samples analyzed.

In the next zone local pollen from Cyperaceae starts to dominate the overall sequence. Whilst this makes interpretation difficult it is clear that total tree pollen declines to under 30% in this zone but there is still the presence of woodland in the catchment. Heathland plants also decline whilst there is a expansion in the values of *Filipendula*, Filicales undiff. and Gramineae indicating some opening and disturbance of the woodland. Palynologically, this may be due to two major causes: one is the removal of woodland under pressure from human activity including the introduction of grazing animals. Alternatively it may be connected to the hydroseral change to a valley marsh from a lake, and a consequent increase in the amount of local pollen representation. However given the available parallels elsewhere on Shetland an anthropogenic cause is certainly possible.

The bulk of the diagram will be familiar to anyone who has looked at Late Holocene pollen diagrams from Shetland. It is dominated by local pollen from Cyperaceae, with a strong Gramineae component, and the other herbs mostly comprising *Potentilla* and *Ranunculus* type. This portion of the diagram in all probability represents the middle-late Holocene. In this zone there is a continuous presence of the *Sporomiella* and occasional records of *Podospora*, *Delitschia* and *Cercophora*, possibly indicating a continuous record of grazing within the catchment.

CONCLUSIONS

These results would tend to point to the rise of selected taxa of fungi in sediments being coincident with a shift in the pollen spectra from a open wooded landscape, to a landscape largely devoid of trees and dominated by grasses and heathland. From the pollen data, although it is difficult to draw conclusions in the absence of radiometric dates, it would appear probable that these events took place in the Middle Holocene. It is notable that the fungal taxa which show the most marked rise are thought to be either obligate or preferentially coprophilous and have been associated with the grazing of large herbivores. In several cases these taxa appear to be absent before the start of this phase. It is tempting to conclude that the arrival and/or increasing representation of these fungal taxa is due to the arrival of human populations and their introduction of grazing herbivores to the island ecosystem.

A word of caution is required, however. These are initial results and form part of a larger study so they may reflect a bias due to small sample size. The ecology of fungal spores is a still developing subject, and the observed changes may be due to stratigraphical changes in the mire. However the results suggest that fungal spores have some potential as indicators of environmental change in archaeology and palaeoecology.

REFERENCES

Ahmed, S.E. and Cain, R.F. (1972). Revision of the genera Sporomia and Sporomiella. *Canadian Journal of Botany.* **50**, 419–477.

Clapham, A.R., Tutin, T.G., and Moore, D.M. (1987). *Flora of the British Isles.* Cambridge: Cambridge University Press.

Clarke, C.M. (1994). *Fungal spores as palaeoenvironmental indicators of anthropogenic activity.* Unpublished Phd. thesis, University of Edinburgh.

Davis, O.K. (1987). Spores of the Dung Fungus *Sporomiella*: Increased Abundance in Historic Sediments and before Pleistocene Megafaunal Extinction. *Quaternary Research* **28**, 290–294.

Dockrill, S. (1992). *The South Nesting Palaeolandscape Project.* Bradford: University of Bradford.

Edwards, K.J., Moss, A.G., and Whittington, G. (1993). A late Glacial pollen site at Grunna water, Nesting, pp. 99–103 in J. Birnie, J., Gordon, J., Bennett, K. and Hall, A. (eds) *The Quaternary of Shetland Field Guide.* Quaternary Research Association.

Ellis, M.B. and Ellis, P.J. (1988). *Microfungi on Miscellaneous Substrates.* London: Croom Helm.

Hawksworth, D.L., Sutton, B.C., and Ainsworth, G.C. (1983). *Ainsworth & Bisby's Dictionary of the Fungi (including the Lichens).* Kew: Commonwealth Mycological Institute.

Johansen, J. (1975). Pollen diagrams from the Shetland and Faroe Islands. *New Phytologist* **75**, 369–387.

Keith-Lucas, M. (1986). Neolithic impact on vegetation and subsequent vegetational development at Scord of Brouster. In *Scord of Brouster.* (A. Whittle, ed.). Oxford University Comittee for Archaeology Monograph No.9, Oxford.

Lundqvist, N. (1972). Nordic Sordariaceae S. lat. *Symbolae Botanicae Upsaliensis* **20**, 1–374.

Moore, P.D., Webb, J.A., and Collinson, M.E. (1991). *Pollen Analysis.* Oxford:Blackwell Scientific Publications.

Spence, D. (1979). *Shetland's Living Landscape.* Sandwick: The Thule Press.

Traverse, A. (1988). *Palaeopalynology.* London: Unwin Hyman.

Van Geel, B. (1978). A palaeoecological study of Holocene peat bog sections in Germany and the Netherlands. *Review of Palaeobotany and Palynology* **25**, 1–120.

Van Geel, B., Bohnke, S.J.P., and Dee, H. (1981). A palaeoecological study of an upper Late Glacial and Holocene sequence from "De Borchert", The Netherlands. *Review of Palaeobotany and Palynology* **31**, 367–448.

Van Geel, B., Hallewas, D.P., and Pals, J.P. (1983a). A late Holocene deposit under the Westfriese Zeedijk near Enkhuizen (Prov of N-Holland, the Netherlands), palaeoecological and archaeological aspects. *Review of Palaeobotany and Palynology* **38**, 269–335.

Van Geel, B., Jurjen, M.B., and Pals, J.P. (1983b). Archaeological and palaeoecological aspects of a medieval house terp in a reclaimed raised bog area in North Holland. *Berichten van de Riijkdienst voor het Oudheidkundig Bodemonderzoek* **33**, 419–444.

5. The Decline of Woodland in Orkney: Early Neolithic to Late Iron Age

Camilla Dickson

Recent pollen analyses from two sites near to the Late Neolithic village of Skara Brae indicate that before the elm decline (5,900 years ago from calibrated radiocarbon dates) extensive woodland covered that part of Mainland, Orkney. Charcoal analyses from Skara Brae show the woodland to have been species-rich. Pollen analyses from several sites demonstrate that after the elm decline woodland greatly decreased, largely, if not entirely, as the result of human activity. The development of widespread blanket bog on the hills during the Bronze Age would have limited the habitats suitable for tree growth. The demands for fuel for Iron Age smelting and smithing probably added to the decline and by the Late Iron Age period trees and tall shrubs in the west of Mainland Orkney seem to have largely disappeared

Keywords: Orkney, woodland, pollen, charcoal, Neolithic, Iron Age.

INTRODUCTION

At the present time the fertile soils of the Orkney Islands are mainly under agriculture, especially pastoral farming. The climate is oceanic and extremely windy; the low relief means that exposure and salt laden winds affect the vegetation throughout the islands. The islands are noted for their lack of trees. The only native woodland is on the island of Hoy. A small relict woodland at Berriedale (Figure 5.1) consists of *Betula pubescens* ssp *tortuosa* (the northern form of the downy birch), two bushes of *Corylus avellana* (hazel), *Populus tremula* (aspen), *Salix* spp. (willows) and *Sorbus aucuparia* (rowan). There is an understorey of tall herbs and ferns as is found in similar ungrazed open woodland in mainland Scotland. The community is described by Prentice and Prentice (1975, Table 12). Grazing ceased on north Hoy in 1950 and it has been shown by Chapman and Crawford (1981) that the woodland is capable of "vigorous and sustained growth with the active establishment of many young trees." Other stands of aspen trees grow on Hoy and other islands and

native willow trees and shrubs are scattered from Rousay southwards (Bullard 1995).

A woodland flora of limited species range on Mainland, the largest island, has been indicated from pollen analyses by earlier authors. Moar (1969) and Davidson *et al.* (1976) suggested that in the mid Flandrian, when woodland reached its maximum development, birch-hazel scrub predominated in western and central Mainland respectively. Donaldson's (1986) analyses from Deerness in the east of Mainland indicated local birch woodland with willow and hazel.

Several tree species, including the above tree types, thrive in plantations and gardens. Other species grown include *Ulmus* (elm), *Fraxinus* (ash), *Prunus* spp. and *Acer pseudoplatanus* (sycamore) (Bullard & Bremner 1990). Sycamore is not a British native but it, and some of the other taxa, sets seed on Orkney. *Quercus* spp. (oaks) will only grow well in the shelter of other trees but *Pinus sylvestris* (scots pine) has not thrived. All need initial protection, such as polypropylene tubes, from wind, voles

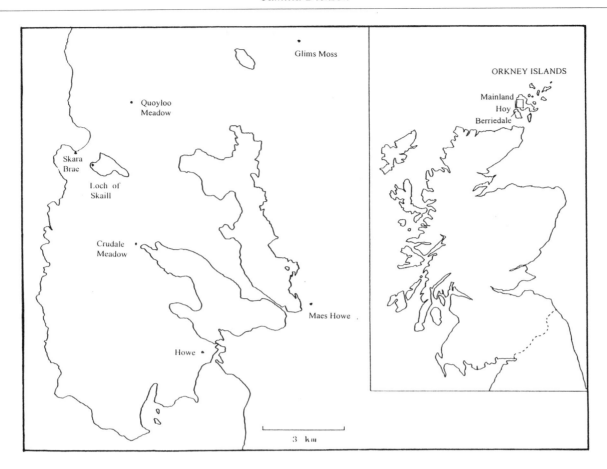

Figure 5.1: West Mainland, Orkney, showing sites referred to in the text.

and rabbits. Rabbits were, however, a Norman introduction into Britain.

It seems then that the present day climate is suitable for tree growth, given adequate shelter which the wind-resistant hazel provides on parts of the exposed western coasts of Scotland at the present time. So the question posed is: why are the islands largely lacking in native woodland? Native trees still grow in adjacent areas of the northern mainland of Scotland and so sources of seed would presumably have been available in the past.

To answer this question we need to go back about 8000 years and trace the history of the Orkney vegetation from pollen and macro-plant analyses.

THE POLLEN SITES

The pollen sites to be considered (Figure 5.1) are all in the west of Mainland which is the largest Orkney island, as are two archaeological sites with wood and charcoal. Skara Brae, a Late Neolithic settlement on the west coast, has been re-excavated recently (Clarke 1976) and the extensive partly waterlogged middens have yielded numerous plant remains. Howe, some 9km southeast of the

Neolithic village, is a multi-period site with domestic settlement lasting over a thousand years of the Iron Age (Ballin Smith 1994).

INTERPRETATION AND DISCUSSION

Discussing the vegetational history of Orkney, Jane Bunting (1994) is concerned with two small basins; the nearest to Skara Brae, Quoyloo Meadows, is only 3km northeast of the Late Neolithic village. It is now a water meadow with arable cultivation on the surrounding land. The pollen diagram goes back to the Late-glacial but we are only concerned with the Post-glacial part of the diagram. This shows that extensive woodland had developed by about 8000 years BP. No radiocarbon dating was carried out because it was considered that the calcareous sediments would make this unreliable. The dating has been estimated from the tephra dating shown on Bunting's diagram as 9200 BP = 10100 cal. BP. The date of the elm decline, which has been shown to be synchronous across Europe, is shown as 5100 BP uncalibrated (Smith & Pilcher 1973), 5900 cal. BP. The woodland was dominated by a *Betula* (birch) and *Corylus* (hazel) scrub with considerable *Pinus* (scots pine) pollen recorded, a little *Ulmus* (elm) and occasional *Salix* (willows), *Quercus* (oak) and *Alnus* (alder), with a fern-rich understorey. Grains rarely recorded are *Sorbus* type (rowan type), *Fraxinus* (ash) and *Juniperus* (juniper). The tree pollen attains about 80% of the total pollen and spore counts and Bunting considers that this represents extensive woodland forming a dense canopy.

This woodland was disturbed, presumably by Mesolithic people, at an estimated date of about 5400 BC. At that time the woodland cover briefly decreased with tree pollen reduced to a minimum of 20%. Ferns and grasses expanded and there was an increase in microscopic charcoal. As woodland regenerated and assumed its former dominance reaching 70–80%, *Pinus*, *Quercus* and *Alnus* all seem to have benefitted at the expense of *Corylus* which never recovered its former high values.

At about 5900 cal. BP, all the trees show a dramatic permanent decline to very low values. This is accompanied by an initial fall then small peak of Filicales (ferns), and an increase in *Empetrum* (crowberry), *Calluna* (heather), *Ranunculus* type (buttercup type), *Rumex* (sorrel/dock type), *Plantago lanceolata* (ribwort) and *P. maritima* (sea plantain) with smaller quantities of *Artemisia* (mugwort) and other herbs. A continuous curve for cereal type pollen begins after the rise in herb pollen. Poaceae (grasses) and Cyperaceae (sedges) show the greatest increase and at Quoyloo and Crudale, Bunting's second site, probably represent local overgrowth and dominate the pollen values to the undated top of both sequences. This transition from woodland to herbaceous dominated vegetation shows the development of diverse habitats; heathland, arable and pasture are all indicated. Bunting ascribes these changes to Neolithic farming and suggests that the decline in tree pollen values took place within just a few hundred years at Quoyloo Meadow.

The pollen diagram from Crudale Meadow, about 4km south east of Skara Brae, shows high tree pollen at 50–70% with a similar decline in trees at the elm decline but this is estimated to have taken about a thousand years. The trees continued to be present in small frequencies and were accompanied by an expansion of understorey vegetation, notably grasses and ferns; heathland developed later. A similar vegetational history is therefore depicted from the two sites, only 3 to 4km from Skara Brae, of a woodland reduced to scrub in less than a thousand years.

Table 5.1 gives summaries of those pollen analyses from the west of Mainland which cover the period of, or just after, the elm decline. Pollen diagrams by Keatinge and J.H. Dickson (1979) from the Loch of Skaill, 1km east and Glims Moss, 9km north east of Skara Brae, both radiocarbon dated, show a comparable sequence to the upper part of Bunting's diagrams. A *Betula-Corylus* (birch-hazel) woodland together with *Pinus* (pine) and small proportions of *Salix* (willow), *Ulmus* (elm), *Quercus* (oak), *Alnus* (alder) and a little *Fraxinus* (ash) are indicated at both sites. Tree pollen values are, however, lower at both these sites. Loch of Skaill is close to the sea and

became more exposed to salt spray at *ca*. 3000 BC when the Bay of Skaill was formed (Keatinge & J.H. Dickson 1979).

Glims Moss supported a less dense woodland, probably reflecting the waterlogged areas in the vicinity unsuitable for tree colonisation. The decline in trees is also less marked at Glims Moss where they seem to have been partly replaced by a more open herbaceous and later heath vegetation.

The analyses from the Loch of Skaill show a well-marked decline in *Betula* (birch) and some reduction in already low values for the other trees excepting *Alnus* (alder) which remains unchanged. The birch was seemingly largely replaced by grasses with the beginning of a continuing presence of *Calluna* (heather), *Plantago lanceolata* (ribwort plantain) and small values for other open ground herbs. Open woodland is suggested by low fern values which declined further as the woodland was progressively removed. Pollen analyses from two Neolithic chambered tombs provide evidence of the vegetation further to the east.

A pollen sample thought to represent the ground surface at the time of the construction of the chambered tomb at Maes Howe, some 10 km south east of Skara Brae, and two samples from the ditch surrounding the tomb, show similar tree values to the above sites (Godwin 1956). The earlier sample shows that heathland had already developed although grassland predominated in the later samples. This was confirmed from a pollen series by R.L. Jones taken through the northern part of the ditch surrounding Maes Howe. A short pollen profile shows a further decline in tree pollen values and a herb dominated landscape with a continuous curve for cereal pollen (Davidson *et al.* 1976).

At Howe, two analyses from the original ground surface beneath a chambered tomb mound show low tree pollen values of about 16% of total pollen and spores, with moderate grass and some ferns (Dickson 1994).

It appears that at all these sites as the trees were progressively removed, the herbaceous vegetation responded in various ways, probably depending on grazing pressure. The decline in tree pollen in Orkney seems to have begun at about the same time as the elm decline in other parts of Britain. The predominantly low tree pollen values at the two chambered tomb sites presumably reflects an almost total tree clearance for the erection of tombs and standing stones at this ceremonial centre of the island.

The main trees on west Mainland seem to have been birch and hazel. These are the trees together with willow which are represented by remains in peat both on Mainland and some of the other Orkney islands (author's unpublished data and E. Bullard pers. comm.). The earliest charcoal evidence we shall be assessing is from Skara Brae. The radiocarbon dates are late Neolithic (Clarke 1976). Clarke suggests that the occupation lasted from 2500 BC until 2000 BC (4450–3950 BP) or from around 3100 BC until 2450 BC (5050–4400 cal. BP). To judge from the analyses we have been considering, woodland in

Table 5.1: Neolithic phases from pollen analyses from west mainland, Orkney.

SITE	DATING	TREES	HEATHS	GRASSES	CEREALS	HERBS EX. CYP	FERNS
CRUDALE	pre-5900	high	+	low	-	v low	low
	c. 5900	mod >	+	v low - mod	+	+	mod
	post-5900	low	v low <	low - mod	+	v low	low - mod
QUOYLOO	pre-5900	high	+	v low - low	-	+	low
	c. 5900	>	+	<	-	v low	>
	post-5900	low - +	+ - low	mod	+	low	v low - low
LOCH OF SKAILL	pre-5900	mod - high	o - v low	low - mod	-	v low	low >
	post-5900	mod >		mod	-	v low <	v low >
GLIMS MOSS	pre-5900	mod	o - v low	v low - low	-	low	low - mod
	post-5900	v low - low	v low - mod	v low - mod	-	mod	+
MAES HOWE '56	pre - & post-tomb	v low - mod	mod - v low	mod	-	low	v low - mod
MAES HOWE '76	post-tomb	v low	v low	low - mod	low	mod	v low
HOWE	pre-tomb	low	v low	mod	-	low	low

ca. 5900 cal. BP = elm decline
Pollen as % total land pollen + spores

Key:
Cyp, Cyperaceae (sedges)
<, rising
>, falling
+, present
v low, very low, less than 10%
low c 10–20%
mod, moderate, c 21–50%
high, c 51–80%

CRUDALE (Bunting 1994) pre-5900, P3a; *ca.* 5900, P3b; post-5900, P4a.
QUOYLOO (Bunting 1994) pre-5900, P3c; *ca.* 5900, P3c (top); post-5900, P4a.
LOCH OF SKAILL (Keatinge & Dickson 1979) pre-5900, LS1; post-5900, LS2a.
GLIMS MOSS (Keatinge & Dickson 1979) pre-5900, GM1; post-5900, GM2.
MAES HOWE (Godwin 1956) OLS & ditch surrounding chambered tomb, 3 counts.
MAES HOWE (Davidson *et al.* 1976) ditch surrounding chambered tomb, MHN-1.
HOWE (Dickson 1994) OLS beneath chambered tomb, 2 counts.

the west of Mainland was declining throughout this period. Table 5.2 shows the number of charcoal fragments identified from bulk sievings on site of both the older and younger midden deposits. Trench 1 contexts 68 to 39 are from older midden deposits and 34 to 10 and Trench 2 are from later middens; small samples have been combined. Only a few grams are represented in total; the weight for each taxon is generally in proportion to the number of fragments.

The conifers *Picea* (spruce), *Larix* cf *laricina* (cf tamarack), *Abies* (silver fir) and *Pinus strobus* type (Weymouth pine type) are all non-native trees but all grow on the eastern coast of North America. It is suggested that they arrived as drift wood. This is confirmed for the spruce

Table 5.2: Skara Brae charcoal expressed as number of fragments.

CALIBRATED DATES BP	TRENCH 1 *ca.* 5050		TRENCH 11 *ca.* 4400	*ca.* 4400
CONTEXT	68	65–39	34–10	13
Alnus (Alder)	62	60	29	176
Betula spp (Birches)	37	57	6	38
Cf *Cornus* (cf Dogwood)	–	–	–	1
Corylus (Hazel)	5	26	2	24
Crataegus/Malus type (Hawthorn/Wild Apple type)	–	2	2	1
Fraxinus (Ash)	–	–	–	1
Juniperus (Juniper)	–	–	–	1
Cf *Juniperus* (cf Juniper)	1	–	2	–
Pinus sylvestris (Scots Pine)	1	14	9	65
Populus (Aspen/Poplar)	1	2	–	6
Prunus avium type (Wild Cherry type)	–	4	1	–
P. Avium/padus type (Wild Cherry/Bird Cherry type)	1	1	–	2
Prunus spinosa type (Blackthorn type)	–	–	–	5
Quercus (Oak)	1	9	15	28
Salix (Willow)	4	10	21	35
Sorbus (Rowan type)	2	10	5	16
Ulmus (Elm)	1	–	–	53
Viburnum (Guelder Rose/Wayfaring-tree)	–	–	–	1
Driftwood				
Abies (Silver Fir)	5	–	–	–
Larix (Larch)	–	–	–	4
Cf *Larix* (cf Larch)	–	–	–	1
Larix/Picea (Larch/Spruce)	4	–	–	13
Picea (Spruce)	25	22	14	34
Pinus strobus gp (Weymouth Pine gp)	–	–	–	1
No. of identified fragments	149	215	105	512

by tunnels made by the ship's worm, a species of *Teredo*, in some of the unburnt wood. These conifer taxa are well known from coastal archaeological sites in Orkney, Shetland and the Western Isles (J H Dickson 1992; 1994).

Most of the other tree taxa represent a species-rich mainly deciduous woodland which is probably the climax vegetation on calcareous bedrock such as that on Mainland Orkney. With the exception of *Cornus*, most of the other taxa can be found growing on base-rich substrata in northwest Sutherland and some in relict woodlands in Caithness (E. Bullard pers. comm.). *Alnus* is restricted to the wetter parts. Native *Pinus* is rarely present although more common in the past; pine showed a general decline in northern Scotland after 3800 BP resulting from increasing wetness (Gear & Huntley 1991). The list of trees is greater than that shown in the pollen analyses because rosaceous trees such as *Crataegus* (hawthorn), *Malus* (apple), *Prunus avium/P. padus* type (wild cherry /bird cherry type), *P. spinosa* type (blackthorn type) and *Sorbus* (rowan type) together with *Viburnum* (guelder-rose/wayfaring-tree) are all insect pollinated and their grains are not sufficiently widely dispersed to be found consistently in pollen cores.

Such rich deciduous woodland has a field layer of ferns and tall herbs with shade tolerant grasses but it has already been noted that fern spores decreased gradually through the Neolithic levels at the nearby Loch of Skaill and grass and heather pollen increased. Midden samples from several levels have also produced little evidence of a shade tolerant ground flora; but instead the vegetation represented by the waterlogged seeds and other plant remains is of a heathy grassland type with *Calluna* (heather), *Empetrum* (crowberry) and *Juniperus* (juniper) as shrub heath elements with many herbs such as *Potentilla erecta* (tormentil) and *Ranunculus acris* and *R. repens* (meadow and creeping buttercup). Grass fruits do not generally preserve well and only *Danthonia* (heath-grass) has been recorded consistently although *Poa* spp. (meadow grasses) and *Agrostis* spp. (bents) are present.

Scrub woodland of a similar type on mainland Scotland is frequently grazed by stock and deer and if the grazing becomes sufficiently intense as to prevent trees from regenerating, a semi-natural calcicolous pasture develops (Rodwell 1991, 166). It is notable that among the many bones in the midden are those of cattle (*Bos*) with a very few red deer (*Cervus elaphus*) also represented. It is well known that both cattle and deer browse eagerly on young saplings and so prevent successful regeneration of trees. Sheep (*Ovis*), with bones also present in quantity, would also profit from the expanding grassland and fairly intensive grazing would prevent the spread of heather. It seems from the results that *Betula* and *Alnus* may have been the woods most used; birch perhaps because it burns well. Both would probably have been locally available, growing by the shores of the nearby Loch of Skaill.

The recovery of such a rich tree and shrub flora is no doubt due in part to the large quantity of midden which

was sieved; but few wooden artefacts were found and unburnt wood was usually present as small pieces, mainly a few cm in diameter. It seems probable that the charred wood represents mainly firewood but this was not necessarily gathered near to the settlement. Preliminary pollen analyses from the middens show very low values for tree pollen (Dickson forthcoming). This charcoal assemblage seems to represent the species-rich woodland already very much in decline in this part of Mainland Orkney. The decline was probably begun by people and their animals but was thought by Keatinge and J H Dickson (1979) to have been hastened in this coastal area by an exceptional sand storm recorded in deposits around the Bay of Skaill. This dates from the period of the elm decline.

The second part of this paper is a brief consideration of the post-Neolithic woodland. The evidence for woodland during the Bronze Age is sparse in the west of Mainland Orkney. Habitation sites have proved elusive and few of the many cremation sites have yet been excavated. One such barrow at Mousland shows birch to have been the sole wood used (Dickson *et al.* 1994) but this may reflect its situation on a bleak moorland hillside.

At *ca.* 3400 BP blanket peat formation began on the hills. This is thought to have been due to a combination of increased wetness and high grazing pressure (Keatinge & J.H. Dickson 1979). Therefore the habitats suitable for trees became increasingly limited, especially on the hillsides. The Iron Age on Orkney is notable for its many broch sites. Some of these massive circular towers remained in use for many centuries and the settlement around the broch site at Howe was inhabited for over a thousand years (Ballin Smith 1994).

Table 5.3 shows wood and heather from the later part of the occupation at Howe. This Table has been extracted from the results in Table 2 given by Dickson (1994). Only the Middle Iron Age (1st to 4th centuries cal. AD) and Late Iron Age (4th to 7th centuries cal. AD) are listed here; the latter corresponds in age to early Pictish but there is a lack of Pictish artefacts at the site and so the author prefers to call it Late Iron Age.

The local woodland seems to have been reduced to alder, birch and willow. Rare finds of other woods could represent artefacts which have been brought in. Spruce and cf tamarack once again represent driftwood.

It is particularly interesting that a furnace of Middle or Late Iron Age date was found still full of willow charcoal used for iron smelting. Evidence for iron working at Howe began in the Early Iron Age and continued through to the Late Iron Age and almost 200kg of ores, slag etc were recovered, mainly from the Middle and Late Iron Age levels. The number of samples containing wood is, in the Late Iron Age, only 84 (out of 235) against 127 (out of 167) of Middle Iron Age date. There is a striking increase in the number of Late Iron Age contexts containing heather. Heather twigs were sometimes accompanied by other heathland species, such as seeds of certain sedges and grasses. These have been shown to be characteristic of

Table 5.3: Wood and heather in Iron Age samples from Howe, Orkney.

CALIBRATED 14C DATES AD	MIA ? 1st/2nd–4th c.	LIA 4th–7th c.
No. of samples	167	235
No. containing wood	127	84
Alnus (Alder & cf Alder)	4	2
Betula (Birch)	4	–
Fraxinus (Ash)	–	1
Larix cf *laricina* (cf Tamarack)	1	–
Picea (Spruce & cf. Spruce)	14	2
Prunus avium/padus (Wild/Bird-cherry type)	–	1
Salix (Willow)	104	78

heathy turf (Dickson 1994) which used to be burnt as back peats on Orkney, to eke out the fuel (Fenton 1978, 207, 212). This suggests that wood was scarce.The possibility that industrial activity finally removed the scrub woodland in southwest Mainland Orkney is strengthened when it is considered that 16 more Iron Age brochs and other settlements have been found on Mainland within a 10km radius of Howe. (Shepherd 1994, Illus. 161). The nearby north coast of Hoy is rich in iron ore so fuel demands may have been high for smelting and smithing, in addition to normal domestic requirements. It is, however, not known how many of these sites were engaged in smithing or smelting as such evidence has either not been fully excavated or not analysed (McDonnell 1994).

CONCLUSION

It appears that in the main people were responsible for changing the landscape of at least this part of Mainland Orkney from well wooded to virtually treeless. This change seems to have begun in the Mesolithic and accelerated during the Late Neolithic. The remaining scrub appears to have been largely removed during the long industrial Iron Age.

The degree of agricultural use on Orkney has never been static. Arable farming has intensified during the last half century but rough grazing sems to have declined (Berry 1985). About half the surface area is occupied by agricultural land at present. Industry has also had an impact on the natural vegetation. Increasing awareness of the environment together with agricultural surpluses may present a better prospect for the future. Trees are being grown from local seed and the time may come when woodland returns once again to Orkney.

Acknowledgements

The Skara Brae work was funded by the National Museums of Scotland and Historic Scotland. I am grateful to Miss E.R. Bullard and to my husband, Dr Jim Dickson, for helpful discussion.

REFERENCES

Ballin Smith, B. (ed.) (1994). *Howe four millennia of Orkney prehistory, excavations 1978–1982*. Edinburgh: Society of Antiquaries of Scotland monograph no. **9**.

Berry, R.J. (1985). *The Natural History of Orkney*. London: Collins New Naturalist.

Bremner, A.H. and Bullard, E.R. (1990). *Trees & Shrubs in Orkney*. Privately published, E.R. Bullard, Toftwood, Kirkwall, Orkney, and A.H. Bremner, Bendigo, St Ola, Orkney, 1–36.

Bunting, M.J. (1994). Vegetation history of Orkney, Scotland, pollen records from two small basins in west Mainland. *New Phytologist* **128**, 771–92.

Bullard, E.R. (1995). *Wildflowers in Orkney, a New Checklist*. Privately published, E.R. Bullard, Toftwood, Kirkwall, Orkney, 1–28.

Chapman, H.M. and Crawford, R.M.M. (1981). Growth and Re-generation in Britain's most Northerly Natural Woodland. *Transactions of the Botanical Society of Edinburgh* **43** (4), 327–5.

Clarke, D.V. (1976). *The Neolithic Village at Skara Brae, Orkney 1972–3 Excavations*. Edinburgh: Her Majesty's Stationery Office.

Davidson, D.A., Jones, R.L. and Renfrew, C. (1976). Palaeo-environmental reconstruction and evaluation: a case study from Orkney. *Transactions of the Institute of British Geographers* N S **1** (3), 346–61.

Dickson, C. (1994). Plant remains, pp. 125–139 in Ballin Smith, B. (ed.) *Howe Four Millennia of Orkney Prehistory*. Edinburgh: Society of Antiquaries of Scotland monograph no. **9**.

Dickson, C., Downes, J., Mckinley, J.I. and Hinton, P. (1994). The contents of the cist, pp. 146–47 in Downes, J. Excavations of a Bronze Age burial at Mousland, Stromness, Orkney. *Proceedings of the Society of the Antiquaries of Scotland* **124**, 141–54.

Dickson, J.H. (1992). North American driftwood, especially *Picea* (Spruce), from archaeological sites in the Hebrides and Northern Isles of Scotland. *Review of Palaeobotany and Palynology* **73**, 49–56.

Dickson, J.H. (1994). Ancient driftwood on the Northern Isles and its origin. *The Orkney Naturalist*, 8–9.

Donaldson, A.M. (1986). Pollen analysis, pp. 5–14 in Morris, C.D. and Emery, N. The setting for the Brough of Deerness, Orkney. *Northern Studies* **23**.

Fenton, A. (1978). *The Northern Isles Orkney and Shetland*. Edinburgh: John Donald.

Gear, A.J. and Huntley, B. (1991). Rapid changes in the range limits of Scots Pine 4000 years ago. *Science* **251**, 544–7.

Godwin, H. (1956). "Report on the peat samples". Appendix, in Childe, V.G. Maes Howe. *Proceedings of the Society of the Antiquaries of Scotland* **88**, 169–72.

Keatinge, T.H. and Dickson, J.H. (1979). Mid-Flandrian changes in vegetation on Mainland Orkney. *New Phytologist* **82**, 585–612.

McDonnell, J.G. (1994). Slag Report, pp. 228–234 in Ballin Smith, B. (ed.) *Howe Four Millennia of Orkney Prehistory Excavations 1978–1982*. Edinburgh: Society of Antiquaries of Scotland monograph no. **9**.

Moar, N.T. (1969). Two pollen diagrams from the Mainland, Orkney Islands. *New Phytologist* **68**, 201–8.

Prentice, H.C. and Prentice, I.C. (1975). The hill vegetation of North Hoy, Orkney. *New Phytologist* **75**, 313–67.

Rodwell, J.S. (1991). *British Plant Communities volume 1 Woodland and scrub*. Cambridge: Cambridge University Press.

Shepherd, A. (1994). Howe: a review of the sequence, pp. 267–90 in Ballin Smith, B. (ed.) *Howe Four Millennia of Orkney Prehistory Excavations 1978–1982*. Edinburgh: Society of Antiquaries of Scotland monograph no. **9**.

Smith, A.G. and Pilcher, J.R. (1973). Radiocarbon dates and vegetational history of the British Isles, *New Phytologist* **72**, 903–14.

6. Post Iron Age Vegetation History and Climate Change on the North York Moors: A Preliminary Report

Richard C. Chiverrell and Margaret A. Atherden

Peat sequences from the blanket mire site at May Moss and the valley mire site at Fen Bogs, on the North York Moors, were analysed using a variety of palaeoecological and sedimentological techniques. The investigation concentrates on peat accumulation which post-dates the Iron Age and Romano-British woodland clearances *ca.* 330 BC. The techniques concentrate on the plant sub-fossils within the peat sediment including pollen analysis, and macro-fossil analysis. A quantitative analysis of the degree of peat humification was also made. These techniques analyse fluctuations in the regional vegetation, local vegetation and surface moisture of the mire at the time of sedimentation.

The pollen diagrams contain evidence of fluctuating degrees of human interference on the regional vegetation, including rapid increases in arboreal pollen after the Roman withdrawal. Subsequent fluctuations in regional vegetation can be linked to political, cultural, and demographic changes, and specifically variations in local land use.

Macro-fossil and humification results from May Moss enable the authors to reconstruct changes in local mire surface moisture. The May Moss site demonstrated at least twelve shifts in mire surface moisture during the last 2000 years, which may reflect changes in effective precipitation given the mire's ombrotrophic nature.

Keywords: Human impact, climate change, peat stratigraphy, vegetation change, North York Moors.

INTRODUCTION

This paper examines the evidence for vegetation and climate change contained within the North York Moors peat stratigraphies of the last 2000 years. Recent research into peat stratigraphies suggests raised mires (Barber 1981; Barber *et al.* 1994a; b) and ombrotrophic blanket peat (Blackford 1993; Blackford & Chambers 1993; 1995) are excellent palaeoclimate archives. Ombrotrophic mire peat stratigraphies are essentially a record of effective palaeo-precipitation, because the only source of moisture for ombrotrophic mires is rainfall. A variety of factors controls the composition of the local blanket mire vegetation, but the abundance of surface moisture is particularly important. Evidence of past vegetation and local hydrology at the time of sedimentation, contained within peat stratigraphies

from ombrotrophic localities allows the reconstruction of mire surface moisture and, by inference, palaeoclimate.

Previous palaeoecological research on the North York Moors includes several complete Holocene sequences (Atherden 1976; 1979; Jones 1977; 1978). However much of the regional palaeoecological research concentrates on the Mesolithic and Mesolithic/Neolithic transition (Innes 1989). The last 2000 years have been comparatively underworked due mainly to the lack of organic profiles covering this period (Simmons 1995).

This paper examines changes within local and regional vegetation records, which are interpreted with reference to established climate (Lamb 1977; Jones & Bradley 1992) and local land-use histories (Spratt 1993; Spratt & Harrison 1989). Fluctuation in the regional arboreal vegetation

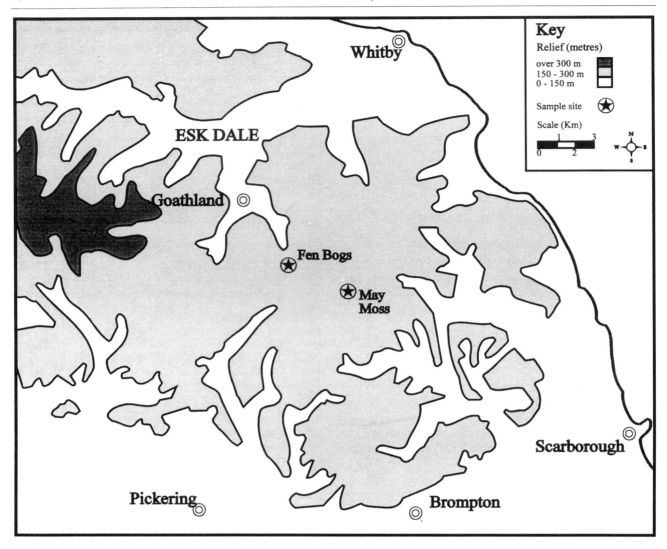

Figure 6.1: Location map for May Moss and Fen Bogs.

provides a record of human exploitation of wood resources and reflects the changes in the political, social, economic and climatic conditions affecting the population of the North York Moors.

SITE DESCRIPTION

The two study sites are on the central eastern watershed of the North York Moors (Figure 6.1). Fen Bogs (SE 853977) is a valley mire at the head of Newton Dale. It is a Site of Special Scientific Interest (SSSI) recognised as an excellent example of an upland mire with rheotrophic and ombrotrophic facies (Atherden 1976). May Moss (SE 876960) is a large area covered by actively forming blanket peat. It is an ombrotrophic water-shedding blanket mire formed on a plateau draining to the north and south. The site is designated an SSSI by English Nature. Atherden (1976; 1979)

extracted virtually complete Holocene pollen sequences from both sites. Both suggest that the top two metres of peat accumulated during the last 2000 years. Therefore both peat sequences might eventually yield fine temporal resolution palaeoclimate and palaeovegetation data.

METHODS

Coring technique

The cores were extracted using a Russian borer. Three replicate 2.70m. cores of peat were extracted from both sites[1]. The three cores were located no further than 1m. apart.

Standard pollen analyses

Sub-samples of 1 cm³ were extracted from the cores using

---

[1] A series of cores has been extracted from May Moss for future research. The core referred to in this paper is Core D of this series.

a volumetric sampler and prepared using a KOH and sieving technique. Acetolysis was avoided to minimise damage to non-pollen palynomorphs. The preparations were stained with safranin and mounted in glycerol. Counts were made along evenly spaced transects, with identification of pollen grains and spores aided by reference to Faegri and Iversen (1993) and Moore *et al.* (1991). Counts continued until at least 150 arboreal pollen grains per sample had been counted, including *Corylus avellana*-type (Bennett *et al.* 1994).

The pollen diagrams (Figures 6.2 and 6.3) were produced using TILIA and TILIAGRAPH computer packages (Grimm 1991). The pollen diagrams are divided into local pollen assemblage zones (LPAZ) using minimum variance stratigraphically constrained cluster analysis implemented through TILIA (Grimm 1991). The LPAZ are prefixed by the site designations FB and MMD for Fen Bogs and May Moss respectively and numbered in Roman Numerals from the base upwards.

Macro-fossil analysis

The relative abundance of the macrofossil components in peat has been widely used to reconstruct fluctuations in past mire surface wetness and palaeoclimate, however much of this research is based on lowland raised mire peat stratigraphies (Barber 1981; Barber *et al.* 1994a, b). The 120μm sieve residues from the pollen preparations for May Moss were analysed to assess the viability of applying similar techniques to an ombrotrophic blanket mire.

At May Moss the macrofossil assemblages are dominated by *Sphagnum* sp., Ericaceae and *Eriophorum vaginatum* remains. Previous macrofossil analysis suggests *Sphagnum* dominated peat indicates wetter conditions, whereas peat dominated by Ericaceae and *Eriophorum vaginatum* is indicative of drier conditions (Barber 1981; Tallis 1994).

Fluctuations in the species composition within *Sphagnum*-dominated peat provides further evidence of changes in surface wetness. *Sphagnum* section *Acutifolia* tends to prefer drier conditions (Daniels & Eddy 1990). *Sphagnum* section *Acutifolia* includes *Sphagnum capillifolium* which currently occupies the top of hummocks at May Moss. *Sphagnum papillosum* and *Sphagnum imbricatum* prefer slightly wetter conditions forming large dense hummocks and covering more extensive lawns (Daniels & Eddy 1990). *Sphagnum* section *Cuspidata* probably consists of *Sphagnum cuspidatum* and *Sphagnum recurvum*, which occupy wet hollow habitats (Daniels & Eddy 1990). This broad ecological framework enables reconstruction of past moisture conditions on the mire surface, consequently providing proxy evidence of palaeoclimate.

Initially the relative abundance of the main peat constituents (Monocotyledons, *Sphagnum*, Ericaceae remains, and Unidentifiable Organic Matter) was estimated by pouring the residue into a petri dish marked with fifty 1cm² grid squares, gauging the relative abundance of each component in each square on a scale of 1 to 10. The abundance scores were then percentaged and plotted as percentages on a composite graph demonstrating fluctuations in the dominant peat components.

The composition of the *Sphagnum* community was quantified using a variation on the "Quadrat and Leaf Count" method (Barber *et al.* 1994). Approximately one hundred *Sphagnum* leaves were randomly selected and identified using the keys of Smith (1978) and Daniels & Eddy (1990). The *Sphagnum* abundances (Figure 6.4) are expressed as percentages of estimated total percentage *Sphagnum* content in the peat sediment.

In addition any other identifiable macro-fossil remains were also counted; these included Ericaceae leaves, various seeds, beetle remains and Oribatid mites. These are expressed on Figure 4 as raw counts.

Degree of humification

The degree of peat humification in ombrotrophic mires reflects changes in the hydrological conditions of the mire surface at the time of sedimentation. Therefore fluctuations in the degree of peat humification through time can be interpreted as an indicator of effective precipitation and by inference climatic change (Blackford & Chambers 1995). Changes or shifts to poorly humified peat indicate increased moisture on the mire surface and suggest a change to a wetter climate.

Colorimetric analysis of the degree of peat humification was undertaken on 2cm thick contiguous sub-samples throughout the May Moss core. Percentage transmission was determined on a Perkin Elmer Lambda 11 UV/VIS Spectrometer following the recommendations and methods of Blackford & Chambers (1993). Essentially 8% NaOH was used to extract the humic acids, the measurement filter wavelength was 540nm and each analysis took 2h. from addition of NaOH to the time of measurement. The humification curve is displayed on Figure 6.5.

PREVIOUS RESEARCH

Geochronology

Unfortunately neither peat sequence has been independently dated. However Atherden (1976) produced a radiocarbon dated profile from Fen Bogs, which contained three dates during the last 2000 years. These dates referred to three particular vegetation changes that are recognisable in the new pollen profiles. Therefore preliminary correlation is made between changes in palynostratigraphy and the radiocarbon dates produced by Atherden (1976) displayed in Table 6.1. Radiocarbon dating of the peat sequences is essential and will eventually remove the problem of correlating dates based on changes in

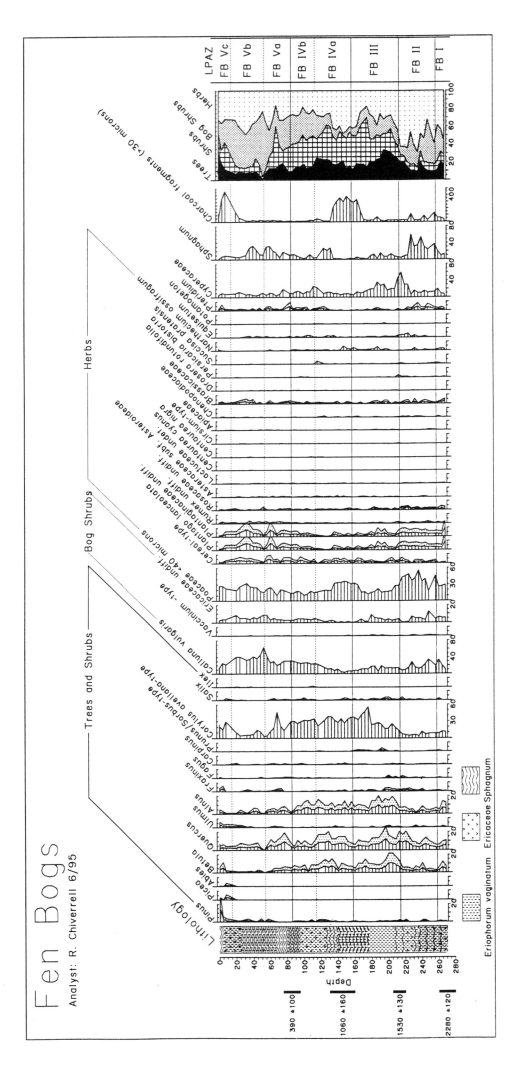

Figure 6.2: Relative pollen percentage diagram from Fen Bogs. Pollen taxa are expressed as a percentage of total pollen. Aquatics and spores are expressed as a percentage of total pollen plus aquatics and spores. The hashed exaggeration curves indicate a 2x exaggeration on selected taxa. The radiocarbon date depth bars indicate the probable location on the profile of the dates obtained by Atherden (1976). These depths are estimations based on palynostratigraphic correlation.

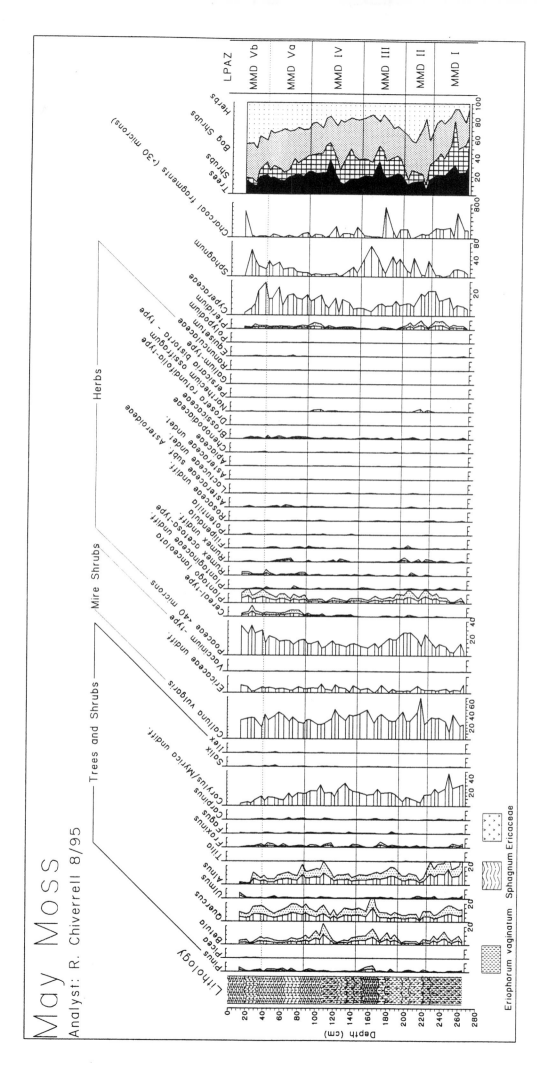

May Moss

Analyst: R. Chiverrell 8/95

Figure 6.3: Relative pollen percentage diagram from May Moss. Pollen taxa are expressed as a percentage ot total pollen. Aquatics and spores are expressed as a percentage of total pollen plus aquatics and spores. The hashed exaggeration curves indicate a 2x exaggeration on selected taxa.

Table 6.1: Palynostratigraphic correlation with radiocarbon dates from a previously published Fen Bogs peat sequence (Atherden 1976).

Depth at Fen Bogs	Depth at May Moss	Palynostratigraphic Event	Radio-carbon Date Code	Radiocarbon Date Years BP	Calibrated age* AD/BC	Calibrated age* AD/BC (±1 σ)	Calibrated age* AD/BC (±2 σ)
75–95 cm	75–85 cm	Before *Corylus*, *Quercus* and *Fraxinus* increase.	T 1151	390 ±100	AD 1486	AD 1432 –1645	AD 1331–1954
130–160 cm	125–140 cm	Base of subsequent increase in arboreal taxa.	T 1087	1060 ±160	AD 995	AD 780 –1185	AD 655 –1283
210–220 cm	185–195 cm	Post-Roman woodland regeneration.	T 1086	1530 ±130	AD 542	AD 412 –651	AD 243 –773
260–280 cm	225–230 cm	Iron Age Romano-British woodland clearance.	T 1085	2280 ±120	376, 370, 364, 265 BC	407 –172 BC	761 –1 BC

* Calibrated using Calib 3.0.3c (Stuiver & Reimer 1993).

palynostratigraphy across a region possibly affected by variations in local vegetation cover.

Vegetation history

Atherden (1976; 1979) produced pollen diagrams from both Fen Bogs and May Moss. These analyses covered most of the Holocene and included interpretation of the period under investigation in this paper. Tables 6.1 and 6.2 provide a summary of :

· The vegetation changes identified in the peat sequences. The sequences are divided into the LPAZ devised by Atherden (1976; 1979)

· The cultural and climatic interpretation of the vegetation changes

· The radiocarbon age determinations carried out on those vegetation changes (Atherden 1976; 1979).

This paper re-examines the post Iron Age vegetation history of both sites and provides detailed interpretation of vegetation changes encountered within the broad palaeoecological /cultural zones identified in Table 6.2.

DISCUSSION

The regional vegetation history of the central eastern North York Moors.

Atherden (1979) suggests the higher parts of the North York Moors were largely deforested by the end of the Iron Age, thereby creating optimum conditions for wind dispersal of pollen throughout the last 2000 years. Consequently it is likely that the arboreal pollen component represents sporadic wooded areas maintained by settlements or landowners, probably located on valley sides and on agriculturally marginal land.

The following discussion concentrates on human exploitation of the landscape, and how this exploitation is

represented in the vegetation history. Reference is made to established knowledge of the archaeology (Spratt 1993) and history (Spratt & Harrison 1989; Musgrove 1990) of the North York Moors.

The basal zones of both pollen diagrams (Figures 6.2 and 6.3) LPAZ FB I and MMD I are characterised by high arboreal pollen frequencies, specifically *Betula, Quercus, Alnus* and *Corylus avellana*-type. These arboreal pollen frequencies decline markedly at the top of FB I and MMD I. Previous research on the regional palaeoecology suggests this arboreal decline marks the beginning of significant Iron Age and Romano-British woodland clearances (Atherden 1976; 1979; 1989). Radiocarbon dating of this event at Fen Bogs (Atherden 1976) and Harwood Dale Bog (Atherden 1989) suggests the clearances began in the fourth century BC.

This major clearance provides a convenient starting point for this study. In order to facilitate interpretation of vegetation changes after the fourth century BC the discussion is divided into four broad historical periods.

The Iron Age and Romano-British period (ca. 330 BC to AD 542)

FB II and MMD II correspond to the Iron Age and Romano-British Period. Initially this period is characterised by declining pollen frequencies of arboreal taxa and these low frequencies continue to the top of FB II and MMD II. The end of the woodland clearance phase is indicated by increases in arboreal pollen frequencies from the top of FB II and MMD II. Previous research at Fen Bogs radiocarbon dates the top of the woodland clearance to *ca.* AD 542, confirming the clearance initiated in the Iron Age and continued throughout the period of Roman occupation of Britain (Atherden 1976). Associated with the low arboreal pollen frequencies are increases in the abundance of herb taxa. The herb taxa include cereals, *Plantago lanceolata* and Brassicaceae.

On the basis of archaeological and palaeobotanical

Table 6.2: A summary of the vegetation history uncovered in previous palynological research at Fen Bogs and May Moss (Atherden 1976; 1979).

May Moss LPAZ	Fen Bogs LPAZ	PERIOD	AGE (Radiocarbon Years BP)	VEGETATION CHANGE	CULTURAL INTERPRETATION
MM 10	FB 10	Modern	150 –	Decline in arboreal population and expansion in Ericaceae. *Pinus* frequencies increase at the top of both profiles.	Modern moorland management for grouse shooting with sheep grazing as a secondary activity. Modern conifer plantations.
MM 9	FB 9	Tudor - Stuart	390 –150	Limited woodland regeneration indicated by increases in *Betula, Fraxinus* and *Corylus* frequencies. Cereal and ruderal species remain abundant.	Dissolution of the Monasteries resulted in a reduced scale of agriculture in upland areas. Intensification of arable farming on lower ground causing increases in ruderals.
MM 8	FB 8	Viking - Medieval	1060 – 390	Woodland clearance phase affecting most tree species. Poaceae, cereals, *Plantago lanceolata* and *Rumex* increase in abundance.	Viking and Medieval economic/demographic expansion on the moors. Medieval felling in the Royal Forest of Pickering. Arable and pastoral activity on the moors.
MM 7	FB 7	Dark Ages	1530 – 1060	Woodland regeneration indicated by increases in *Quercus, Ulmus, Alnus, Betula* and *Corylus* frequencies. Continued presence of cereal and	Roman withdrawal from Britain. Continuing arable and pastoral farming by native population, supplemented by Anglo-Scandinavian colonisation
MM 6	FB 6	Iron Age - Romano-British	2280 – 1530	Significant regional woodland clearance with declines in most tree species. Poaceae and ruderal pollen dominate the assemblages.	Iron Age cultural expansion and pastoral farming. Romano-British pastoral and arable activity, particularly on the southern hills.

evidence, Spratt (1993) suggests the Iron Age population of the North York Moors was expanding markedly, especially in coastal areas, upland valleys and the southern limestone hills. Additionally there is evidence of population expansion in the lowland areas surrounding the moors in the Vale of Pickering and the Cleveland lowlands (Spratt 1993). The agricultural activities of this expanding population are a probable cause of increased Iron Age woodland clearance. Cereal pollen is present at Fen Bogs throughout the Iron Age suggesting continuous arable activity.

Set against this background of population and agricultural expansion palaeoecological evidence of the arrival of the Romans is absent. Musgrove (1990) suggests Northern Britain thrived economically under Roman occupation. He also suggests the Romans encouraged grain production in Yorkshire by romanised and native farmers, with the Vale of Pickering contributing grain to feed legions stationed in Malton and York.

This economic expansion has implications for interpretation of palaeoecological records on the North York Moors. There is evidence of cereal pollen at both sites suggesting extra-local arable activity. There is also archaeological evidence of cattle stockades on Levisham Moor (Spratt 1990), which suggests a mixed agricultural economy persisted on the North York Moors during the Iron Age and Romano-British Period. Spratt (1993) suggests settlements were widespread on the southern Tabular Hills during the period of Roman occupation, with arable farming concentrated on the better soils of the Tabular Hills and other areas peripheral to the central moorland (Spratt 1993). Throughout the Roman period arboreal pollen frequencies although lower than during the early Iron Age are relatively abundant at both Fen Bogs and May Moss, including increased abundance of *Betula* and *Fraxinus* at Fen Bogs. This may reflect concentration of arable activity on the better soils at the expense of agricultural activity on the upland moor allowing limited colonisation by invader tree species in marginal areas.

Associated with the Iron Age/Romano-British woodland clearances are high frequencies of Cyperaceae pollen in FB II and MMD II. These may reflect increases in sedge abundance on the bog surface, possibly as a result of the development of a wetter climate during the late Iron Age (Simmons *et al.* 1993).

The Anglo-Scandinavian period (AD 542 to AD 1066)

The Anglo-Scandinavian Period occurs within FB III and MMD III. The beginning of this period is characterised by marked increases in arboreal pollen frequencies specifically *Betula, Alnus, Fraxinus* and *Corylus avellana*-type. *Quercus* frequencies also increase however at May Moss this occurs after the increase in frequency of the other arboreal taxa. Associated with this woodland regeneration is a decline in non-arboreal pollen frequencies, although there are still continuous records of cereals, *Plantago lanceolata* and Brassicaceae.

These changes suggest the Romans' departure had a greater impact on the palaeoecological record than their arrival. It is possible that the removal of this demand for grain combined with a reduction in population, may have reduced the need for cash crops and forced a return to subsistence and local market farming. A reduction in agricultural demand would have reduced pressure on wooded areas and allowed marginal agricultural land to return to scrub woodland dominated initially by heliophytic trees, such as *Betula* and *Fraxinus*.

The remainder of FB III and MMD III is characterised by a gradual decline in arboreal pollen frequencies which suggest the post-Roman woodland regeneration was relatively short-lived. Lang (1989) suggests the distribution of settlements during the Anglo-Scandinavian period changed little from that encountered in Roman Britain, being concentrated mainly on the southern limestone hills and in the coastal region.

The population of North Yorkshire was supplemented by continuous immigration of Germanic and Scandinavian people throughout the fifth to tenth centuries AD (Musgrove 1991; Lang 1989). Yorkshire was a centre for Scandinavian occupation of Britain with a Scandinavian king in York until AD 954. It is possible that a growing population applied pressure on woodland areas causing a decline in arboreal pollen through increased arable and pastoral agriculture and exploitation of wood supplies for building materials and fuel. This view is re-enforced by the continuous presence of cereal and arable weed pollen throughout FB III and MMD III.

The medieval period (AD 1066 to AD 1500)

Atherden (1976a, b; 1979) described the Viking-Medieval Period as a broad clearance phase; however examination of the vegetation changes indicated in Figures 6.2 and 6.3 suggests the picture is more complex. The base of FB IV and MMD IV are characterised by low arboreal pollen frequencies and by high frequencies of cereal and arable weed pollen. This indicates sparse woodland cover and the presence of agricultural activity representing the culmination of land-use trends which began in the Anglo-Scandinavian Period (Harrison & Roberts 1989). It is impossible in the absence of radiocarbon dating of these profiles to link definitively the vegetation changes encountered here with historical events in the landscape history of the North York Moors, however some of the changes warrant further comment.

At both Fen Bogs and May Moss there is a recovery in arboreal pollen which extends towards to the top of FB IVa and MMD IV. The impact of King William's 'harrying of the North' which devastated much of North Yorkshire in the winter of 1069–70 and the period immediately after in which landowners moved populations to encourage economic and agricultural recovery on the better soils of the lowland areas (Harrison & Roberts 1989), probably resulted in the woodland regeneration encountered in FB IVa and MMD IV.

Harrison and Roberts (1989) suggest that after the Norman devastation, the lowlands around the North York Moors experienced a major recovery, which implies the renewal of pressure on woodland areas. However at Fen Bogs the arboreal revival is not short-lived, this may be a function of ample valley-side woodland between Pickering, Brompton and Goathland, an area which became the Royal Forest of Pickering (Harrison & Roberts 1989). However a decline in arboreal pollen frequencies occurs across the FB IVa/FB IVb boundary reaching a minimum at 105cm which may be a product of continued regional agricultural and economic growth. This is supported by records of woodland clearance for agricultural use and extensive illegal felling in the Royal Forest of Pickering (Turton 1894) and specifically in the northern part of the Forest around the settlement of Goathland (Harrison & Roberts 1989; Hollings 1970).

After the minimum at 105cm there is a small recovery in arboreal pollen frequencies followed by a further decline extending to the top of FB IVb. The arboreal recovery in FB IVb maybe a product of demographic collapse caused in part by the Black Death which decimated the population of Yorkshire in 1348–1349 and in further epidemics in the 14th century, reducing land-use pressure on woodland areas (Stamper 1988). The decline in arboreal pollen frequencies to the top of FB IVb suggests the reduction in land-use pressure was relatively short-lived due to a renewal of economic growth. Additionally fluctuations in climate from the 14th century onwards (Lamb 1977; Jones & Bradley 1992) may have encouraged increased wood exploitation for fuel in the Late Medieval Period.

The post-medieval period (AD 1500 to the present day)

The base of FB Va is characterised by increases in arboreal pollen frequencies particularly *Quercus, Alnus* and *Fraxinus*. This arboreal regeneration is associated with the period following the Dissolution, when monastic estates were divided amongst lay farmers, which resulted in a reduction in agricultural activity on the moors.

A significant feature of FB V and MMD V is the increase in abundance of pollen spectra indicating arable activity, specifically Cereal-type and Asteraceae subf. Asteroideae. Hollings (1970) detailed land-use developments around the settlement of Goathland during the Post-Medieval Period. These included increased arable activity

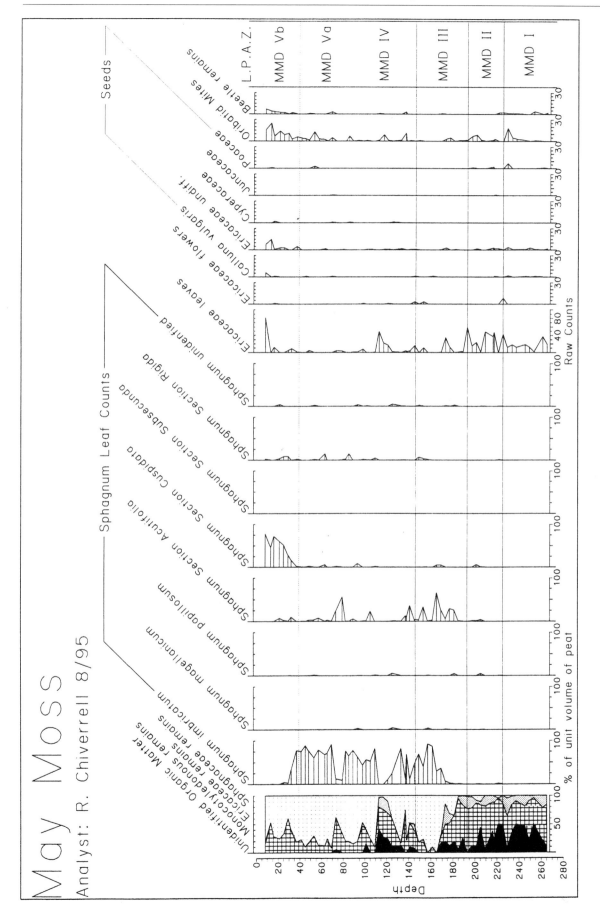

Figure 6.4: Macrofossil diagram from May Moss. The LPAZ are taken from Figure 6.3.

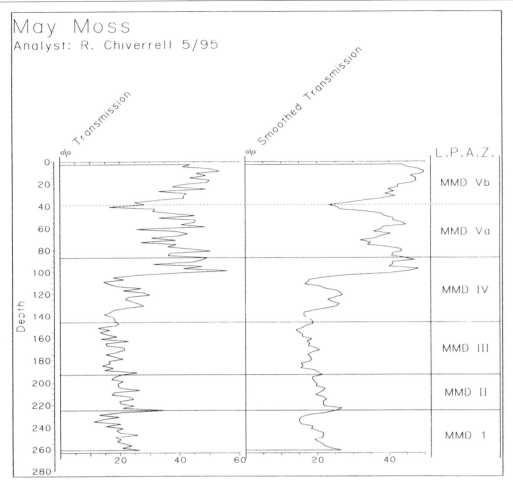

Figure 6.5: Humification diagram from May Moss. The % Smoothed Transmission curve was obtained by taking the three point running mean of the raw data. The LPAZ are taken from Figure 6.3.

within the boundaries of the Royal Forest during the Tudor period and productivity improvement associated with increased private land ownership. *Plantago lanceolata* and *Rumex acetosa* frequencies also increase which may be a product of increased grazing of livestock on the moors during the post-Medieval period (Hollings 1970). Towards the top of FB Va arboreal pollen frequencies decline, which is probably a function of increased agricultural activity. The climatic fluctuations associated with the Little Ice Age may have encouraged a demand for wood as a fuel, although turf was also a local fuel source (Hollings 1970).

FB Vb is characterised by increases in *Calluna vulgaris* and Ericaceae undiff. frequencies, which represents 19th and 20th century management of the moors for grouse shooting alongside sheep farming (Statham 1989). Charcoal peaks at the top of both FB V and MMD V provide further evidence of the heather burning activities involved in modern moorland management.

Finally in FB Vc and at the top of MMD V there is evidence of the impact of modern forestry, specifically

increases in *Pinus* and *Picea* pollen frequencies. Forest planting by the Forestry Commission began in the 1920s in the Dalby, Bickley and Hackness areas (Statham 1989).

Local Blanket Bog Vegetation and Hydrological change during the last 2000 years.

The results of the macrofossil and humification analyses from May Moss identify a number of shifts between dry and wet mire surface conditions. To facilitate comparisons of the evidence for climate change the LPAZ are indicated on both the macrofossil diagram (Figure 6.4) and the humification diagram (Figure 6.5). The palynostratigraphy is used to infer a preliminary chronology for the peat sequence. Charcoal layers indicating local moorland fires (see Figure 6.3) may provide additional evidence of dry mire surface conditions.

Climate changes between wet and dry conditions identified in previous peat-based palaoeclimate research are summarised in Figure 6.6. The surface moisture changes identified at May Moss are discussed in relation to the

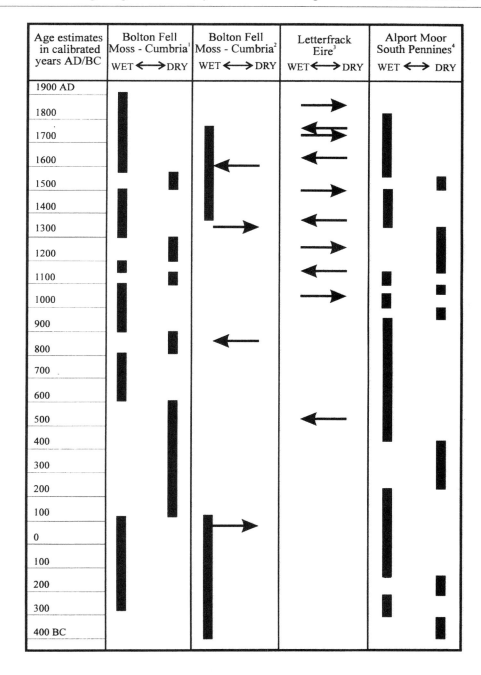

Figure 6.6: Surface moisture shitfs from two blanket mires [3,4] and a raised mire [1,2] from the British Isles. [1]Bolton Fell Moss, Cumbria (Barber 1981). [2]Bolton Fell Moss, Cumbria (Barber et al., 1994a). [3]Letterfrack, western Eire (Blackford & Chambers 1991; 1995). [4]Alport Moor, southern Penines (Tallis 1994).

changes summarised in Figure 6.6, highlighting similarities and differences. The shifts in mire surface conditions and inferred climatic changes at May Moss are summarised in Table 6.3.

LPAZ MMD I (270–225 cm)
At the base of MMD I the peat is well humified and dominated by Monocotyledon and Ericaceae remains,

which suggests the mire surface was relatively dry during the late Bronze Age and early Iron Age. However towards the top of MMD I at 230cm there is a marked shift to less well humified peat and *Sphagnum* leaves are present, indicating the development of a wetter mire surface during the Iron Age.

This Iron Age climate deterioration corresponds with the classic Sub-Boreal/Sub-Atlantic climate change

Table 6.3: Changes in moisture conditions at May Moss inferred from fluctuations in the degree of peat humification and the ecological interpretation of the mire vegetation history uncivered in the plant macrofossil analysis.

SHIFT	DEPTH	PERIOD	HUMIFICATION CHANGE	VEGETATION CHANGE
WET	35 cm	Post Medieval	Well humified to very poorly humified peat	*Sphagnum imbricatum*, replaced by *Sphagnum* section *Cuspidata* at 35 cm
DRY	45 cm	Post Medieval	Very poorly humified to well humified peat	Dominated by *Sphagnum imbricatum* with some *Sphagnum* section *Acutifolia*
WET	65 cm	Early Post Medieval	Well humified to very poorly humified peat	Dominated by *Sphagnum imbricatum*
DRY	80 cm	Early Post Medieval	Very poorly humified to well humified peat	Dominated by *Sphagnum* section *Acutifolia*
WET	110 cm	Late Medieval	Well humified to very poorly humified peat	*S. imbricatum*/Ericaceae/Monocotyledon replaced by *Sphagnum imbricatum*
DRY	125 cm	Medieval	Poorly humified to well humified peat	*Sphagnum imbricatum* replaced by *Sphagnum imbricatum*
WET	135 cm	Early Medieval	Well humified to poorly humified peat	Ericaceae/Monocotyledon replaced by *Sphagnum imbricatum*
DRY	155 cm	Anglo-Scandinavian	Well humified peat	*Sphagnum imbricatum* replaced by *Sphagnum* section *Acutifolia*
WET	170 cm	Anglo-Scandinavian	Well humified to poorly humified peat	Ericaceae/Monocotyledon replaced by *Sphagnum imbricatum*
DRY	180 cm	Anglo-Scandinavian	Gradual regression to well humified peat	Monocotyledon/*Sphagnum* section *Acutifolia* to Ericaceae/Monocotyledon
WET	185 cm	Anglo-Scandinavian	Well humified to poorly humified peat	Ericaceae/Monocotyledon to Ericaceae/Monocotyledon/*Sphagnum*
DRY	200 cm	Romano-British	Poorly humified to well humified peat	Dominated by Ericaceae and Monocotyledon remains
WET	226 cm	Late Iron Age	Well humified to poorly humified peat	Dominated by Ericaceae and Monocotyledon remains

(Sernander 1908). Previous palaeoclimate research on peat stratigraphy from sites across northern Europe suggests the Iron Age climatic deterioration is a regional event (Kilian *et al.* 1995). Evidence of wet mire surface conditions has been recorded *ca.* 285 BC in the southern Pennines, in Cumbria *ca.* 520 BC (Barber *et al.* 1994a) and between *ca.* 736–13 BC (Dickinson 1975). At May Moss the climate signal is complicated by the macrofossil stratigraphy, which suggests the possibility of fluctuation in mire surface wetness during the Iron Age.

LPAZ MMD II (225–193cm)
Well humified peat dominated by Ericaceae and Monocotyledon remains characterises the early part of this zone, suggesting dry mire surface conditions during the Late Iron Age / Romano-British period. There is conflicting evidence of a change in mire surface conditions towards the top of this zone. The peat is well humified, but *Sphagnum* leaves are present in the macrofossil assemblage which suggests a wetter mire surface. However, the *Sphagnum* is mostly *Sphagnum* section *Acutifolia* which includes drier hummock species (Daniels & Eddy 1990). This wetter phase is relatively short-lived, because

at the top of MMD II Sphagnum remains are absent.

This evidence suggests the period of Roman occupation of Britain was characterised by a predominantly dry climate, which supports historical evidence of a warmer climate in north-west Europe during this period (Lamb 1977). Evidence of dry mire surface conditions during this period has been recorded elsewhere in Britain including Cumbria (Barber 1981) and the southern Pennines (Tallis 1994).

LPAZ MMD III (193–146cm)
The base of this zone is characterised by a major change in macrofossil stratigraphy with *Sphagnum* section *Acutifolia* increasing in abundance from 186cm. Subsequently there is a brief dry regression at 175cm followed at 169cm by a massive expansion in the abundance of *Sphagnum* remains, initially *Sphagnum* section *Acutifolia*, but *Sphagnum imbricatum* dominates the assemblage from 165cm onwards. Evidence of this Dark Ages change to a wetter mire surface is less convincing in the humification record which contains minor shifts to poorly humified peat at 190cm and 165cm. These shifts in humification nonetheless correspond with the changes in the macrofossil stratigraphy. A charcoal layer containing charred Ericaceae

leaves suggests the occurrence of local moorland fire during the brief dry regression at 175cm.

The palynostratigraphy suggests this climatic deterioration occurred after the woodland regeneration synonymous with the Roman withdrawal from Britain. The presence of a Dark Ages climate deterioration has been demonstrated at a number of mires across the British Isles (Barber *et al.* 1994a; Blackford & Chambers 1991; Tallis 1994). Previous investigations into the Dark Ages climatic deterioration identify a single change in mire surface wetness, whereas at May Moss the moisture change is staggered. This staggered change could be a function of local autogenic controls, however local climatic variability is also a possibility. The North York Moors are one of the driest areas of moorland in Britain, consequently it is possible the region's peat stratigraphies may be advantageously placed to identify drier periods.

LPAZ MMD IV (146–86cm)

The macrofossil stratigraphy of MMD IV is dominated for the most part by *Sphagnum imbricatum* remains suggesting a predominantly wet mire surface. However there are two layers where Ericaceae remains increase in abundance suggesting a drier mire surface.

At the base of MMD IV between 155–138cm *Sphagnum imbricatum* abundances decline and there is a minor increase in the abundance of Ericaceae, which is followed by a return to dominance by *Sphagnum imbricatum*. Subsequently between 125–110cm Ericaceae remains dominate the macrofossil assemblage. Above 110cm *Sphagnum imbricatum* dominates the assemblage, suggesting a return to a wetter mire surface.

The humification record supports the changes in mire surface wetness indicated in the macrofossil record. The base of MMD IV is well humified with a shift to poorly humified peat between 135–115cm. Between 115–107cm the peat is well humified, after which there is a shift to very poorly humified peat. Charcoal layers at 145 and 115cm including charred Ericaceae leaves indicate local moorland fires and are synchronous with macrofossil and humification evidence suggesting dry mire surface conditions.

It is difficult to interpret this sequence in the absence of radiocarbon dating, however the palynostratigraphy suggests the oscillations in mire surface wetness occurred during the early Medieval Period. The dry mire surface between 125–110cm provides evidence of a Medieval dry (warm) period and climatic deterioration in the late Medieval Period possibly *ca.* AD 1300. Evidence of dry mire surface between 155–138cm suggests a dry (warm) period occurred somewhere between AD 700–1300.

An AD 1300 climatic deterioration has been widely recognised in peat stratigraphies across Northern Europe (Barber 1981; Blackford & Chambers 1991; Tallis 1994). Additionally evidence for a Medieval dry period has also been recorded in the peat stratigraphies at several sites

indicated in Figure 6.6 and in historical sources (Lamb 1977).

The earlier period between 155 and 138cm is interesting because, whilst earlier work has recorded evidence of a dry phase within this period (Barber 1981; Tallis 1994), there is conflicting evidence regarding its age (see Figure 6.6). The evidence may be further complicated by this earlier dry period consisting of two drier phases separated by a short wetter phase.

LPAZ MMD V (86–0cm)

The macrofossil assemblages for the post-Medieval period are dominated by *Sphagnum* remains, and the peat is mainly poorly humified, which suggests wet mire surface conditions throughout this period. However within this period of predominantly wet conditions there is evidence of two drier phases between 80–65cm and 45–33cm.

Sphagnum section *Acutifolia*, which for the most part occupies relatively dry sites (Daniels & Eddy 1990) replaces *Sphagnum imbricatum* between 80–65cm, which combined with a shift to more humified peat suggests a drier mire surface. Subsequently between 45 and 33cm there is a shift in the humification record indicating a change to a drier mire surface, which is supported by increased abundance of *Sphagnum* section *Acutifolia*. Both dry phases are associated with small charcoal peaks.

The other noteworthy event in the macrofossil stratigraphy is the replacement at 30cm of *Sphagnum imbricatum* by *Sphagnum* section *Cuspidata*. *Sphagnum imbricatum* was a common peat forming moss across Britain during the late Holocene, however in the upper sections of many peat profiles there is a dramatic reduction in its abundance (Stoneman *et al.* 1993). A variety of reasons has been proposed to explain its demise, including climatic change (Barber 1981), human interference through burning (van Geel & Middeldorp 1988) and changes in the ecological niche occupied by *Sphagnum imbricatum* (Stoneman *et al.* 1993).

Predominantly wet conditions during the post-Medieval period are a product of the climatic deterioration associated with the Little Ice Age. There is considerable historical evidence of wetter climatic conditions between AD 1300–1800, with a drier period *ca.* AD 1500 (Lamb 1977). Recent reconstruction of northern hemisphere temperatures during the post-Medieval Period identifies warmer periods *ca.* AD 1500–1550 and *ca.* AD 1750–1820 which may account for the two moisture shifts to drier conditions identified at May Moss (Bradley & Jones 1993).

Blackford and Chambers (1995) identified two post-Medieval drier phases on humification profiles from western Ireland, and Tallis (1994) identified a drier phase *ca.* AD 1550 in the south Pennines; these are indicated on Figure 6.6.

SYNTHESIS

Palaeoecological analysis of the peat stratigraphies at May Moss and Fen Bogs reveals a complex picture of human and climatic impact on the central eastern North York Moors.

1. The pollen profiles from both sites provide a detailed analysis of the regional vegetation history. They demonstrate how fluctuations in woodland cover and indicators of arable or pastoral activity associated with population and culture changes are manifested in sub-fossil vegetation records. This study identified vegetation fluctuations that could be attributed to varying degrees of human interference associated with:

- Political, demographic and cultural changes associated with Anglo-Scandinavian colonisation of Britain
- The impact of William's 'harrying of the north' and subsequent Medieval agricultural and economic growth. Land-use changes and felling in the Royal Forest of Pickering affected the pollen profiles at Fen Bogs and May Moss.
- Demographic collapse associated with the Black Death and further epidemics in the 14th century, combined with poor harvests caused by a climatic deterioration (Harrison & Roberts 1989). A climatic deterioration is indicated in the mire palaeohydrological record from May Moss *ca.* AD 1300.
- The impact of modern moorland land-use, specifically for grouse shooting and forestry plantations.

2. The peat stratigraphy at May Moss contains a strong climatic signal. Humification and plant macrofossil evidence suggests there have been *ca.* 13 fluctuations in mire surface wetness since the Iron Age.

- These include several changes in mire surface wetness which support previous peat-based palaeoclimate research (Barber 1981; Barber *et al.* 1994a; Blackford & Chambers 1991; 1995; Tallis 1994), specifically an Iron Age climatic deterioration, warm dry conditions during the Roman occupation of Britain, a Dark Age climatic deterioration, the Medieval warm period and a climatic deterioration *ca.* AD 1300 associated with the beginning of the Little Ice Age.
- The palaeoclimate signal also identifies several areas that require further clarification, specifically:
  a) The Iron Age appears to contain several fluctuations in surface wetness.
  b) The Dark Age climatic deterioration appears to be staggered at May Moss.
  c) The age and duration of the Anglo-Scandinavian/early Medieval dry phase or phases.
  d) The chronology of the moisture fluctuations identified within the Little Ice Age.
- If these moisture fluctuations are cross-mire or regional phenomena, then given the temporal resolution available at May Moss, the site is potentially an excellent palaeoclimate archive. May Moss has the distinct advantages of being an ombrotrophic water-shedding bog with relatively rapid accumulation of peat. Fen Bogs provides an excellent archive of regional vegetation change (Atherden 1976), however its potential as a palaeoclimate archive can be questioned due to the likelihood of receiving surface run-off from surrounding slopes.

3. This paper presents some preliminary results and conclusions from a palaeoclimate research project on the North York Moors, and consequently represents research that is in progress and further work may affect the conclusions reached here. The preliminary results identify areas requiring further analysis, specifically:

- Independent dating of the peat profiles is essential and hopefully will enable correlation of palaeoecological and historical evidence of both climatic and anthropogenic changes.
- Further analysis at May Moss and surrounding sites will improve the spatial/temporal understanding of and confidence in the climate changes identified.
- In addition to the macrofossil and humification analyses discussed in this paper, other techniques are being applied with the aim of reconstructing mire surface wetness. These include analysis of sub-fossil testate amoebae populations and analysis of sub-fossil fungal remains. The application of several techniques, a multi-proxy approach, has the advantage that the confidence in the climatic changes identified is increased.
- Evidence for land-use and climate changes contained within local historical documents is currently being researched by a document historian, parallel to the palaeoecological analysis. Eventually it is hoped that the historical and palaeoecological evidence can be amalgamated to provide a post-Iron Age climate and land-use history of the North York Moors.

Acknowledgements

Research was carried out during the tenure (RC) of a University College of Ripon and York St John studentship. The authors are grateful to: Yorkshire Wildlife Trust and English Nature for allowing access to Fen Bogs Reserve (SSSI), and to English Nature and Forest Enterprise specifically David Jardine, Charles Critchley and David Clayden for their continued support of research on May Moss SSSI. Our sincere thanks are also due to an anonymous referee for valuable comments on an earlier manuscript.

REFERENCES

Atherden, M.A. (1976). Late Quaternary vegetational history of the North York Moors. III. Fen Bogs. *Journal of Biogeography* **3**, 115–124.

Atherden, M.A. (1979). Late Quaternary vegetational history of the North York Moors. VII. Pollen diagrams from the eastern central area. *Journal of Biogeography* **6**, 63–83.

Atherden, M.A. (1989). Three pollen diagrams from the eastern North York Moors. *Naturalist* **114**, 53–63.

Barber, K.E. (1981). *Peat Stratigraphy and Climate Change – a Palaeoecological Test of the Theory of Cyclic Peat Bog Regeneration*. Rotterdam: A.A. Balkema.

Barber, K.E., Chambers, F.M., Dumayne, L., Haslam, C.J., Maddy, D. and Stoneman, R.E. (1994a). Climatic Change and Human impact in North Cumbria: peat stratigraphic and pollen evidence from Bolton Fell Moss and Walton Moss, pp. 20–49 in Boardman, J. and Walton, J. (eds.) *The Quaternary of Cumbria: Field Guide*. Oxford, England: Quaternary Research Association.

Barber, K.E., Chambers, F.M., Maddy, D., Stoneman, R. and Brew, J.S. (1994b). A sensitive high-resolution record of late Holocene climatic change from a raised bog in northern England. *The Holocene* **4** (2), 198–205.

Bennett, K.D., Whittington, G. and Edwards, K. (1994). Recent plant nomenclatural changes and pollen morphology in the British Isles. *Quaternary Newsletter* **73**, 1–6.

Blackford, J.J. (1993). Peat bogs as sources of proxy climatic data: past approaches and future research, pp. 49–56 in Chambers, F.M. (ed.) *Climate Change and Human Impact on the Landscape*. London: Chapman and Hall.

Blackford, J.J. and Chambers, F.M. (1991). Proxy records of climate from blanket mires: evidence for a Dark Age (1400 BP) climatic deterioration in the British Isles. *The Holocene* **1** (1), 63–67.

Blackford, J.J. and Chambers, F.M. (1993). Determining the degree of peat decomposition in peat-based palaeoclimatic studies. *International Peat Journal* **5**, 7–24.

Blackford, J.J. and Chambers, F.M. (1995). Proxy climate record for the last 1000 years from Irish blanket peat and a possible link to solar variability. *Earth and Planetary Science Letters* **133**, 145–150.

Daniels, R.E. and Eddy, A. (1990). *Handbook of European Sphagna*. London: HMSO.

Dickinson, W. (1975). Recurrence surfaces in Rusland Moss, Cumbria (formerly north Lancashire). *Journal of Ecology* **63**, 913–936.

Faegri, K. and Iversen, J. (1989). *Textbook of Pollen Analysis*. 4th Edition, (eds: Faegri, K. Kaland, P.E. and Krzywinski, K.). Chichester: John Wiley.

Grimm, E.C. (1991). *TILIA and TILIAGRAPH*. Springfield: Illinois State Museum.

Harrison, B.J.D. and Roberts, B.K. (1989). The Medieval Landscape, pp. 72–112 in Spratt, D.A. and Harrison, B.J.D. (eds.) *The North York Moors: Landscape Heritage*. London: David and Charles Publishers.

Hollings, A. (1971). *A History of Goathland*. North York Moors National Park.

Innes, J.B. (1989). *Fine resolution pollen analysis of Late Flandrian II peats of North Gill, North York Moors*. Unpublished Ph.D. thesis: University of Durham.

Jones, P.D. and Bradley, R.S. (1992). Climatic variations over the last 500 years, pp. 649–665 in Bradley, R.S. and Jones, P.D. (eds.) *Climate since AD 1500*. London: Routledge.

Jones, R.L. (1977). Late Quaternary vegetational history of the North York Moors, V, The Cleveland Dales. *Journal of Biogeography* **4**, 353–362.

Jones, R.L. (1978). Late Quaternary vegetational history of the North York Moors, VI, The Cleveland Moors. *Journal of Biogeography* **5**. 81–92.

Kilian, M.R., Van der Plicht, J. and Van Geel, B. (1995). Dating raised bogs: New aspects of AMS ^{14}C wiggle matching, a reservoir effect and climatic change. *Quaternary Science Reviews* **14**, 959–966.

Lamb, H.H. (1977). *Climate, Present, Past and Future*. London: Metheum.

Lang, J.T. (1989). Anglo-Saxons and Vikings, pp. 55–71 in Spratt, D.A. and Harrison, B.J.D.(eds.) *The North York Moors: Landscape Heritage*. London: David and Charles Publishers.

Moore, P.D., Webb, J.A. and Collinson, M.E. (1991). *An Illustrated Guide to Pollen Analysis*. 2nd Edition. Oxford: Blackwell Scientific.

Musgrove, F. (1990). *The North of England. A History from Roman Times to the Present*. Oxford: Blackwell.

Rackham, O. (1990). *Trees and Woodland in the British Landscape*. London: J.M. Dent.

Sernander, B. (1908). On the evidence of post-glacial changes of climate furnished by the peat mosses of Northern Europe. *Geologiska Föreningens i Stockholm Förhandlingar* **30**, 365–478.

Simmons, I.G. (1995). The history of the early human environment, pp. 15–51 in Vyner, B. (ed.) *Moorland Monuments: Studies in the Archaeology of North-east Yorkshire in Honour of Raymond Hayes and Don Spratt*. York: Council for British Archaeology Research Report no. 101.

Simmons, I.G., Atherden, M., Cloutman, E.W., Cundill, P.R., Innes, J.B. and Jones, R.L. (1990). Prehistoric environments, pp. 15–50 in Spratt, D.A. (ed.) *Prehistoric and Roman Archaeology of North-East Yorkshire*. London: Council for British Archaeology Research Report no. 87.

Smith, A.J.E. (1978). *The Moss Flora of Britain and Ireland*. Cambridge: Cambridge University Press.

Spratt, D.A. (ed) (1993). *Prehistoric and Roman Archaeology of North-East Yorkshire*. London: Council for British Archaeology Research Report no. 87.

Spratt, D.A. and Harrison, B.J.D. (eds.) (1989). *The North York Moors: Landscape Heritage*. London: David and Charles Publishers.

Stamper, P. (1988). Woods and Parks, pp. 128–148 in Astill, G. and Grant, A.(eds) *The Countryside of Medieval England*. Oxford: Blackwell.

Statham, D.C. (1989). Modern times, pp. 199–222 in Spratt, D.A. and Harrison, B.J.D. (eds.) *The North York Moors: Landscape Heritage*. London: David and Charles Publishers.

Stuiver, M. and Reimer, P.J. (1993). Extended ^{14}C database and revised CALIB radiocarbon calibration program. *Radiocarbon* **35**, 215–230.

Tallis, J. (1995). Pool-and-hummock patterning in a southern Pennine blanket mire II. The formation and erosion of the pool system. *Journal of Ecology* **82**, 789–803.

Turton, R.B. (1894). *Honor and Forest of Pickering*. North Riding Record Society. Vols I-IV.

van Geel, B. and Middeldorp, A.A. (1988). Vegetational history of Carbury Bog (Co. Kildare, Ireland) during the last 850 years and a test of the temperature indicator value of ^{22}H/^{1}H measurements of peat samples in relation to historical sources and meteorological data. *New Phytologist* **109**, 377–392.

7. Conservation or Change? Human Influence on the Mid-Devon Landscape

C. J. Caseldine, B. J. Coles, F. M. Griffith and J. M. Hatton

Mid-Devon has been neglected by archaeologists and palaeoenvironmentalists attracted to the more obvious survival of evidence on Dartmoor and Exmoor. The authors came to be interested in the area for different reasons: a. cropmarks indicated likely prehistoric activity near Bow, enough to affect the natural vegetation cover; b. analysis of river and place names indicated, on the other hand, survival of forest; c. the palaeoenvironmental evidence was thought to be poor and with no time depth, providing a challenge to locate deposits suitable for resolving the clearance vs. thick forest scenarios of the archaeological approaches.

In 1993 we began fieldwork and identified locations for excavation and pollen analysis. The results have expanded the questions rather than resolved the conflict, and they indicate that the area has greater potential than we had anticipated for studying long-term settlement and vegetation change in the lowland (but not wetland) region.

Keywords: mid-Devon, cropmarks, palaeoenvironment, place-names, clearance.

INTRODUCTION

South-western Britain has been well-studied by archaeologists, and a number of detailed palaeoenvironmental projects have been carried out in the region. In Devon and in Somerset, work has to a certain extent focused on particular areas within the counties, namely Dartmoor and the Somerset Levels. Whilst providing good opportunities for combined archaeological and palaeo-environmental investigations, and results of more than local significance, neither Dartmoor nor the Levels can be said to represent the norm of settled land in the region, the one being a block of marginal upland and the other until recently a peat-filled wetland basin.

North of Dartmoor, there lies an area of relatively unimproved farmland, known as the Culm Measures, suitably located to fill the gap in our knowledge of past lowland environments and their use (Figure 7.1). It is an area which has seen little previous archaeological research and virtually no palaeoenvironmental work. Comparatively few surviving archaeological sites have been recognised in this area until recently.

Separate strands of interest led the authors of the present paper to join forces to examine this area more closely, with the aim of establishing whether the perceived sparsity of settlement over time was apparent or real; the product of site selection in past periods, or of subsequent factors affecting site visibility in this area (discussed in more detail in Griffith forthcoming). It was felt that the study area could be susceptible to a combined archaeological and palaeoenvironmental approach.

Two of the authors (C.J. Caseldine and J.M. Hatton) have had a long-standing general interest in lowland Devon, being well aware that their own fieldwork in the county has taken place mainly on Dartmoor, where results might not be representative of the wider region. Human influence on the course of environmental change on

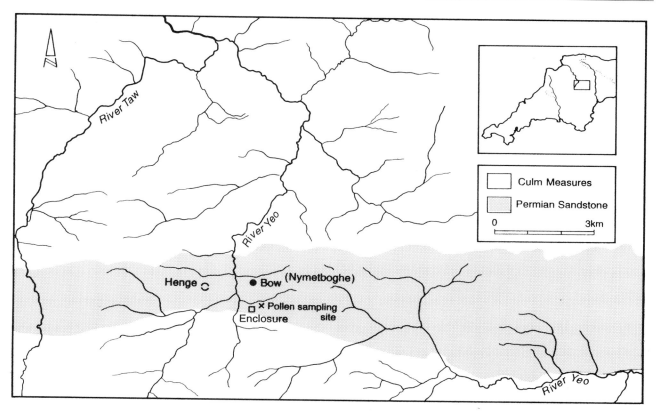

Figure 7.1: Location map and local geology.

Dartmoor has been recognised for some time: it is generally accepted as being critical to the developments of later prehistory, when the marginal character of the granite upland became fully evident. In mid-Devon on the Culm Measures, though close to Dartmoor and bounded to the north by Exmoor, permanent settlement and mixed farming have endured. Would this 'normal' context reveal a different long-term environmental history to the marginalised upland blocks and, if so, with greater or with less human influence on the trajectory?

Within the potential study area, a spit or peninsula of Permian sandstone cuts across the Culm Measures. It was anticipated that this variation in geology, and hence soils, might have affected patterns of land use in the past. It is also likely to have affected the survival of evidence to the present, and through variation in present-day land use it exerts an influence on patterns of discovery.

The paucity of archaeological evidence from the Culm Measures and other areas of lowland Devon had led another of us (FG) to establish in 1983 a programme of systematic aerial reconnaissance in Devon, carried out through Devon County Council. Work has been undertaken in every subsequent year, and has yielded large numbers of 'sites' to occupy some of the former blank areas (Griffith forthcoming; Griffith & Quinnell forthcoming). Within the study area, one Roman fort (Fox 1959) had long been known, and others have subsequently been identified in

the general area (Griffith 1984; Todd 1985). However, to the strictly limited number of settlement sites of earlier periods, aerial reconnaissance has been able to add numerous enclosure sites (of uncertain date), while the few upstanding barrows have been augmented by the recognition of others in the form of ring ditches. A high proportion of those in the study area were seen on the Permian ridge, with its greater susceptibility to the production of cropmarks. One objective of the present study was to seek to determine whether the apparent concentration of earlier landuse on the sandstone soils was 'real' or a product of variable visibility.

Among the rich harvest of cropmarks in 1984 was the site of a Class II henge at Bow, the first definite example of its type in southwest England (Figure 7.2; Griffith 1985a). Subsequent fieldwalking produced a large assemblage of lithics, predominantly of neolithic date though with some evidence of mesolithic activity.

The henge at Bow lies in the midst of a concentration of placenames incorporating the element 'nymet', the Celtic *nemeton* which has the meaning of 'sacred place' or 'sacred grove'. This concentration of names was used in 1959 by Lady Fox in her proposed identification of the Roman fort at North Tawton with the *Nemetotatio* (or '*Nemeto-statio*') of the Ravenna Cosmography (Fox 1959, 174–5). In 1976, the late C.E. Stevens drew attention to the Nymet names and to the placename 'Morchard' ('Great

Figure 7.2: The henge at Bow. Photo F.M.Griffith Devon County Council 6 July 1984. Copyright reserved.

Wood'), to postulate that the area was covered by a great forest of possibly sacred character until the post-Roman period (Stevens 1976). In 1985 FG proposed an alternative explanation, namely that the henge itself could have been the 'sacred place' in reference to which the various Nymets were named (Griffith 1985b). Clearly this question, offering two strongly different intepretations of the intensity of landuse on the basis of placename evidence, was one that the present project might illuminate.

The third strand of enquiry that fed into the present investigations also turned upon place-names, and upon the names of rivers. The remaining author (B.J.Coles) was investigating the possibility that Celtic river-names might provide a clue to the perception and use of rivers at the time of naming. The names are known to us largely from Roman sources, and the researches of Ekwall (1928) and Rivet and Smith (1979) in particular have shown that many present-day river-names in Britain can be traced back to a Celtic form recorded by the Romans. The Thames, for example, is **Tamesis** in Caesar and **Tamesa** in Tacitus (Rivet & Smith 1979, 45). The name is derived from the Celtic ***tam***, as too are the river-names Tamar, Thame, Tame, Team and Tean. What does ***tam*** mean, and what do the rivers have in common that they were given essentially the same name? The answer, it was suggested, might have something to say about the former character of the river and the way in which it was perceived

and used by prehistoric peoples. There are a number of other groups of river-names with Celtic origins, in addition to the ***tam*** group, and for the Trent – Tarrant group an interpretation has been suggested (Coles 1994). Identifying the rivers and interpreting the names is by no means an exact science, and using river-names is a matter of suggestion rather than proof.

In mid-Devon, there are two occurrences of a particular river-name with connotations of oak-woods, within the area of Stevens' postulated 'great wood' and the concentration of Nymet place-names. The Dart flows east to the Exe, and the Little Dart west to the Taw. Neither should be confused with the Dart that flows south off Dartmoor, although all three probably derive from the same Celtic river-name ***derventio***, meaning "oak river" or "river in an oak wood". On the basis of what little is known of Celtic religion this might imply a sacred wood.

Several other water-courses in the mid-Devon area may previously have been named Nymet, in addition to the places with that name (Ekwall 1928, 304–305). One of them is the present Yeo which flows west of Bow, close to the henge cropmark. Figure 7.3 maps the river and place-names suggestive of woods and sacred areas and, as with Griffith's and Stevens' earlier maps, it should be noted that such a concentration is unusual. Interpretation in terms of a prehistoric sacred wood blanketing the mid-Devon landscape is, however, highly speculative. This particular

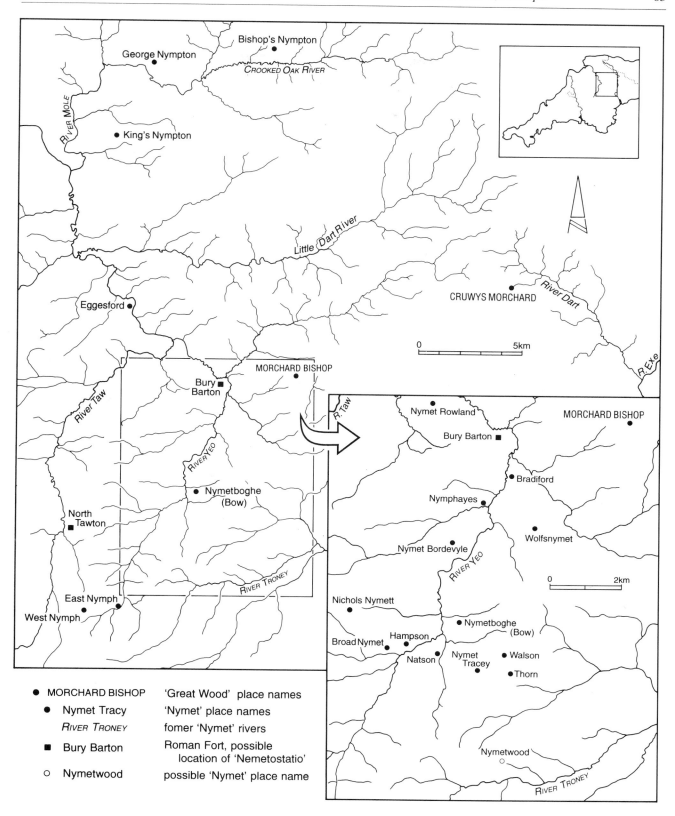

Figure 7.3: Mid-Devon river-names and place-names suggestive of woods and sacred areas. Based on Ekwall 1928, Griffith 1985b, Stevens 1976 and Whale 1903.

Figure 7.4: Nymet Barton Marsh and enclosure. The enclosure ditch can be seen to the right (east) of the central hedge with trees; the pollen sampling site lies in the marshy ground on the upper right. Photo F.M.Griffith Devon County Council 6 July 1984. Copyright reserved.

line of investigation could go no further without supporting evidence.

The award of a University of Exeter Research Grant in 1993 funded a pilot fieldwork programme, the main aim of which was to determine whether or not evidence survived to answer the questions arising from the different approaches outlined above. In particular, we sought deposits suitable for pollen analysis and evidence that would help to establish an outline chronological framework for human activity in the area.

Several earthwork sites were identified through field-walking, most notably two barrows close to the Yeo. Upstream of these, along a small tributary of the Yeo, a wetland area was selected for sampling. A nearby enclosure, recorded as a cropmark during aerial reconnaissance by FG in 1984, was chosen for a trial excavation, partly to recover material for dating, and also in the hope that its ditch might be waterlogged. Both sites were on Nymet Barton farm (Figure 7.4).

NYMET BARTON MARSH: POLLEN

The pollen sampling location is within an SSSI, and lies in an area of alluvial silty clays derived from the Permian sandstone, the soils being moderately base-rich. The catchment area for the drainage basin is small and comprises relatively low-angled slopes, currently under pasture, with cultivation on the higher and better drained land, and includes the cropmark site selected for excavation as well as one or two others. The SSSI is a small *Carex paniculata* valley mire characterised by well developed *Carex* tussocks, with some willows and occasional oaks. Samples were taken where there are no surface tussocks and little evidence for tussock formation in the stratigraphy.

The waterlogged sediments were 125cm deep where sampled. A wood fragment from the base was taken for radiocarbon dating and gave the following result:

2220 ± 60BP [AMS BETA 82197 CAMS – 20448].

When calibrated, this gives ranges of 375–185BC(1s) and 395–100BC(2s), hence a likely date of somewhere between 300 and 200BC. No attempt was made to derive younger dates by extrapolation as it seems probable that the accumulation rate has varied.

Pollen zones (Figure 7.5)

Zone NB1a: This is dominated by Gramineae (>50%). This may include some *Phragmites* but there is little macrofossil evidence for a reedswamp deposit. A wide range of herbs is present especially Compositae lig., *Plantago lanceolata, Rumex spp., Trifolium,* Umbelliferae, Chenopodiaceae, Compositae tub., Ranunculaceae and *Pteridium*. There is also a continuous curve for Cerealia.

This zone is remarkable, considering its age, in having such low levels of tree pollen. There is some local development of alder fen and scattered oak and hazel, but the figures represent a largely deforested landscape similar to the outlook at present. Herb taxa indicate both cultivation and pasture, and the high levels of inwash, indicated in the low moisture/loss on ignition figures, probably derived from the surrounding slopes.

Zone NB1b: This is a transitional zone with relatively minor pollen changes, the main change being an increase in *Cyperaceae* (sedges-probably *Scirpus sylvaticus* which is there today) and reduced values for Gramineae.

This zone represents a largely local change in the bog as it became more organic and less minerogenic. Overall there is little indication of any change in the landscape as a whole with continuous human occupation and no shrub or woodland regeneration.

Zone NB2: This relects the presence of a mire comparable to that of the present with much less alder, the loss of *Pteridium* and increasing Filicales. There is little change in the herb flora, apart from lower *Plantago* and Compositae lig. but still continuous Cerealia and the presence of taxa of field margins such as *Valeriana* and *Succisa*.

Human occupation and especially local cultivation is continuously indicated. Field margin taxa such as *Valeriana* and *Succisa* may represent the more widespread use of permanent field boundaries.

Overall the pollen results show that the immediate landscape was already very open by 300BC with clearance probably having taken place well before this date. Despite the small nature of the site, the lack of tree pollen must show considerable openness, for the amount of pollen deriving from herb taxa would not have been sufficient to 'swamp' longer-travelled tree pollen. For the last two millennia the area has been kept open and continuously used for agriculture with no evidence at all for any periods of lessened activity, which would have led to shrub and woodland regeneration.

The results of the pollen analysis raise two important questions. Firstly what, in this small catchment, caused sediment accumulation to begin in the 3rd century BC? The evidence for an open landscape is well-established from the base, and thus it seems unlikely that forest clearance was a cause. It is possible that there was a change in land use or precipitation patterns, leading to increased erosion and siltation around shrubby growth in the valley bottom. Accidental damming of the small watercourse

downstream is another possible event leading to deposition of sediment; many partial dams consisting of fallen trees and bushes and autumn leaves were observed during field-walking. Deliberate damming of the stream by beaver would have a similar effect. Alternatively, a change in local hydrology leading to enhanced spring activity might have led to the conditions observed. Of all these possibilities, damming downstream is preferred, probably associated with increased agricultural activity on the surrounding slopes.

Secondly, what caused the change from silty deposit to organic mire? There is a possibility of autogenic change as sediment thickened and expanded and continued input of silts could no longer expand over the growing mire. Alternatively, some event in the catchment may have cut off the supply of silty material. Possibilities here are a barrier appearing upstream, or the construction of field boundaries providing a series of sediment traps across the slopes. On balance, the latter explanation is preferred since pollen preservation is not suggestive of reworking of the pollen down valley but rather of sediment input from immediately adjacent slopes. Furthermore, there is a large field boundary just above the edge of the mire.

NYMET BARTON ENCLOSURE EXCAVATION

In the dry summer of 1984, three sides of a sub-rectangular enclosure had been recorded in cropmark form at SS723007 in a field adjacent to Nymet Barton Marsh. Parts of the north and south sides were visible, with a maximum length of 45m, and on the east side 50m with a fairly central entrance gap. The western side of the enclosure was not seen, and may coincide with a field boundary. No part of it was visible in the field to the west, but this may solely be a function of different cropping. The present, and Tithe Map, fieldname is Kittywell Field.

In 1994 it was decided to sample this enclosure by excavation. The work was undertaken by Exeter Museums Archaeological Field Unit, supervised by Steve Reed, with the help of members of the Devon Archaeological Society. The following paragraphs summarise results to date.

A trench 17m x 1m was excavated across and at right angles to the northern or downslope ditch as recorded in aerial reconnaissance. The aim was to section the ditch and any vestigial bank, to recover artefactual and palaeo-environmental material for dating and for comparison with the material from the pollen sampling site, and to test the interior of the enclosure for the survival of any internal features. Ploughsoil was removed using a small mechanical excavator; thereafter excavation was by hand.

The results from the excavation differed from those anticipated. The ditch (505; Figure 7.6), and the remains of its ploughed-down bank (503), were identified, but no primary dating material came from these contexts (detailed context descriptions are available in the site archive). The ditch itself was shallower and broader than is usual for

NYMET BARTON

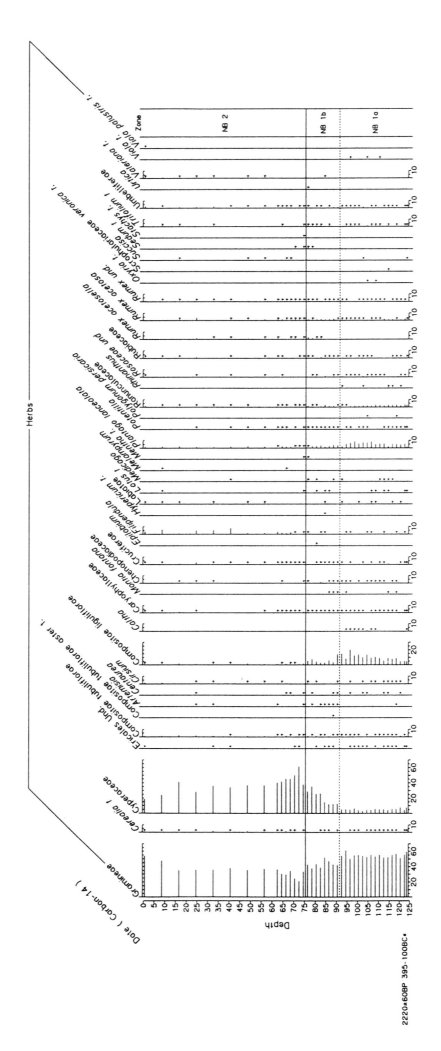

Figure 7.5: Pollen diagram from Nymet Barton. All taxa are expressed as a percentage of Total Land Pollen (T.L.P.). (Continued below).

NYMET BARTON

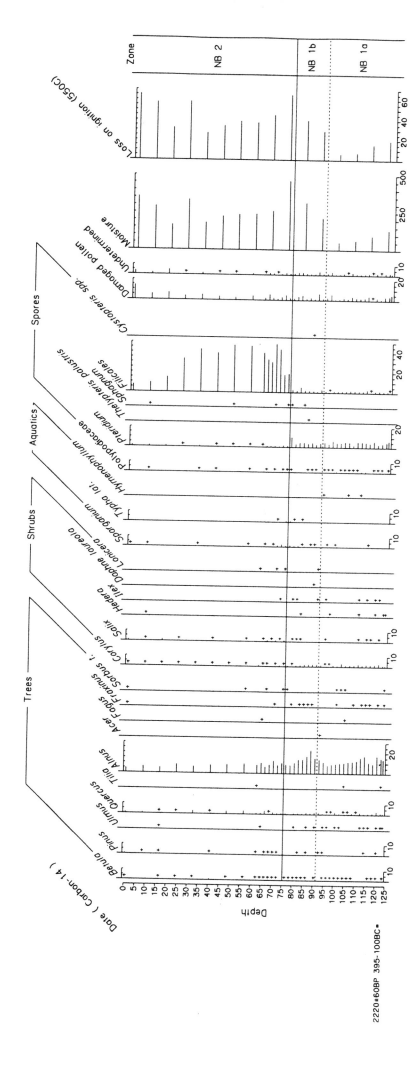

Figure 7.5: Pollen diagram from Nymet Barton. All taxa are expressed as a percentage of Total Land Pollen (T.L.P.). (Continuation of above).

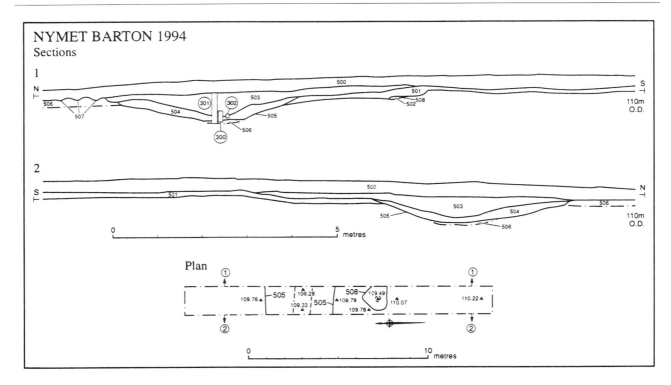

Figure 7.6: Nymet Barton enclosure. Sections of 1994 excavation trench. Circled numbers identify palaeoenvironmental samples, plain numbers archaeological contexts. Drawn by S.Reed and T.Dixon, Exeter Archaeology.

enclosures of this type so far excavated in Devon; it had as its lowest fill a layer of clay (504) whose profile suggested that it had been deliberately used to line the ditch rather than that it derived from natural depositional processes. Neither this nor the putative bank, which spread over and sealed the clay layer infilling the ditch, contained any artefactual material, though some charcoal fragments were found.

Below the spread bank was a layer (501) differentiated from it by a change in texture and a higher charcoal content, which was cut by the ditch. This layer extended beyond the limit of 503, but was progressively less easy to identify beneath the ploughsoil (500). All the soils in this area are of an open structure and the likelihood of inter-migration of material through biogenetic action is great. Root action was apparent, particularly in 500 and 501, and earthworms were plentiful. A small pit (508; fill 502) was sealed beneath 501.

Artefactual material of Neolithic date was recovered from 501 and 502. An assemblage of lithic material was recovered, of good quality black flint in very fresh condition, along with a number of unabraded potsherds. This material is discussed further below.

The results of the small trench do not clarify the original question but pose interesting new ones. No evidence firmly tied the features recorded on the air photograph with the material excavated from the site, and a minimalist explanation is that the enclosure overlay a pre-existing Neolithic site of unknown but possibly unusual character. This suggestion is to some extent supported by the discussion below of the deposition of the artefactual material. However, the nature of the enclosure ditch is in itself unusual, both in profile and in the clay lining, not paralleled at any other subrectangular enclosure so far sampled, and so some relationship between the two cannot be ruled out, particularly given the complete absence of any dating material from the ditch. The anticipated date range of the enclosure, from the topographical and morphological evidence available before excavation, would have been in the later prehistoric or, most likely, the Romano-British period (cf. Simpson *et al.* 1989,24). If this had been the case, the existence and survival of some contemporary ceramic material within the area of the excavation would have been expected.

The interpretation of the layer below the bank poses problems. The well preserved nature of the pottery and flint from the context (501) militates against an interpretation either as a ploughsoil or as an occupation horizon, since the freshness of the flintwork and the very survival of the ceramics indicate that the layer could never have been subjected to cultivation and must indeed have been protected from disturbance almost immediately after its deposition. Quinnell has examined the ceramic material and commented on its possible "special significance". The possibility of this layer being a carefully laid down, and covered, deposit must be entertained, although the limited nature of the excavation means that this line of reasoning cannot be taken further at the moment.

The ceramic assemblage itself is of importance, both in its internal characteristics and in its contribution to the wider picture of the Neolithic in Devon, a subject which has for many years languished but which achieved a fresh impetus in 1994 with the results of work not only at Nymet Barton but also at two newly identified major hilltop sites, at Raddon and Haldon. The Nymet Barton assemblage comprised 39 sherds, 30 from context 501, and nine from pit 502. All appeared equally fresh and unabraded. Quinnell (1994) has identified, through macroscopic examination, three different fabrics – quartz-gritted, granitic and gabbroic. The gabbroic is a fabric familiar from other south western sites, though the sherds from this site are among the thinnest so far recognised. The other two fabrics could be of quite local manufacture, since Nymet Barton lies down river from the Dartmoor granite, and on Permian geology which might furnish the quartz. Nymet Barton was the first site in Devon at which neolithic granitic fabrics have been recognised. Six quartz-gritted sherds came from 501, none from 502; 17 granitic sherds from 501 and one from 502; seven gabbroic sherds came from 501 and eight from 502.

Quinnell draws attention to more complex aspects of the fabrics represented and suggests that the inclusions within the pottery may themselves have been of significance, both through the use of large quartz grits for show rather than practicality, and perhaps through the mixture of different inclusions during manufacture for possibly non-functional reasons. In view of recent work (Cleal 1991) on the contextual significance of carinated bowls, the fact that all the gabbroic sherds may be from such vessels is of particular interest. Further work is at present in progress on the assemblages from other neolithic sites, notably Raddon and Haldon, and all three types of fabric have now been recognised elsewhere. Material such as this is not closely datable within a south western neolithic context, but Nymet Barton makes an important contribution to the current study of this material and has provided very timely additional material for this work.

The flint assemblage from this one trench is likewise too small (42 pieces) for detailed analysis, and it contains no diagnostically datable pieces. Hurcombe, who has kindly examined the material, writes: 'The assemblage would not be out of keeping with a neolithic date but is too small for any positive date. It is all in excellent condition, with fresh and undamaged edges. In addition, very small flakes are present (the smallest is 19x19x8mm and the largest 71 x 43 x 19mm). Both these features indicate that the assemblage is present in its entirety and undamaged by past depositional processes, and this is borne out by the condition of the pottery (although some movement in the loose soil is thought likely by the excavator). Despite the freshness of the assemblage there are five pieces which show evidence of burning in the form of surface crazing, potlid and heat fractured areas.

This may have been caused by a prehistoric event; the possibility that these pieces could be failed examples of heat treatment is intriguing. One of the heat-damaged pieces is a broad flake, large enough to have formed a blank suitable for pressure flaking after heat treatment had occurred. On the other hand, another of the burned pieces has a large proportion of cortex, which would have made it unsuitable for such use. Some of the pieces could be seen as trimming flakes as they have scars on the dorsal side indicating that they came from cores or worked tools. Three pieces had more than 50% of the dorsal surface as cortex, with smaller amounts of cortex in a further 12 cases. This indicated that flint was being worked at the site. Some of the individual pieces may come from a single nodule, though further work is required to verify this. Overall, the assemblage suggests a site of considerable potential interest, with lithic material in good condition and with evidence of reduction techniques and lithic exploitation strategies.'

DISCUSSION

Results to date have been of considerable interest, yet without any clear temporal link between the pollen evidence and that provided by the excavation across the enclosure ditch. In both areas of investigation, more questions have been raised than answered.

The archaeological evidence points to Neolithic activity close to the small watercourse, long before sediments started to accumulate at the pollen sampling site. The rapid burial of pot-sherds and flints is probably not directly related to natural processes associated with the watercourse and the artefacts lie just far enough up from the present valley bottom to be on land that one would assume was cultivable in the past. Pollen evidence from Roadford Reservoir some 30km to the west of Bow is indicative of Neolithic clearance (V. Straker pers. comm.), and Roadford is close enough to Nymet Barton to argue that the Neolithic life-style of the latter area also involved tree clearance and maybe ploughing. One might argue that the Nymet Barton site lay just within the boundary of cultivable land, yet was not itself cultivated. However, it was perhaps rapidly sealed due to cultivation in the immediate vicinity. The Neolithic period lasted for well over a millennium and the chronological relationships between the different sets of evidence referred to here are altogether uncertain. For the present, we should only note that the artefactual material was rapidly buried and thereafter lay undisturbed until the 1994 investigation.

The pollen evidence indicates that clearance was extensive by about 300 cal BC and has remained so ever since. There is evidence for a change within the catchment area at some stage, resulting in a switch from silts to more organic deposits, probably due to the building of field boundaries, but the open character of the landscape does not alter. One can therefore argue that, within the catchment of the pollen site, there was no "Great Wood" in later prehistoric times nor subsequently. The distribution of cropmark evidence for enclosures of presumed later prehistoric or Romano-British date would support this. Either the "Great Wood" was to the north, further into the Culm Measures, or the place-names which point to its existence came into use before clearance, or the place-name and river-name evidence has been mis-interpreted: FG's alternative explanation of the *nemeto* names should be remembered. It is too early to say which of these is the most likely answer, but it would be of interest to locate suitable pollen sites covering the late Mesolithic to Romano-British period, both within the Culm Measures and near Nymet Barton Marsh. Before the present project began, we would have held out little hope of finding such sites, but the results reported here indicate that local wetlands can have a long history, and pollen preservation can be good.

To conclude, human activity in the area has been shown to be more diverse than previously known. The emerging picture appears to be different to that from Dartmoor, and the evidence for a locally cleared landscape by the later Iron Age, with continuous cultivation from then on contrasts with the marginalisation of the upland granite by this time. Survival of good quality evidence, both archaeological and palaeoenvironmental, has been demonstrated, albeit within a problematic chronological framework. It suggests that there is considerable potential for the long-term investigation of human activity, land-use and vegetation change in this south-western agricultural lowland. Change, in the sense of clearance and cultivation, has been identified in one part of the study area. Whether or not we will locate conservation, in the sense of enduring forest cover, elsewhere in the region remains to be seen.

Acknowledgements

Finance was provided by a grant from the University of Exeter Research Fund. and by the British Academy. Aerial reconnaissance was grant-aided by English Heritage, RCHME, Devon County Council, the Devonshire Association and private donors. Landowners kindly allowed access to their fields, and we are particularly grateful to the Pickard and Tylor families in this respect.

Graham Langman carried out the initial work on the pottery with subsequent work by Henrietta Quinnell; Linda Hurcombe examined the lithic assemblage; Tim Quine helped in the field and commented on aspects of the palaeoenvironmental work. Art Ames prepared the pollen samples and the pollen diagram. Sue Rouillard drew the maps and Tina Tuohy typed the text. We are grateful to all the above for their help with the project.

REFERENCES

Cleal, R. (1991). Earlier prehistoric pottery, pp. 171–184 in Sharples, N. *Maiden Castle: Excavations and Field Survey 1985–6*. London: English Heritage.

Coles, B.J. (1994). *Trisantona* rivers: a landscape approach to the interpretation of river names. *Oxford Journal of Archaeology* **13**(3), 294–311.

Ekwall, E. (1928). *English River-Names*. Oxford: Clarendon Press.

Fox, A. (1959). 25th report on archaeology and early history. *Report Transactions of the Devonshire Association* **91**, 166–77.

Griffith, F.M. (1984). Roman Military Sites in Devon: Some Recent Discoveries. *Proceedings of the Devon Archaeological Society* **42**, 11–32.

Griffith, F.M. (1985a). Some Newly Discovered Ritual Monuments in mid Devon. *Proceedings of the Prehistoric Society* **51**, 310–315.

Griffith, F.M. (1985b). A *nemeton* in Devon? *Antiquity* **59**, 121–124.

Griffith, F.M. (forthcoming). Changing perceptions of the context of prehistoric Dartmoor *Proceedings of the Devon Archaeological Society*. (Dartmoor Conference Proceedings 1994)

Griffith, F.M. and Quinnell, H. (forthcoming). The South West in prehistory, in Kain, R. and Ravenhill, W.(eds.) *Historical Atlas of South West England*. University of Exeter.

Quinnell, H. (1994). *Neolithic Pottery from Nymet Barton: an Interim Report* (unpublished report in site archive).

Rivet, A.L.F. and Smith, C. (1979). *The Place Names of Roman Britain*. London: Batsford.

Simpson, S.J., Griffith, F.M. and Holbrook, N. (1989). The prehistoric, Roman and early post-Roman Site at Hayes Farm, Clyst Honiton. *Devon Archaeological Society Proceedings* **47**, 1–28.

Stevens, C.E. (1976). The sacred wood, pp. 239–244 in Megaw, J.V.S. (ed.) *To Illustrate the Monuments: Essays on Archaeology Presented to Stuart Piggott*.

Todd, M. (1985). The Roman fort at Bury Barton, Devonshire. *Britannia* **16**, 49–55.

Whale, T.W. (1903). Analysis of the Exon Doomsday in Hundreds. *Transactions of the Devonshire Association* **35**, 662–712.

8. Remains of Mites as Indicators of Human Impact on Past Environments: Dwelling Mounds and Marine Incursions in the Netherlands

Jaap Schelvis

Mites (Acari) are far from popular creatures. Like their larger arachnid relatives, the spiders and scorpions, they usually get a very bad press. This is caused mainly by a handful of obnoxious species such as housedust-mites, chiggers and ticks. The vast majority, however, of the more than 60,000 described species of mites are not harmful at all and in fact many are involved in such essential biological processes as decomposition and soil-formation.

Mites form a highly successful group within the phylum Arthropoda; they are found in virtually every available habitat from the arctic to the tropic and from the deep sea to the highest mountains. A number of species have also found their way to that small strip of biotope between the land and the sea known as the littoral zone.

Where the influence of the sea has been variable the remains of these littoral mites can be used to reconstruct this marine influence. In some cases these fluctuations can be explained by the traditional model of sea level fluctuations known as transgressions and regressions. In other cases, however, these changes are caused by human activities such as the building of dykes and the reclamation of land.

Keywords: Mites, palaeoecology, littoral, dwelling mounds.

INTRODUCTION

At the 1995 annual meeting of the Association for Environmental Archaeology in Bradford I happened to be the only speaker from the Netherlands. Therefore, I decided to speak about something typically Dutch which would cover that year's theme: People as an agent of environmental change. Thinking about environmental changes I started to think about typical Dutch environments and their origin and then I realised that every environment, every bit of landscape in the Netherlands is in fact the result of some sort of human intervention in the past. Nearly 70% of the Netherlands would be referred to as The North Sea if it had not been for people changing their environment.

This anthropogenic character is also obvious in our nature reserves and national parks which are all the result of human activities. In fact, we have become so used to controlling our own environment that we actually try to minimise natural influences even within nature reserves. So when the small uninhabited island of Griend, in our largest national park the Waddensea, was threatened by currents and other natural aspects of the dynamics of an intertidal ecosystem, it was decided that we had to rescue it and preserve it by the construction of a protective dam twice the size of the island. My conclusion is therefore straightforward: the Netherlands is the most artificial country in the world. This of course made it very easy for me to pick a subject for this paper; practically every study in environmental archaeology in the Netherlands reflects in one way or the other people as an agent of environmental change.

There are many different ways of reconstructing past environments and the changes brought about by people in

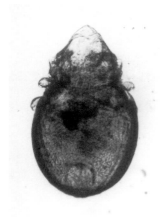

Figure 8.2: A medieval individual of the oribatid mite
Phauloppia lucorum *(CL Koch 1841) (length: 650 µm).*

Figure 8.1: A recent individual of the oribatid mite
Phauloppia lucorum *(CL Koch 1841) (length: 650 µm).*

these environments. In this paper I would like to (re-?)
introduce you to my personal favourite: the use of mite
remains (Schelvis 1992).

MITES

Mites are small spider-like creatures with eight legs, no
wings, no antennae and no segmented eyes to mention just
some of the obvious differences with insects (Figure 8.1).
On the other hand they do share some important characteristics with insects such as their exoskeleton composed of
chitin, the enormous number of known species (at the
moment some 60,000 spp. of mites have been described)
and the fact that these species have spread into every
conceivable habitat.

In an archaeological or paleontological context mites
can in fact be treated as small insects. The method of
extraction is the same (the Paraffin Flotation Method as
described by Kenward *et al.* 1980) and it does not really
matter whether the subject of your study originally had 6
legs or 8 legs, because they lose their legs anyway (Figure
8.2). Identification also gives the same sort of problems
as in insects, although with mites you do tend to find more
complete individuals instead of all the disarticulated insect
sclerites. But still, the identification keys starting with the
number of claws on the first pair of legs are useless so you
really need a reference collection.

The interpretation of 'archaeological' mite remains is
also comparable to interpreting insect finds although there
are some differences. Mites, for instance, are so small that
we are not aware of their presence. This means on the one
hand that people would never try to collect or destroy the
mites in their environment so you can exclude any con-

scious human selection but on the other hand people could
move mites around without knowing it by simply moving
soil or fodder. Which brings us to the second difference
with insects: the fact that mites never have wings. This
means that in theory their remains should reflect the strictly
local ecology of any sampled site because their dispersal
capacity is restricted to a maximum of 1 or 2 metres.
Unfortunately, this is not true because mites have developed several methods to move about.

One of these methods is *anemochory* in which the mites
use aircurrents. Some species have evolved large wing-
like structures, appropriately known as pteromorphs, which
enable them to be blown about passively by the wind.

Another, somewhat more predictable way of getting
around is known as *phoresy*. Phoretic mites use other
animals, mostly flying insects, to get where they want.
Sometimes there are specific developmental stages, usually
referred to as wandernymphs, which are specially prepared
to do so. They do not have functional legs or mouthparts
but just a large ventral sucker used to cling to, for instance,
a dung-fly or dung-beetle visiting the cow-pat in which
they were born and hoping, of course, that they will be
able to get off again at another pleasant place with enough
food to complete their development.

In other cases the adults are phoretic and they lay their
eggs alongside the eggs of the fly or beetle which brought
them there. Then a race against the biological clock starts
with a very high selection pressure for rapid development,
because whoever develops faster can use the other as food.
As a result of such mechanisms some mite species living
in excrement can go from egg to adult in less than 72
hours.

It is clear that mites are not as sedentary as they appear
and of course post-mortem transport can complicate things
even further.

Only a small minority of all mite species, less than two
percent, has developed a parasitic life-style. Some taxa,

for instance, are exclusively found in the cloacas of marine turtles, the nostrils of the capibara or in the hair-follicles of your eyelashes (Karg 1970). Practically all mites, however, are not parasitic and they can be found in a wide variety of habitats ranging from the tropics, where there are probably at least another 60,000 spp. to be discovered, to the high arctic and from the deep sea to the highest mountain tops. Of course, we do not have such extreme environments in our artificial country but we do have a coast and along this coast we have a littoral zone. This narrow strip between the land and the sea consists of an unique ecosystem with many characteristic plants and animals including mites. The remains of these mites can be used to reconstruct the position and movements of this littoral zone.

DWELLING MOUNDS

Nowadays the coastline in the north of the Netherlands is more or less in a fixed position, moving north very slowly as a result of continuous reclamation of land. However, it has not always been like this; the first people to settle on these coastal plains must have had a really hard time keeping their feet dry. On present knowledge this first colonization took place during our middle Iron Age around 500 BC (Waterbolk 1979). People living on the nearby Pleistocene sand started to colonize new areas probably because of a growing population and a reduction of inhabitable land area as a result of bog-development. The same sea-level rise or transgression which caused a rise of the groundwater level and thereby the spreading of the bogs also resulted in deposits of clay along the coast. This new land provided excellent grazing opportunities for the domestic animals of the Iron Age people as well as good hunting grounds and possibilities for fishing.

So what may have started as an experiment of coastal transhumance (van Gijn & Waterbolk 1984), taking your cattle to graze on the saltmarshes during the summer, rapidly developed into real settlements. Apparently, this land had so much to offer that it was worth the risk of the nearby sea and it was worth the effort of constructing the first dwelling mounds during this period. These dwelling mounds provided a safe place for both the people and their animals during periods of high water. We should not overestimate the effect of an occasional flood during this initial phase of settlement as is demonstrated by two pictures in Koehn (1939). The first picture, taken on the 20th of September 1935 at Knudswarf near Gröde on the intertidal mudflats in the north of Germany, shows a dwelling mound surrounded by a seemingly endless sea. On the narrow strip of land around the farmhouse some thirty cows are packed together. The next picture shows the same dwelling mound just one day later: all the land is dry and accessible again, the cattle are grazing and the children are playing.

For a long time these dwelling mounds survived during all the regressions and transgressions of the sea, steadily growing with the dirt and excrement of their inhabitants. Then, at around 1000 AD, people started to build dykes to assure a more permanent protection of their land and livestock. Of course these first primitive dykes were very low and did not give any real security. Gradually the number of dykes grew, the dykes got higher and the marine influence diminished. During spring-tide and with storms these dykes often gave way to the sea and the higher the dyke the more dramatic the effect. So once there are dykes we should not underestimate the effect of an occasional flood: the last serious flood in the Netherlands as a result of a dyke burst as recent as 1953 killed more than 1800 people.

Nowadays, a lot of these dwelling mounds have disappeared. Their fertile soil was used as manure to improve the very same Pleistocene sands from which their original inhabitants once came. After the First World-War the growing Dutch population needed more and more potatoes and the digging of 'terpaarde' that is the soil of dwelling mounds developed into an important industry employing hundreds of labourers. Along with the soil the dwelling mounds yielded large numbers of archaeological objects including numerous animal bones. In fact the study of these bone assemblages by van Giffen (1913) can be seen as the birth of archaeozoology in the Netherlands.

At the moment all remaining dwelling mounds or what is left of them are protected, or should be protected by law as monuments. However, there are always cases in which a new road is considered more important than a monument and there is no law against drilling small scientific holes into dwelling mounds. In these cases dwelling mounds offer very good opportunities for environmental studies. The quality of preservation of organic material is usually very good and some dwelling mounds have been inhabited for more than 2000 years.

To reconstruct the environment, and in this case more specifically the marine influence, mites are very useful. Their remains are usually well preserved and they can be found in high densities. Several taxonomic groups of mites can be found near the sea shore: some astigmatic mites (Order Acaridida) occur only in intertidal pools where they feed upon marine algae but their remains are highly unlikely to be found in archaeological samples because they have a very flimsy exoskeleton. Other groups such as the predatory Gamasida also have representatives which are found exclusively in the littoral zone. Single individuals of this group such as *Phaulodinychus repleta* occasionally turn up in archaeological samples but the most frequently found group are the Oribatids which in English are known as beetle-mites or moss-mites. This order is particularly useful for environmental reconstructions because their ecology is relatively well studied, they never exhibit phoresy and their remains are always the best preserved mite remains in a sample because of their robust build (Figure 8.3).

To measure the marine influence we can use the general

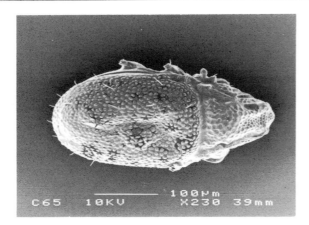

Figure 8.3: A medieval individual of the oribatid mite Carabodes schatzi *Bernini 1976.*

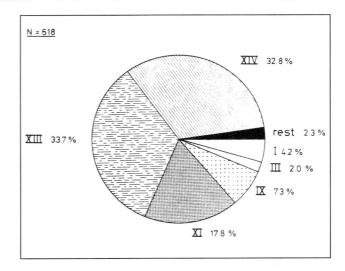

Figure 8.4: Spectrum of the ecological groups of oribatid mites found in an 11th century sample from the dwelling mound of Oldeboorn.

method for environmental reconstruction on the basis of oribatids in which the species are allocated to one of 20 ecological groups (Schelvis 1990). Each of these groups is optimally represented in a specific habitat or a combination of habitats. One of these 20 ecological groups is group XIV which consists of 7 species which are frequently found together in salty grassland only.

Figure 8.4 presents an example of the results of the mite analysis of an 11th century sample taken from the dwelling mound of Oldeboorn in the north of the Netherlands. A sample of only half a litre yielded more than 700 remains of mites in the first flotation, including 644 oribatids. More than 96% of these oribatids could be allocated to one of the ecological groups. Among these mites were 5 species which belong to ecological group 14. Because the method of environmental reconstruction on the basis of oribatid mites takes into account not only the number of individuals of each species, but also the completeness of the ecological groups, group XIV, with 5 out 7 spp. present, is well represented in this sample. The other ecological group that is well represented in this sample is group XIII whose members are to be found in any wet grassland, either fresh or salty. Ecological group XI is optimally represented in constantly soaking wet mosses, especially *Sphagnum* in moorland and group IX is indicative of both soaking wet moorland and grassland as well as swamp woodland. Those groups which are more or less characteristic of drier and more wooded environments such as groups III and I are only marginally represented. Unfortunately, there was only one sample available from this small excavation. A larger series of samples would have allowed the marine influence to be monitored over the ages. This single sample, however, provided the only environmental data on the site and its analysis was therefore of unquestionable importance.

CONCLUSIONS

The remains of mites are powerful tools in the reconstruction of past environments. Their species distribution in archaeological samples reflects the past ecological conditions as well as the possible presence of people as an agent of environmental changes. The changes in the frequency of those species of mites which occur in salty grassland only can be used successfully to monitor past changes in marine influence.

REFERENCES

Giffen, A.E. van (1913). *Die Fauna der Würten.* Ph.D. thesis, University of Groningen.

Gijn, A.L. van and Waterbolk, H.T. (1984). The colonization of the salt marshes of Friesland and Groningen: the possibility of a transhumant prelude. *Paleohistoria* **26**, 101–122.

Kenward, H.K., Hall, A.R. and Jones, A.K.G. (1980). A tested set of techniques for the extraction of plant and animal macrofossils from waterlogged archaeological deposits. *Science and Archaeology* **22**, 3–15.

Koehn, H. (1939). *Die Nordfriesischen Inseln, Die Entwicklung ihrer Landschaft und die Geschichte ihres Volkstums,* Hamburg.

Krantz, G.W. (1970). *A Manual of Acarology.* Corvallis, Oregon: O.S.U. Book Stores, Inc.

Schelvis, J. (1990). The reconstruction of local environments on the basis of the remains of oribatid mites (Acari; Oribatida). *Journal of Archaeological Science* **17**, 559–571.

Schelvis, J. (1992). *Mites and Archaeozoology. General Methods; Applications to Dutch sites.* Ph.D. thesis, University of Groningen.

Waterbolk, H.T. (1979). Siedlungskontinuität im Küstengebiet der Nordsee zwischen Rhein und Elbe. *Probleme der Küstenforschung im südlichen Nordseegebiet* **13**, 1–21.

9. Disappearance of Elmid "Riffle Beetles" from Lowland River Systems in Britain – the Impact of Alluviation

David Smith

Recent sedimentological work in the lowland river valleys of Britain has indicated that there was a widespread change in their fluvial and depositional environments in the Iron Age. There was a change from lateral deposition in a stable anastomosing and multichannelled system to that of overbank deposition of alluvium across the floodplain. Often this has been linked to woodland clearance, changes in farming practice and/or climatic factors.

It has been speculated that one of the results of this change is the disappearance of many of the elmid or "riffle beetles" from the lowland river systems due to the periodic flushing of the river channels with silts. However, bulk samples associated with the 11th century AD bridge at Hemington, Leicestershire, contained fossil elements of many elmids, including the now very rare *Stenelmis canaliculata* (Gyll.) *and Macronychus quadrituberculatus* Müll. This would appear to suggest that the elmids may have disappeared in the lowlands after the onset of alluviation, and perhaps only during relatively recent times. However, both local conditions on the Trent during the 11th century and a number of problems concerning the circumstances of river deposition may cloud this overly simple model.

Keywords: Palaeoentomology, alluviation, elmid, Trent valley, Holocene.

INTRODUCTION

On occasions, samples from the most mundane of circumstances, those which have sat in the back of the store cupboard whilst more interesting matter is examined, can produce the best and most thought provoking results. Such is the case presented here. In many ways the insect faunas from the Hemington bridges are unremarkable, just what you would predict from a medieval channel fill deposit running beside wet meadowland and pasture (Smith 1995).

However, one element of the fauna was unpredicted and unexpected. This was the large number of elmid or riffle beetles: in particular considerable numbers of two of Britain's rarer water beetles. This paper discusses the implications of their presence "at the wrong time and in the wrong place", and indeed whether this really is "the wrong time and the wrong place".

The changing sedimentology of Britain's lowland rivers

Within the last twenty years a number of studies have changed the way we view the Holocene development of both channel systems and the flood plains of lowland rivers. The dating, implications and causes of this change in hydrology, and the differing sedimentological regimes that have resulted, have been discussed extensively (Shotton 1978; Limbrey 1987; Needham & Macklin 1992; Macklin & Needham 1992).

Although there are clear differences between dates of inception and the circumstances involved, many lowland rivers appear to develop in a broadly similar way during the Holocene (Brown 1991). The lowland rivers of England today show a gross underfit between the river channels, their associated meander belts, and their large floodplains (Brown 1987; Brown *et al.* 1994; Salisbury 1992). This is probably a result of a combination of low gradient and low stream flow in the Holocene. This means that some rivers cannot erode laterally due to the resistance of banksides and terraces to erosion (Brown *et al.* 1994). The rivers therefore have relatively stable channels with little lateral movement, and are narrow in comparison to the width of their floodplains (Brown 1987).

It is suggested that these present river systems developed from the incised channels formed by actively meandering braided rivers in the late glacial, whilst stream flow was high. During the early and mid Holocene these multichannelled river systems persist as anastomsing rivers (Brown *et al.* 1994). Anastomosing river systems have multiple but stable channels, which show little lateral migration. Most deposition of fluvial material occurs within the channel itself rather than across the flood plain as a whole (Smith 1983). Where channel change occurs it is often by avulsion, a sudden and catastrophic change in course, rather than by the gradual lateral movement common in most meandering systems (Smith 1983). The potential role of both human and / or beaver activity in initiating such changes should not be forgotten (Coles 1992). These factors can often result in channels being cut off from the main river system. Within anastomosing river systems vegetated stable and long lived ground surfaces develop between the channels. Often areas of infilling backswamps develop within abandoned channels. Anastomosing river systems therefore produce a series of stable but complex environments across considerable areas of their potential flood plains. Among the major lowland river systems which appear to show this channel pattern during the early and middle Holocene are the Severn (Brown 1987), Trent (Knight & Howard 1994; 1995; Salisbury 1992), Nene (Brown & Keogh 1992), Welland (French *et al.* 1992), and possibly the Thames (Robinson & Lambrick 1984; Robinson 1992). It is also commonly asserted that anastomosing river systems are characterised by a relatively low silt load.

Many lowland rivers appear to show a major and dramatic change in both their fluvial and depositional behaviour relatively late in the Holocene. At differing times, from the Late Bronze Age onwards, the rivers systems move towards being single channelled and begin to deposit fine clays and silts over extensive areas of their flood plains away from the channel (Brown 1987; Brown *et al.* 1994). This contraction of the river system is usually portrayed as resulting from the flooding of the river system with large amounts of fine sediment. This increase in fine sediment load is often though to result from increased soil wash from the surrounding valley slopes due to anthropogenic activity (woodland clearance, expansion of cultivation or changes in farming regime (Buckland & Sadler 1985); these factors may be also be related to long-term climatic change (Bell 1992). As Macklin and Needham (1992, 16) state: "*the British Holocene fluvial record can be considered to be an alluvial sequence that*

has been climatically driven but culturally blurred"

Whatever, the cause of this change in the river systems of Lowland Britain, its effects on the river beds themselves is fairly clear. It would suggest a move from a stable stony bed to one which is periodically flushed and blanketed with clay and silt sediments. This appears to be the situation in most of the Lowland rivers at present. As will be seen below, it is this change within the channel which is important, rather than the effects of alluviation across the flood plain as a whole.

The impact of alluviation on water beetles

In a paper on the Coleopterous faunas recovered from deposits associated with the Bronze Age river Avon at Bidford upon Avon, Warwickshire, Peter Osborne (1988) suggested that the onset of alluviation could have affected the beetle fauna. In these deposits from Bidford, along with the "normal" mix of species characteristic of slower waters, there were a relatively large number of elmid species. Amongst these were considerable numbers of *Oulimnius* species and lesser numbers of *Esolus paralellepipedus* (Müll.) and *Limnius volckmari* (Panz.). Although not rare today, these species have a distinct distribution. At present they are limited to upland streams or the headwaters of the larger rivers, and are not found in the lowlands (Holland 1972). In addition, Osborne also found three species of elmid which are rare and endangered at present in this country. These are *Stenelmis canaliculata* (Gyll.) (Red Data book Status 2), *Macronychus quadrituberculatus* Müll. (RDB 3) and *Normandia nitens* (Müll.) (RDB 2) (Shirt 1987; Hymen 1992). All of these species live in clear, well oxygenated waters were they cling to the underside of stones and gravels.

Osborne (1988) argued that this was the nature of the river bed at Biford during the Bronze Age. He suggested that there were good reasons to think that these individuals were present in the lowland river, rather than carried from its headwaters during periods of flood scour (an argument which had been advanced previously when considering interglacial and early post glacial faunas which contained these species (Shotton & Osborne 1965; Osborne 1974)). He cited modern work on flood refuse collected below the Cuttle Brook Nature Reserve which produced no elmids despite their presence upstream (Shotton & Osborne 1986). This suggested that despite dramatic flood activity the elmids had "*hung on grimly to their holds despite the flow of water.*" (Osborne 1988, 722). Osborne argued that their presence at Bidford at this date indicated a major difference between the Bronze Age Avon, where a gravel based rifle and pool system was present, and its modern form, where the river bed is blanketed with a considerable depth of silt and mud. This situation has also been repeated at a number of other sites in other river catchments of a similar date, which suggests that this pattern was widespread (Osborne 1974; Robinson 1991; 1992; 1993). Osborne (1988) suggested that the disappearance of the

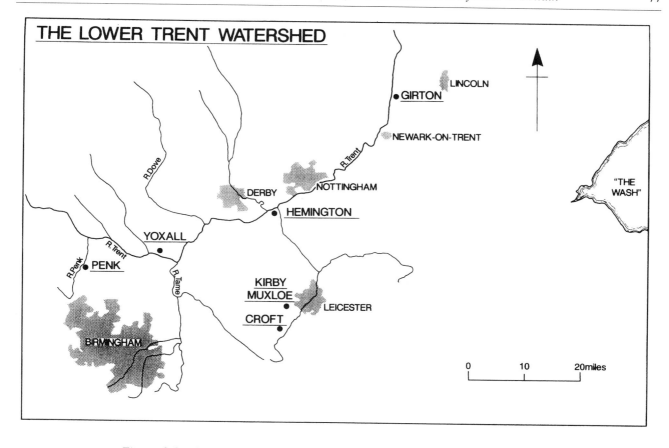

Figure 9.1: The Lower Trent Valley, showing locations referred to in the text.

elmids from the lowland rivers was probably linked to the increase in fine grades of material in the water during and after the main phases of alluviation, and that the artificial straightening of water courses and the establishment of dams, weirs and locks on the lowland river system might function to stop the growing blanket of silt being cleared from the channel beds.

Osborne's incisive work led to the opinion amongst palaeoentomologists that, at least as a working hypothesis, the elmid species should not be present in lowland rivers after the onset of alluviation. However, new data from the site of Hemington on the Trent permits an assessment of the validity of such an hypothesis.

HEMINGTON

During mineral extraction at Hemington, Leicestershire (Figure 9.1) a number of medieval bridges were discovered and excavated by the Leicestershire County Council Archaeology Unit (Cooper *et al.* 1994). The remains of 11th century AD bridge consisted of four large stone filled wooden caissons. Three samples of a sandy silt were collected for insect analysis from below collapsed caisson timbers or from under wooden hurdles. All three samples

appeared to be in contexts that were contemporary with, or post-dated, the bridge. In addition, the horizontal mats of material contained in the sediments suggested that they were laid *in situ* and were not clasts.

The majority of the rich terrestrial fauna that was retrieved from these samples is not unexpected for the medieval period, and indicated that the landscape was cleared and contained wet bankside pastures and meadowlands. However, similar to Osborne's Bidford samples, the water beetles contained a mix of indicators of both fast and slow flowing waters. In the case of species indicating the former conditions there were again large numbers of elmids. This includes considerable numbers of *Elmis aenea* (Müll.), *Oulimnius* species, *E. parallelepipedus*, and *L. volckmari*. In addition, 17 individuals of *S. canaliculata* and 28 individuals of *M. quadrituberculatus* were also recovered. This in itself confirms that the distribution of these species in the past was more widespread than at present. Two other elmid species of note found in these samples are 6 and 16 individuals respectively of *Riolus cupreus* (Müll.) and *R. subviolaceus* (Müll.). Both of these species are Red Data book Notable A (Hymen 1992) and are thought to be restricted to calcareous waters (Holland 1972). In total the elmids accounted for 72.9% of the water beetles recovered. In addition to these species others are present which are also indicative of fast flowing or clear waters such as the Dytiscidae *Sticthotarsus duodecimpustulatus* (F.) and *Potamonectes depressus* (F.) and the Hydraenidae *Hydraena riparia* Kug.. This clearly shows that at medieval Hemington river conditions were similar to those suggested for Bronze Age, pre alluvial, Bidford (Osborne 1988).

DISCUSSION

The implications of this fauna appear to be quite clear; the indication is that the elmid faunas in the lowland rivers are present much later than has been previously assumed, that the fauna was a much longer lived phenomenon than expected, and moreover that the species could occur after the onset of alluviation. Osborne is without doubt right in his assertion that these species can not live in permanently cloudy waters or where there is silt on the channel beds. Perhaps, despite the periodic flushing of the river systems with large amounts of fine mineral silts and clays, these species continued to live in sections of the river course where silt did not collect or where the bed was scoured? Perhaps the elmid species were able to re-colonise some areas of these rivers as they cleared the deposited clays and silts between the differing periods of alluvial behaviour. Their disappearance in modern times would have to be explained by other factors. Perhaps, as Osborne (1988) notes, recent canalisation and straightening of water courses, and the use of weirs, locks and dams, may be responsible for the permanency of thick blankets of silts within the river channels? Equally, pollution may have had an effect on the distribution of these species.

Such assertions, however, may serve only to simplify a complicated picture. A number of additional factors may be important: there is good reason to believe that medieval river conditions at Hemington are exceptional for a lowland river in England, but may be exceptional for the Trent catchment as a whole.

Examination of a number of sections in gravel quarries in this area of the Trent have suggested that the river was not behaving in the same way as the other lowland rivers during the medieval period. As Knight and Howard (1995, 18) note *"It is worth emphasising ... the remarkable character of the Holocene sediments in certain stretches of the Trent Valley, noticeably in the vicinity of Hemington, Leicestershire and Colwick, Nottinghamshire. These deposits consist of coarse grained sands and gravels such as are usually associated with the Devensian or earlier cold stages"*. It would appear from this that the river Trent was reworking considerable depths of coarse sands and gravels more of less up to modern times (Salisbury 1992; Knight & Howard 1995). The Hemington bridges themselves were buried under two and half metres of coarse sands and gravels. This fact, and other historical evidence, may suggest that the river continued to anasto-

mose in some stretches until a similarly late date (Salisbury 1992; Knight & Howard 1995). The reason for this is some what unclear, but Brown (1992) has suggested that it may result from the exceptional one sided nature runoff in the catchment. In addition it is notable that three main tributaries (the Dove, the Derwent and the Soar) all join the Trent in this five mile stretch (Salisbury 1992).

In terms of the insects at Hemington this may explain the presence of this elmid fauna at such a late date. Shifting sands and gravels, with fast flowing waters, are the optimum environments for these species. In addition, the presence of *S. canaliculata* and *M. quadrituberculatus* at the Hemington bridges may be explained by even more local factors. Both above and below the bridges there are the remains of large and deep scour pools. There are suggestions that both of these species commonly occur in the scour pools below weirs and other river implacements on the continent (Steffan 1979). *M. quadri-tuberculatus* is also thought to be associated with fallen or submerged timbers in water courses (Holland 1972; Steffan 1979). Therefore, its relatively high numbers at Hemington may be due to the presence of the bridges themselves. In addition, *M. quadrituberculatus* was taken from the river Trent, at Burton on Trent, in 1867 (Holland 1972). This suggests that these river conditions may have persisted more or less up to modern times.

Both of these situations raise doubts that the presence of these species on the Trent implies that they would be present in the other lowland river systems at this date as a matter of course. In terms of Osborne's (1988) suggestion that the elmids would not survive in these alluviated rivers after the Iron Age, the Trent may be the exception that proves the rule.

Taphonomic factors relating to site location and archaeological period may be equally significant and introduce bias into the palaeoentomological record. There is a temporal problem resulting from the paucity of work on river deposits that demonstrably date to the Roman, Dark Age and medieval periods. This results not from a lack of interest by the palaeoentomologist, but rather because these late channels tend to be located in areas of deep alluvial deposition, where prospecting for them can be problematic (Clark 1992; Salisbury 1992). In addition, channels from these later dates are rarely cut by quarry sections, since they are seldom underlain by the sands and gravels which are sought for extraction but rather by alluvial or colluvial deposits.

Another factor that must be considered is the position of the sampling site within in the watershed as a whole. This is clearly shown when the elmid faunas from a number of differing quarry sites in the Trent watershed are examined. Three sites from headwater locations were analysed: these were Neolithic and Bronze Age Croft and Bronze Age Kirby Muxloe, Leicestershire, and Penk, Staffordshire (Figure 9.1). Two further Bronze Age sites are actually from the flood plain of the Trent itself. These are the infilling reed bed at Yoxal, Staffordshire, and the damp

Table 9.1: The distribution of the Elmid species from archaeological deposits in the Lower Trent Watershed.

	Head water				Flood plain			Main channel
	Kirby Muxloe	Croft	Penk		Yoxal	Girton		Hemington
Helichus substriatus (Müll.)		√						
Stenelmis canaliculata (Gyll.)								•
Elmis aenea (Müll.)	•	•	•					•
Esolus parallelepipedus (Müll.)		•	√		√			•
Oulimius spp.	√	•	•		√			•
Limnius volckmari (Panz.)	√	•	√					•
Riolus cuprus (Müll.)		√						√
R. subviolaceus (Müll.)			√					•
Macronychus quadrituberculatus (Müll.)								•

few individuals present √

> 10 individuals present •

mire beside the burnt mound at Girton, Nottinghamshire (Figure 9.1). The various elmids present at these sites and Hemington are presented in Table 9.1. The pattern seen from this table appears to be the converse of what had been hypothesised. There is a more restricted range of species before the Bronze Age than after it. However, this pattern can easily be explained by the nature of the deposits and their location within the watershed rather than by any recourse to temporal and external changes within the rivers regime such as the onset of alluviation. The lack of elmid species at both Yoxal and Girton is not surprising. Neither the in-filling reed bed nor the damp mire are environments conducive to the elmids. Equally, the elmid species that are present in small numbers are those which are believed to the most tolerant of mud and silts (Blackburn *pers. com*). The sedimentology of sites from the headwaters suggests these streams are relatively shallow and clearly ran across clear sands and gravels at this time, and so were able to support a relatively large and diverse elmid fauna. Water depth may be the factor that explains the difference between these head water sites and Hemington. Hemington is clearly in the main channel of a relatively deep river. Indeed, both *S. caniculata* and *M. quadrituberculatus* are thought to be species with a preference for deep waters (Steffan 1979; Blackburn pers. comm.).

This discussion of elmid faunas from Trent clearly shows that an explanation of the differences between the sites need not solely rely on changes of the river regime over time, but may result from the location of the site within the landscape of the river catchment as a whole. This would suggest that the presence or absence of elmids in deposits such as these should not be used as an indicator for the occurrence of alluviation within the river system by themselves.

CONCLUSIONS

It is probable that Osborne's suggestions about the timing and cause of the disappearance of the elmid species in Britain's lowland rivers are still applicable only at an individual catchment scale, but obviously the pattern of alluviation and the link to the elmid fauna is a complex phenomenon. There is a clear need for the examination of post Roman deposits in other catchments to confirm or deny this.

Acknowledgements

I would like to thank the Leicestershire County Council Archaeology Unit for collecting the samples from Hemington. The work was carried out as part of the Hemington Bridges post excavation program which was funded in part by Ennemix Construction Materials and English Heritage. I would also like to thank both Jessica Winder and John Blackburn from the river laboratory, Institute of Fresh Water Ecology for their helpful comments. In addition Jon Sadler made many helpful comments on this paper.

REFERENCES

Bell, M. (1992). Archaeology under alluvium: human agency and environmental process. some concluding thoughts, pp. 271–276 in Needham S. and Macklin, M.G. (eds.) *Alluvial Archaeology in Britain*. Oxbow Monograph 27. Oxford: Oxbow books.

Brown, A.G. (1987). Holocene floodplain sedimentation and channel response of the lower River Severn, United Kingdom. *Zeitschrift für Geomorphologie*, (Neue Folia), **31**, 293–310.

Brown, A.G. (1991). Hydrogeomorphological changes in the Severn Basin during the last 15000 years: orders of change in a maritime catchment, pp. 11–169 in Starkel, L. Gregory K.J. and Thornes,

J.B. (eds.) *Temperate Palaeohydrology*. John Wiley and Sons Ltd: Chichester and New York.

Brown, A.G. (1992). Soil erosion and colluviation at the floodplain edge, pp. 77–87 in Boardman J. and Bell, M. (eds.) *Soil Erosion Past and Present*. Oxbow Monograph 77. Oxford: Oxbow books.

Brown, A.G., and Keough, M.K. (1992). Palaeochannels and palaeolandsurfaces: the geoarchaeological potential of some Midlands floodplains, pp. 185–196 in Needham S. and Macklin, M.G. (eds.) *Alluvial Archaeology in Britain*. Oxbow Monograph 27. Oxford: Oxbow books.

Brown, A.G., Keough, M.K. and Rice, R.J. (1994). Floodplain evolution in the east Midlands, United Kingdom: the lateglacial and Flandrian alluvial record from the Soar and Nene Valleys. *Philosophical Transactions of the Royal Society of London* **A.348**, 261–293.

Buckland, P.C., and Sadler, J. (1985). Late Flandrian alluviation in the Humberhead levels. *East Midland Geographer* **8**, 239–251.

Coles, B. (1992). Further thoughts on the impact of beaver on temperate landscapes, pp. 93–99 in Needham S. and Macklin, M.G. (eds.) *Alluvial Archaeology in Britain*. Oxbow Monograph 27. Oxford: Oxbow Books.

Cooper, L., Ripper, S., and Clay, P. (1994). The Hemington bridges. *Current Archaeology* **140**, 316–321.

French, C.A.I., Macklin, M.G. and Passmore, D.G. (1992). Archaeology and palaeochannels in the Lower Welland and Nene Valleys: alluvial archaeology at the fen-edge, eastern England, pp. 169–176 in Needham S. and Macklin, M.G. (eds.) *Alluvial Archaeology in Britain*. Oxbow Monograph 27. Oxford: Oxbow Books.

Holland, D.G. (1972). A key to the larvae, pupae and adults of the British species of Elminthidae. *Freshwater Biological Association Scientific Publication* **26**.

Hyman, P.S. (1992). *A Review of the Scarce and Threatened Coleoptera of Great Britain*. No 3. part 1. U.K. Nature Conservation. Peterborough.

Knight, D. and Howard, A.J. (1994). The Trent Valley Survey. *Transactions of the Thoroton Society* **98**, 126–129.

Knight, D. and Howard, A.J. (1995). *Archaeology and Alluvium in the Trent Valley. An Archaeological Assessment of the Floodplain and Gravel Terraces*. Nottingham: Trent and Peak Archaeological Trust.

Limbrey, S. (1987). Farmers and farmland: aspects of prehistoric landuse in the Severn basin, in Gregory, K.J., Lewis, J. and Thomas, J.B. (eds.) *Palaeohydrology in Practice*. John Wiley and Sons: Chichester and New York.

Macklin, M.G. and Needham S. (1992). Studies in British alluvial archaeology: potential and prospect, pp. 9–23 in Needham S. and Macklin, M.G. (eds.) *Alluvial Archaeology in Britain*. Oxford: Oxbow Monograph 27. Oxbow Books.

Needham S. and Macklin, M.G. (1992). *Alluvial Archaeology in Britain*. Oxbow Monograph 27. Oxford: Oxbow Books.

Osborne, P.J. (1974). An insect assemblage of early Flandrain age from Lea Marston, Warwickshire and its bearing in the con-

temporary climate and ecology. *Quaternary Research* **4**, 471–486.

Osborne, P.J. (1988). A late Bronze Age insect fauna from the River Avon, Warwickshire, England: its implications for the terrestrial and fluvial environment and for climate. *Journal of Archaeological Science* **15**, 715–727.

Robinson M.A. (1991). Neolithic and late Bronze Age insect assemblages, chapter 17 in Needham S. (ed.) *Excavation and Salvage at Runnymede Bridge 1978*. London: British Museum Press and English Heritage.

Robinson, M.A. (1992). Environment, archaeology and alluvium on the river gravels of the South Midlands, pp. 197–208 in Needham S. and Macklin, M.G. (eds.) *Alluvial Archaeology in Britain*. Oxbow Monograph 27. Oxford: Oxbow Books.

Robinson M.A. (1993). The Iron Age environmental evidence, pp. 101–120 in Allen, T.G. and Robinson M.A. *The Prehistoric Landscape and Iron Age Enclosed Settlement at Mingies Ditch. Hardwick-with-Yelford, Oxon*. Thames Valley Landscapes: The Windrush Valley Volume 2. The Oxford Archaeological Unit.

Robinson, M.A. and Lambrick, G. H. (1984). Holocene alluvation and hydrology in the Upper Thames Basin. *Nature* **308**, 809–814.

Salisbury, C.R. (1992). The archaeological evidence for palaeochannels in the Trent Valley, pp. 155–162 in Needham S. and Macklin, M.G. (eds.) (1992) *Alluvial Archaeology in Britain*. Oxbow Monograph 27. Oxford: Oxbow Books.

Shirt, D.B. (1987). *British Red Data Books: 2. Insects*. London: Nature Conservancy Council.

Shotton, F.W. (1978). Archaeological inferences from the study of alluvium in the Severn / Avon valleys, pp. 27–32 in Limbrey S. and Evans, J.G. (eds.) *The Effect of Man on the Landscape: the Lowland Zone*. London: Council for British Archaeology Research Report 21.

Shotton, F.W. and Osborne, P.J. (1965). The fauna of the Hoxian interglacial deposits at Nechells, Birmingham. *Philosophical Transactions of the Royal Society of London*. Series **B 248**, 353–378.

Shotton, F.W. and Osborne, P.J. (1986). Faunal content of debris left by an exceptional flood of the Cuttle Brook at Temple Balsall nature reserve. *Proceedings of the Coventry Natural History and Scientific Society* **V**, 359–363.

Smith D.G. (1983). Anastomosed fluval deposits: modern examples from western Canada, pp. 155–168 in Collinson, J.D. and Lewin J. (eds.) *Modern and Ancient Fluvial Systems*. Oxford: International Association of Sedimentologists, Special Publications, Blackwell.

Smith, D.N. (1994). *The Coleoptera Associated with the 11th. Century Bridge at Hemington*. Unpublished Report to Leicester County Coucil Archaeology Unit.

Steffan, A. W. (1979). Familie: Dryopidae. In Freude, H., Harde, K. W. and Lohse, G. A. *Die Käfer Mitteleuropas*. Band 6. Krefeld: Goecke and Evers Verlag.

10. Palaeoenvironmental Reconstruction in the Central Mexican Highlands: A Re-Appraisal of Traditional Theory

Georgina H. Endfield, Sarah L. O'Hara and Sarah E. Metcalfe

Interdisciplinary research into long term environmental change in the highlands of central Mexico is providing new evidence as to the extent and nature of environmental degradation in the pre-and post-Conquest period. The widely held belief that the indigenous population lived in harmony with their environment and that the introduction of new farming techniques by the Spanish conquerors caused widespread environmental destruction is being challenged on a number of fronts. Palaeolimnological investigations indicate that periods of accelerated erosion occurred throughout the highlands of central Mexico following the introduction of sedentary agriculture *ca.* 3,500 years ago, reaching a maximum in the period immediately prior to the Conquest. Furthermore there is a growing body of evidence to suggest that following the Conquest there was a period of environmental recovery with a subsequent decrease in erosion rates. Archival evidence indicates that the Spanish were well aware of the problems of intense grazing and took measures to reduce land use pressure and hence environmental degradation. Thus, contrary to the belief that the Spanish introduced harmful land management practices, it would appear that they acted in an environmentally conservative manner. The two basic ideas which have guided much environmental research in Mexico appear to be losing ground and it is clear that a we need to adopt a more objective approach in our attempts to unravel the relative impacts of different cultures in the New World.

Keywords: Mexico, erosion, agriculture, palaeolimnology.

INTRODUCTION

Any attempt to reconstruct past environments necessitates a degree of discretion and assumption, for there are inevitable lacunae and inconsistencies in whatever resources we, as contemporary observers of the past, choose to exploit. At best, all we can hope for is a *hypothetical* scenario or course of events, be they "natural" or cultural, and one could argue that it is the "unknown" quantity that precludes a definitive palaeoenvironmental reconstruction of any one area. A degree of contention in any study of environmental change is, therefore, to be expected. Despite much debate, for example, there is still no consensus over the cause of widespread land degradation in the central Mexican highlands. The key issue concerns the relative impacts of pre-and post-Conquest societies and their respective agrosystems, although in this climatically-sensitive area, the implications for the influence of small-scale climatic fluctuations on cultural activity and consequent environmental degradation, have recently been highlighted (O'Hara *et al.* 1994).

With a growing awareness of the need for conservation measures in a context of increasing population pressure and climatic change, there are moves by environmental agencies in Mexico and elsewhere for a return to traditional forms of agriculture. Supported by a mounting body of evidence of prehispanic soil erosion, however (Garcia-Cook 1986; O'Hara 1991), theories of pre-Conquest degradation are gaining acceptance and it may well be the case that a return to indigenous agricultural systems is not the most environmentally-sensitive policy. Less attention has to date been paid to the precise nature of agricultural activity and the environmental impacts of post-Conquest societies, though palaeolimnological and archival evidence would suggest that the impact of the Spanish imposed agricultural systems in this area may well have been more conservative than is traditionally appreciated. In addition, preliminary archival investigations are establishing that there was a good deal of continuity rather than change in terms of settlement and land use following the arrival of the Spanish (Butzer 1991).

MYTHS AND MISCONCEPTIONS

It has recently been suggested that many of the accepted theories regarding New World environments and people were fostered by the Europeans themselves as a result of the Romanticised ideals of the 18th and 19th centuries (Pagden 1994). Metaphors regarding the deity-like status of the European Conquistadores, for example, were not, it is now argued, promulgated by the indigenous peoples, but flowed naturally from the concepts of Renaissance and Enlightenment (Harris 1995). Such themes were, moreover, enhanced by the enduring Romantic genre of the "noble American savage", epitomised in the writings of 18th century French authors such as Voltaire, Rousseau and Montesquieu (Wilson 1995).

It is this "othering" of indigenous peoples (Harris 1995) by Europeans and the "progressive mythologisation" of New World environmental and cultural history that continues today in a number of modern academic approaches. Bowden (1992) suggests that major American beliefs regarding the pre-American environment were all created successively as myths once settlement had been established in a particular area. It has been claimed, for example, that New World peoples lived in harmony with nature and refrained deliberately from altering their environment while Europeans had a "ruthless land ethic" and introduced an agrosystem that was by definition environmentally destructive (Butzer 1992). Such long-held theories, constituting "The Pristine Myth" (Denevan 1992), whereby the nature of the environment at the time of European contact was undisturbed, have proved to be particularly pervasive and have recently been revived by a group of American militant ecologists. Sale (1990), for example, claims that it was the Europeans who transformed the environment of the New World, and champions the widely-held dichotomy of the benign Indian landscape and its devastated colonial counterpart. Similarly, it has recently been suggested that "pre-Columbian America was the first Eden – a pristine natural kingdom" (Shelter 1991, 226).

It cannot be doubted that the arrival of the Europeans led to both profound immediate – and more protracted, though equally significant – changes in the New World. Historians now agree that the European discovery of the Americas touched off waves of epidemics and indigenous depopulation *en masse,* given the lack of immunity of the native population to introduced Old World diseases, though debate rages over the size of pre-Columbian populations, and the magnitude, rate and timing of what can be seen as a hemispheric depopulation (Roberts 1989). While it has been suggested that the population decline amongst the highland communities was not as severe as that of the lowlands (Newson 1994) there is evidence to suggest a population decimation in the Purepechan controlled areas of the central Mexican highlands (Gorenstein & Pollard 1983). Dramatic cultural and societal change, therefore, immediately followed and in some cases even preceded[1] European contact in parts of the New World.

In addition to the more immediate impacts of European contact, however, there occurred more prolonged, and what were to be long-term economic changes. The Conquest basically entailed a translocation of European systems of production, lifestyles and ideals, so that with the arrival of the Spanish came a new crop complex and, perhaps most significantly, the arrival of herd animals such as sheep, pigs and goats. The Mediterranean plough also made its first appearance in the New World, only digging sticks (*coas*) being employed to till the ground previously. The detrimental environmental impacts of European agrosystems has long been a forum of debate and controversy, with the suggestion that the heavily-eroded and deeply dissected landscape of the Mediterranean was a consequence of overgrazing, deforestation and the use of the plough, enabling deeper tillage and the cultivation of previously unexploited marginal tracts of land (van Andel *et al.* 1990). That the introduction of herd animals and the cultivation of new crops, combined with the use of the ox-drawn plough, to a supposedly "pristine" environment might result in degradation seems, therefore, conceptually feasible.

Following an argument raised by Chevalier (1970, 103–104), Melville (1990; 1994) has suggested that during the 1570's sheep herds multiplied beyond the capacity of the available land to support them. Moreover, based on archival evidence she concluded that the impact of stock-raising in the Valle del Mesquital, Hidalgo State, "was a rapid and profound process of environmental degradation caused by overstocking and indiscriminate grazing of sheep in the post-Conquest era" (Melville 1990, 24).

It is unlikely, however, that such a dogmatic and mono-causal model provides an adequate explanation of the degradation we can observe in the area today. For the most part, these investigations were based largely on the exploitation of a single line of evidence, which can result in erroneous conclusions being drawn (O'Hara & Metcalfe in press). The exploitation of a range of physical and cultural sources of evidence have, however, provided a more detailed record of environmental change in the area, and have helped redress what has become a distinctly colonial outlook. Our purpose here is not so much to

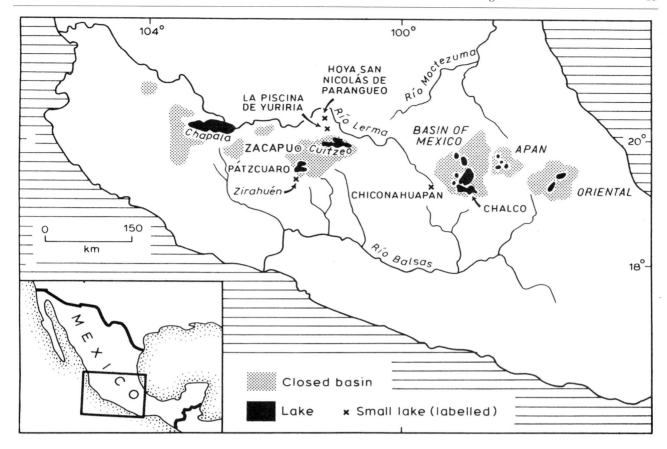

Figure 10.1: The Neovolcanic Axis of Central Mexico, showing the location of major lakes.

discuss the methodological approaches and results of some of the more recent multi-disciplinary investigations carried out in the central Mexican highlands, which in any case are discussed in detail elsewhere (O'Hara 1991; O'Hara *et al.* 1993; 1994; Metcalfe *et al.* 1994), but to employ the evidence emerging from these projects as a basis for a re-appraisal of environmental history in central Mexico.

THE ENVIRONMENTAL CONTEXT: THE AREA OF INVESTIGATION

The volcanic uplands of central Mexico, crossing Mexico at around 19°N (the neovolcanic axis, NVA) (Figure 10.1) represent a distinctly eroded and degraded environment. Establishing the relative importance of climate and humans as factors causing this degradation has, however, proved problematic, for the area has been subject to climatic change on a range of timescales, as well as long-term human activity.

The NVA represents an area of summer rainfall with only 5% of the annual precipitation falling during the winter months. Lying at the northern end of the tropical summer rain belt rainfall decreases sharply along a south-north gradient from 1000 mm in the highlands to <400

mm towards the northern sub-tropical desert (Metcalfe *et al.* 1994). In addition, changes in the strength and location of the dominant atmospheric circulation systems have rendered the area sensitive to periodic drought (Wallen 1955; Metcalfe 1987) and a concomitant extension southwards of the more arid realm. The lake basins of the volcanic area, with their temperate humid climate and fertile alluvial soils have, nevertheless, provided an attractive focus for human settlement (Metcalfe *et al.* 1994), and there is evidence to indicate that sedentary agriculture was widespread in this area at least 3,500 years ago, although sedentary settlements are known to have existed in the Basin of Mexico some five thousand years earlier (Niederberger 1987). It has been suggested, however, that the more arid, northern frontier of settlement has oscillated between phases of expansion and contraction during wetter and drier periods respectively (Armillas 1969), though the simplicity of this hypothesis has been questioned (Brown 1985; 1992).

Multi-disciplinary investigations in Michoacan and neighbouring Guanajuato, both highland states in west-central Mexico (O'Hara 1991; O'Hara *et al.* 1994; Metcalfe *et al.* 1994), have been used to elucidate the link between climate, human settlement and landscape degradation. It has, for example, been suggested that periodic drought has influenced settlement scenarios, and that degradation resulting from overuse of the landscape coupled with drought-induced soil erosion, has precipitated abandonment. In this way humans could be considered as mediators in a climate-landscape degradation equation. That a complex relationship exists between climatic change, human settlement and exploitation and environmental degradation in the area cannot, it seems, be doubted, and it remains questionable whether any simple model can be used to explain what is clearly a very complex inter-relationship.

THE PALAEOLIMNOLOGICAL RECORD: A SEDIMENTARY HISTORY OF ENVIRONMENTAL CHANGE

Certain natural attributes of the physical environment in the NVA have facilitated the reconstruction of environmental change. Many of its basins, for example, contain or contained lakes which have remained closed for all or part of their histories. The sediments which have accumulated in these lakes can provide an important record of catchment change, stability or instability.

The value of palaeolimnological investigation for the reconstruction of past environments in Mexico has long-been recognised. Early palaeolimnological studies attempted to elucidate the relationship between climate, palaeoecology and human activity (Deevey 1944; Sears & Clisby 1955), although the lack of chronological resolution and problems of distinguishing the climatic signal from basins subject to tectonic, volcanic and anthropogenic activity, have limited the value of these investigations. What they did highlight, however, was the possibility of employing palaeoecological and palaeo-limnological evidence for the reconstruction of past cultural events. In consequence, more recent investigations of lake sediment records have focused on establishing a long-term history of human impact on the landscape of Mesoamerica (Deevey *et al.* 1979; Metcalfe *et al.* 1989; 1994; O'Hara 1991; O'Hara *et al.* 1993; 1994).

Traditionally palaeolimnological investigations in Mexico have been based on the analysis of a single core, most commonly taken from the deepest part of the lake. A number of investigations have noted an increase in sediment accumulation at the core site during the late Holocene period, which has been attributed to human disturbance within the catchment (Bradbury 1971; Metcalfe *et al.* 1989; 1994). The use of a single core for the reconstruction of sediment accumulation rates and hence rates of erosion within a catchment has been criticised (Bloemendal *et al.* 1979; Dearing *et al.* 1981; Davis *et al.* 1984) as processes such as sediment focusing, can introduce a discrepancy between changes in accumulation rates measured directly from sediment cores and the actual changes in the influx in sediment. Multi-coring approaches in conjunction with high resolution dating allow a reconstruction of the spatial and temporal influx of sediment to the basin and can provide a more accurate picture of the environmental impacts wrought by different culture groups.

LAKE PATZCUARO CASE STUDY

Physical and cultural background

Lake Patzcuaro lies in a small (927km^2), closed, intermontane basin located in the volcanic highlands of Michoacan. The distinct C-shaped lake, stands at an elevation of 2,035 metres above sea level and covers an area of 110km^2 (Figure 10.2). The depth of the lake varies from a maximum of 12m. in the north of the basin to 1–2m. in the south, with an average water depth of 4.9m. (Chacon Torres 1989). It is surrounded by steep, deeply dissected slopes to the north and west, and gentle, largely ungullied alluvial and colluvial deposits to the south and east. The lower slopes are covered in a thorny scrub, though pine and oak forests are common on the steeper slopes (Bassols-Barrera 1986). The archaeology of the area is poorly documented. The oldest known archaeological site is found to the west of San Francisco Uricho, located on the western shore of the lake (Figure 10.2) and dates to the late Classic period (*ca.* AD 800, Pollard 1994). During the late Postclassic the Basin of Patzcuaro was the focal point of the Purepechan culture who held sway over much of west-central Mexico. The area has been the subject of a number of recent socio-economic, anthropological, historical (Gorenstein & Pollard 1983) and biological (Chacon Torres 1993), investigations and has been used to provide us with a record of the environmental impacts of human activity in this area (O'Hara 1991).

The spatial and temporal record of erosion

Twenty short cores, 1.42 to 2.85m. in length, together with a 14.2 m core taken from the lake during a previous investigation (Watts & Bradbury 1982; Figure 10.2), have been analysed for their physical and chemical properties. In conjunction with radiocarbon dating of suitable organic material, it has been possible to reconstruct temporal and spatial variations in sediment inputs to the lake, and so to provide estimates of long-term soil erosion rates in the area (O'Hara 1991).

Analysis of the cores revealed that there have been four distinct periods of catchment instability of varying intensity during the past 4000–5000 years (Figure 10.2). The earliest event predates the appearance of maize (*Zea mays*) one of the three main Mesoamerican cultivars in the palaeoecological record, coinciding with a shift to drier climatic conditions, while subsequent erosion events have been associated with human induced changes in the landscape. For example, a period of erosion dated to between *ca.* 3,600 and 3,050 BP coincides with the first

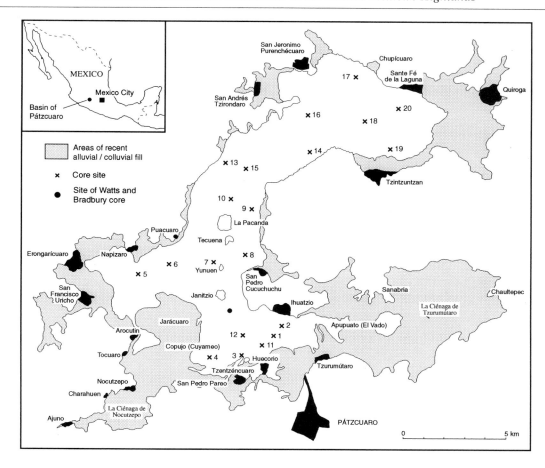

Figure 10.2: Lake Patzcuaro, showing the location of core sites.

appearance of *Zea mays* in the pollen record and has been attributed, as has a similar erosion event recognised in other lakes in the area[2], to the arrival of sedentary agriculturists. The most intense period of erosion began approximately 2,500 BP and occurred in two main phases, the first (phase 3) associated with an agricultural and artisan cultural group known as the Chupicuaro dates to 2,500–1,200 BP and the second (phase 4) with Postclassic and Hispanic settlers.

The cores allow a comparison of sedimentation rates over the last 4,050 years to be made and highlight marked spatial and temporal variations in sediment loading to the lake (Table 10.1). The accumulation of mineral sediment between 3,600 and 3,050 BP is estimated to have been $29.2 \pm 13.6 \text{ g m}^{-2} \text{yr}^{-1}$ with a total of 2.3 million tonnes of sediment being deposited in the lake. During the third erosional phase a total of 13.4 million tonnes of sediment accumulated in the lake, at an average rate of $10,300 \text{ t yr}^{-1}$. What is significant, however, is the fact that this sediment influx is concentrated in the northern basin (Table 10.1). The same trend appears to have been followed in most recent phase of erosion during which time a total of 24.6 million tonnes of sediment accumulated at an average rate of about $29,000 \text{ t yr}^{-1}$.

Terrestrial evidence lends support to the trends illustrated in the sediment accumulation data given in Table 10.1, with the thickness of colluvium being greatest in the northern part of the catchment. Accumulations in excess of 25m., for example, have built up in the vicinity of Quiroga (Figure 10.2), located on the northeastern shore of the lake, while in much of the southern basin sediment accumulations are rarely in excess of 2m. (O'Hara 1991). Although it is possible that the thickness of these deposits may be a reflection of the degree of human-induced degradation, it is more likely that steeper slope gradient in the northern basin resulted in greater erosion.

Converting the sediment accumulation data into erosion rates indicates that there has been a progressive increase in erosion over the last 4,050 years, with rates being at their highest during the last 850 years (Table 10. 2).

It is important to note that the rates of erosion given are in fact minimum estimates as they assume that all sediment eroded from the slopes is deposited in to the lake and that all the catchment is contributing sediment. The build-up of colluvial and alluvial deposits around the lake indicates that this is not the case and it is estimated that over 60% of material eroded from the slopes is held in storage (O'Hara 1991), suggesting significantly higher erosion

Table 10.1: Variations in the rate of sediment accumulation for selected core sites from Patzcuaro over the last 4,050 years. Sediment influx was assessed on inorganic, carbonate and biogenic opal free dry weight basis (after O'Hara et al. 1993). The second phase of erosion is recorded only for the southern parts of the basin, the cores in the northern basin being of insufficient length to cover this episode.

| | South Basin | | Central Basin | North Basin | |
Years BP	core 11 $g\ m^{-2}\ yr^{-1}$	master core $g\ m^{-2}\ yr^{-1}$	core 10 $g\ m^{-2}\ yr^{-1}$	core 19 $g\ m^{-2}\ yr^{-1}$	erosion phase
850–0	118	153	130	553	4
1200–850	40	37	77	66	
2500–1200	49	115	162	131	3
3050–2500	41	47	N/A	N/A	
3600–3050	46	76	N/A	N/A	2
4050–3600	51	47	N/A	N/A	

Table 10.2: Rates of erosion within the Lake Patzcuaro Basin since ca. 4,050 yr BP. Rates of erosion are based on the sediment delivery from the catchment to the lake being 100% (A,C,E,G) and 40% (B,D,F,H) respectively and assume 100% (A,B), 75% (C,D), 50% (E,F) and 25% (G,H) catchment disturbance (from O'Hara et al. 1994).

Years BP	A $kg\ ha^{-1}\ yr^{-1}$	B $kg\ ha^{-1}\ yr^{-1}$	C $kg\ ha^{-1}\ yr^{-1}$	D $kg\ ha^{-1}\ yr^{-1}$	Erosion phase
850–0	362	905	483	1207	4
1200–850	55	137	73	183	
2500–1200	129	323	171	429	3
3050–2500	46	115	61	154	
3600–3050	64	160	85	212	2
4050–3600	51	127	68	170	

Years BP	E $kg\ ha^{-1}\ yr^{-1}$	F $kg\ ha^{-1}\ yr^{-1}$	G $kg\ ha^{-1}\ yr^{-1}$	H $kg\ ha^{-1}\ yr^{-1}$	Erosion phase
850–0	725	1812	1450	3625	4
1200–850	110	275	220	550	
2500–1200	257	644	515	1287	3
3050–2500	92	231	185	462	
3600–3050	127	319	255	637	2
4050–3600	102	256	205	512	

rates. Furthermore, the assumption that erosion occurred throughout the entire basin seems unlikely since the extent of forest clearance and catchment disturbance would vary through time (Table 10.2).

Based on sediment accumulation rates it is not possible to discern any increase in erosion following the contact, indeed a comparison of sediment influx above and below a date of 480±60 years BP (AD 1405–1450) from core 12, indicates that there may well have been a decrease in erosion rates following the arrival of the Spanish (O'Hara 1991; O'Hara *et al.* 1993a). Chemical analysis, however, does suggest that the introduction of the plough may have had some environmental impacts. For example, a shift in the type of sediment entering the lake (from weathered or

surface material, to unweathered material, implying deep gullying) has been noted (O'Hara 1991).

EXPLAINING THE RECORD

Garcia-Cook (1986) claims that "agriculture and settlements......have been endangered by erosion since the beginning of a sedentary way of life". Settlement of agricultural communities in central Mexico led to widespread forest clearance for agricultural purposes, but also for supplies of wood for fuel and timber. Such deforestation is thought to have contributed to the removal of top soil. Fine charcoal fragments dispersed through much of the colluvium around Lake Patzcuaro suggests that burning was, indeed, widespread during the accumulation of these sediments. As this area is not susceptible to natural fires, it is likely that burning was deliberate and probably associated with slash and burn farming techniques (O'Hara 1991). Cook (1949) was one of the first to equate environmental degradation in central Mexico with population pressure suggesting that "the intensive habitation must be the cause of the serious land destruction". Archaeological evidence in the Basin of Mexico indicates a sustained population growth at an annual rate of 1% during the 150 years or so prior to the Conquest (Butzer 1992). Such population increases represent a veritable "demographic explosion", and it has been suggested that the population carrying capacity of the basin had actually been reached by the time the Spanish arrived in 1519 (Williams 1989). This demographic changes would have required considerable expansion, and intensification, of agricultural land use as well as exploitation of more marginal land. Certainly there is evidence to suggest that in the 150 years leading up to the Spanish Conquest there was an increase in the amount of irrigation works, and the terraces and semi-terraces (*metepantli*) of central Mexico encountered by the Europeans implies a need for extra cultivable land, although the terraces could equally reflect the indigenous preference for steeper lands[3]. Williams (1972) has suggested that during periods of population pressure, marginal lands such as that covered with hard baked carbonate crust or *tepetate,* itself an indication of erosion (the carbonate accumulation forming a subsurface horizon in a soil profile), were brought under cultivation, a practice that continues today in some areas of central Mexico. Butzer (1990) has recently expressed scepticism regarding the effectiveness and resilience of prehispanic agrosystems, with the suggestion that there was little in the way of evidence of land improvement. Given such pressures, it is questionable whether environmental stability could have been maintained, in the period immediately prior to Spanish contact.

The timing of the final and most intense period of erosion recognised in the Patzcuaro Basin coincides with the arrival of the Purepechan culture group to the area and it is no coincidence that the greatest influx of sediments to the basin can be correlated with the period of high population pressure in Tzintzuntzan, the capital of the Purepechan empire, located on the northern shores of the lake (Figure 10.2).

Evidence from investigations of other closed lake basins in the NVA have lent support to these findings (Metcalfe *et al.* 1994; Figure 10.3). Data from La Piscina de Yuriria, in Guanajuato State, for example, provides evidence of four phases of disturbance, over the the past 4000 to 5000 years. The timing of these events is largely coincidental with those that are documented in the Patzcuaro Basin (Figure 10.3). The second phase of erosion has been attributed to the arrival of sedentary agriculturalists in the area, while a phase of erosion has also been associated

with the activities of the Purepecha during the Postclassic period, though inverted radiocarbon dates in the top of the sediment core used for analysis have precluded any accurate dating for this later event. A similar problem has confounded the accurate dating of the uppermost part of a sediment core retrieved from La Hoya de San Nicolas de Parangueo, Guanajuato (Metcalfe *et al.* 1994). Despite this two phases of erosion have been recognised (Figure 10.3). The first *ca.* 3210 ± 120 to 2350 BP coincides with palynological evidence of deforestation (Brown 1985) and has been associated with sedentary agriculturalists. The second is again thought to be associated with dense Postclassic settlement of the area (Metcalfe *et al.* 1994). Both erosion events therefore, have been attributed to anthropogenic interference.

These findings highlight the fact that there have been several periods of erosion predating the arrival of the Spanish, contrary to the traditional theories which highlight the benign indigenous impact on the landscape. It has become clear that there have been distinct spatial and temporal variations in the rate of influx of sediments to the lakes and hence in the rate of erosion from the catchment. In sum, what these findings illustrate is that the Spaniards encountered a distinctly humanised and already degraded landscape. It seems that romanticised ideals regarding the harmonious relationship between Indian and environment in the New World cannot now be supported with any confidence.

BEYOND CONVENTIONAL "WISDOM": REVOLUTION IN PROCESS

If multi-disciplinary investigations have served to dismiss one of the more salient and pervasive misconceptions regarding the pre-Contact environment, their contribution to the investigation of post-contact change is likely to be even more complete. Where palaeo-limnological analysis can provide detailed evidence of environmental change in a purely physical sense, archaeological and archival investigations can be used to shed light on the nature of agrosystem dynamics following the arrival of the Spanish (Butzer 1991) and has been used to provide more indirect evidence of environmental change over the last six hundred years (Butzer & Butzer 1993; Butzer & Butzer in press; O'Hara, 1993; O'Hara & Metcalfe 1995).

As discussed above, the palaeolimnological record from the Basin of Patzcuaro suggests that not only was there a change in the nature of material being eroded but that there may have been a decrease in actual erosion rates. Archival sources support these findings and indicate that during the immediate post Conquest period there was increased environmental stability. Drawings in the *Relacion de Michoacan,* for example, depict the area around Tzintzuntzan as being treeless, with the slopes being covered by thorny scrub. Whether vegetation throughout the entire basin was similarly degraded is

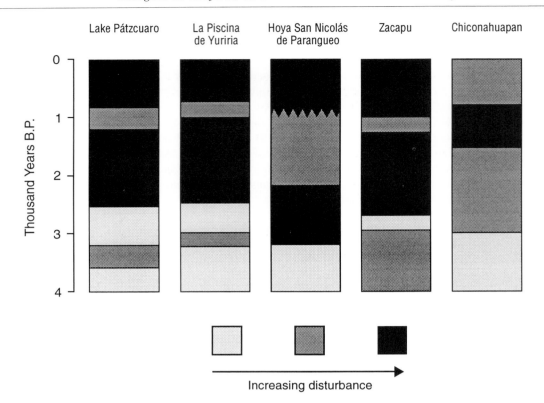

Figure 10.3: Periods of anthropogenic disturbance in selected lake basins of the Neovolcanic Axis over the last c.4000 years.

difficult to determine, although in Cortes' third letter to Charles V it is stated that the Basin of Patzcuaro *'was not very satisfying for them for colonizing'* (Cortes 1522). Furthermore, it is noted in the *Relacion de Michoacan* that when Patzcuaro was settled in the fourteenth century it was necessary to clear the slopes of forest.

By the mid-1700s, however, it appears that the forests within the catchment has been reestablished. Writing in 1748, Villasenor y Sanchez (1748) described Patzcuaro as being '.. *surrounded by large and closely growing trees'* while Alcedo y Bexarano, 1786–1789 noted that the slopes around Lake Patzcuaro were *'...covered by very tall trees'*. Certainly historical sources suggest that the forests in the Basin of Patzcuaro remained relatively intact until the latter part of the 1800s. In 1886 the railway arrived in the Basin of Patzcuaro, heralding renewed exploitation of the forests in this region. Manuel Stillman wrote that:

> 'While the lines of communication were difficult and scarce these forests remained intact over the years, but as soon as the railway cut distinct tracts into the centre of this part of the national territory exploitation of the forests began.' (cited in Guzman Avila 1982).

A North American traveller who visited the area shortly after the arrival of the railway also commented that:

> '..it is not only the journey that has suffered changes, the

destruction of the forest, the drying of mountain springs and the climate of the region including the regularity of rains...' (La Libertad 1894, cited in Ramirez 1988).

Examination of archival documents such as the *Relaciones, Mercedes* and *Tierras*[4] pertaining to other areas has served to corroborate evidence of prehispanic deforestation and degradation. Such archives suggest that there had been considerable deforestation in the Lake Cuitzeo Basin (Figure 10.1) by the time the Spanish arrived in the area. The *Relaciones Geograficas* of 1579, for example, indicates that the nearest stands of woodland were located 20km away from the lake (Acuña 1987).

Significantly, it is archival documentation in the form of the land grant deeds or *Mercedes* that supports the findings from palaeolimnological investigations which suggest that there was no discernible impact of the Spanish. Butzer & Butzer (1993) have, for example, highlighted the significant evidence contained within the *Mercedes* to suggest that the Spanish had no immediate and negative impact on the central Mexican landscape and that the general patterning of the vegetation in the Bajio during the 16th century was similar to that of today. Though the documents are open to subjectivity, they provide a clear indication that the initial impact of Spanish introduced agrosystems have been overstated. Clearly, this is not to say that there was no disturbance or ecological degradation wrought by the Conquest, for the evidence we have to date reflects only what was going on in select regions of central Mexico. Moreover, there is evidence to suggest that with the population recovery of the 1700s there was renewed intensified pressure on resources (Butzer & Butzer in press).

Given the introduction of livestock such as pigs, sheep, goats and cattle, hitherto absent from the Mexican environment the lack of evidence of degradation on a significant scale is perhaps surprising. Yet when one considers some of the antecedent Iberian policies and agricultural customs that were translocated more successfully into the New World, some explanation can be forwarded. Long distance transhumance treks and sheep walks (*cañadas*) were commonplace in Spain since the 12th century formation of the sheep grazers union (the *Mesta*) (Glick 1979). That such strategies had been translocated to New Spain soon after Conquest is indicated by references to long distance sheep treks and livestock mobility in some of the early colonial documents[5]. It is such policies that have been used to explain the apparent conservative nature of Spanish agrosystems, and can be used to weaken the arguments currently being raised by the political ecologists mentioned earlier.

The benefits of Mediterranean-type pastoralism have frequently been overlooked in much of the research completed or in progress to date. Lewthwaite (1986) has, for example, highlighted the value of combining livestock raising and cultivation. Not only do livestock provide a valuable source of "indirect storage" in times of food shortage, perhaps during a drought period (Halstead 1989), but they are also of particular use as pack animals, crucial for the transportation of foodstuffs, and later for minerals as the mining industry began to escalate (although the poor state of the road systems and *caminos* were later to place restrictions on the amount of goods that could be transported in this way (Miller 1994). Moreover, the value of readily available fertiliser, it has been argued, will have more than compensated for the crop losses resulting from field depredations by animals, one of the key criticisms of the political ecologists (Butzer & Butzer 1993).

These findings appear to contradict the belief that the Spanish caused widespread environmental devastation in the highlands of central Mexico. To date, however, there is still a lack of empirical evidence to ascertain the full impacts of Spanish agrosystems. The decline in soil erosion could be a consequence of more benign agricultural impacts, but could equally reflect the impact of depopulation and land abandonment with a subsequent renewal of landscape stability. Such a theory seems acceptable when one considers the rapidity with which secondary vegetation is thought to have regenerated (Denevan 1992). Depopulation will have been sufficient to significantly reduce the amount of land under cultivation and thus could have influenced sediment yields; if less land was cultivated, reduced erosion is to be expected. Based on the results from the Lake Patzcuaro, however, it

is also clearly important to recognise the spatial variations in terms of sediment influx from the catchment to the lake according to land use, and that apparent reductions in sediment influx to the lake may not be representative of the whole basin. Clearly, there is a need for more detailed investigation to establish the relationship between population levels, the amount of land under cultivation, and sediment yields in the immediate post-Contact period. Recent archival work has, however, provided some enlightening evidence in this respect and has highlighted some potential lines for future investigation.

CONTESTING THE IMPORTANCE OF "CONQUEST"

That European contact was to result in significant socio-economic and political changes in Mexico cannot be doubted. With the Spanish came the dual purpose of resource exploitation and the diffusion of and conversion to Christianity, both achieved with lesser or greater success during the three centuries following the arrival of the Spanish and prior to Mexico's Independence. Yet what tends to be overlooked in the literature is the very gradual process whereby these challenges were eventually met and, moreover, the degree of syncretism and mutual interaction that took place between the two respective cultures. From an indigenous stance, the prolonged process of acculturation and mutation following contact, in social and agricultural terms at least, detracts somewhat from the traditional European ethos of dramatic change and adjustment in the New World immediately following Conquest. Arguably to begin with the Spanish could control and exploit the peoples of the highland states and chiefdoms by modifying the existing native institutions[6], but despite such intervention, substantial components of the indigenous population in Spanish America did survive on their traditional lands in both biological and social terms. Butzer (1991), for example, cites examples of societies in Michoacan, Hidalgo, Tlaxcala and Oaxaca whose language and culture was little changed by those of the colonial period, though it should be noted that in a long-term context, even these societies were significantly different from their pre-Colombian counterparts in that some selective adoption of Spanish traits was inevitable (Zeitlin 1989, 24). The once accepted scenario of Spanish "takeover" has recently come into question and with it a need has been recognised to identify more precisely the nature of change wrought by the European colonists.

It seems, therefore, that the study of Mexican environmental history will soon face revolution. That the Spanish encountered a distinctly humanised landscape has been proved (Denevan 1992) and what is only now becoming clear is the environmentally destructive nature of indigenous exploitative economies. In contrast, the imposition of Spanish type agrosystems, long regarded as the cause of widespread degradation in the New World, seem to have had little immediate impact on the landscape. It is suggested that further multi-disciplinary investigations could well support these recent findings. This being the case, the two allied and pervasive "myths", that have dogged much of the research on Mexican historical study would, therefore, face refutation, thereby heralding the introduction of a new era of more objective approaches to New World historical investigations.

Acknowledgements

The authors would like to thank an anonymous referee for comments made on the original draft of the paper.

NOTES

1. It has been suggested that Old World diseases may have actually been dissipated along trade routes, European contact not necessarily being implicated in the transfer (Gerhard 1982; Roberts 1989).
2. A similar erosion episode at La Piscina de Yuriria (50km Northeast of Patzcuaro) is also associated with the first appearance of Zea mays *ca.* 3200 BP (Metcalfe *et al.* 1994).
3. Steeper lands are thought to have been preferred by the Purepecha because of the reduced risk of frost but also for the capacity of such lands to capture drainage water for irrigation purposes (O'Hara 1991).
4. All three archival sources date back to the Colonial period. The *Relaciones* represent the results of a survey, designed in Madrid to elicit basic information on the environmental and social characteristics of the diverse regions of New Spain. The *Mercedes* represent land grant documentation and deeds related to tracts of land, detailing information on the characteristics of the land area in question. The *Tierras* represent body of litigation records spanning the whole of the Colonial era. Since most disputes related Indigenous and Spanish acquisition of and access to tracts of land, these documents contain valuable information that can be used for palaeoenvironmental reconstruction.
5. Relacion de Queretaro: Acuña 1987, and documents housed in the Ayer Collection of the Newbury library, Chicago, or published in Paredes *et al.* (1995) *Y por mi visto.* Colegio de Michoacan; documents housed in the Archivo General de la Nacion, Mexico City: e.g. Ramo Indios volumes 4, expediente 567, expediente 587.
6. New World historians tend to attribute Spanish policies in the Americas to Iberian antecedents, established during the reconquest of Islamic Iberia. Yet the Tribute system adopted in colonial New Spain, whereby a landlord could demand goods and provisions from the indigenous peoples under his jurisdiction, represents a mutation of an Aztecan administrative system.

REFERENCES

Acuña, R. de (ed) (1987). *Relaciones Geograficas del Siglo XVI.* Mexico City: Serie Antropologia, UNAM, 10 volumes.

Alcedo y Bexerano, A. (1786–1989). *Diccionario geografico historico de las indias occidentales o America.* 5 volumes, Madrid.

Armillas, P. (1969). The arid frontier of Mexican civilization. *Transactions of the New York Academy of Sciences,* section of anthropology, 697–704.

Bassolls-Barrera, N. (1986). *La sistema geografica de la cuenca de Patzcuaro, Michoacan.* Tesis Profesional, Instituto de Geografia, UNAM, 486pp.

Bloemendal, J., Oldfield, F. and Thompson, R. (1979). Magnetic measurements used to assess sediment influx at Llyn Goddiondon. *Nature* **280**, 50–51.

Bowden, M.J. (1992). The invention of the American tradition. *Journal of Historical Geography* **18**, 3–26.

Bradbury, J.P (1971). Palaeolimnology of Lake Texcoco, Mexico: evidence from diatoms. *Limnology and Oceanography* **16**, 180–200.

Brown, R. B. (1985). A summary of the late-Quaternary pollen records from Mexico west of the Isthmus of Tehuantepec, in Bryant, V.M. and Holloway, R.G. (eds), *Pollen records of Late Quaternary North American Sediments.* American Association of Stratigraphic Palynologists, Dallas.

Brown, R.B. (1992). *Arqueologia y Paleoecologia del Norcentro de Mexico.* Coleccion Cientifica, Instituto Nacional de Antropologia e Historia.

Butzer, K.W. (1990). Ethno-agriculture and cultural ecology in Mexico: historical vistas and modern implications, *Benchmark 1990, Conference of Latin Americanist Geographers* **17/18**, 139–153.

Butzer, K.W. (1991). Spanish colonisation of the New World: cultural continuity and change in Mexico. *Erdkunde*, Band **45**, 205–219.

Butzer, K.W. (1992). The Americas before and after 1992: an introduction to current geographical research, pp. 345–368 in Butzer, K.W. (ed.): *The Americas Before and After 1492.* Cambridge, MA: Blackwell.

Butzer, K.W. and Butzer, E.K. (1993). The sixteenth-century environment of the Central Mexican Bajio: archival reconstruction from colonial land grants and the question of the ecological impact, pp.? in Matthewson, K. (ed.) *Culture, Form and Place*, Baton Rouge, LA: Louisiana State University, Geoscience and Man.

Butzer, K.W. and Butzer, E.K. (1997). Archival documentation of a sixteenth century savanna environment re-opening the issue of "natural" vegetation in the Mexican Bajio". *Quaternary International* **43/44**, 161–172.

Chacon Torres, A. (1989). *A Limnological Study of Lake Patzcuaro, Michoacan, Mexico.* Ph.D. thesis, University of Stirling.

Chevalier, F. (1970). *Land and Society in Colonial Mexico.* Berkeley: University of California Press.

Cook, S. F. (1949). Soil erosion and population in central Mexico. *Ibero-Americana* **34**. University of California Press: Berkely.

Cortes, H. (1522). Third letter to Charles V in Cortes, H. *Cartas de Relacion.* Reprinted 1985 by Editores Mexicanos Unidos.

Davis, M.B., Moeller, R.E. and Ford, J. (1984). Sediment focusing and pollen influx, pp. 261–293 in Harworth, E.Y. and Lund, J.W.G. (eds.) *Lake Sediments and Environmental History.* Leicester : Leicester University Press.

Dearing, J.A., Ellner, J.K. and Happey-Wood, C.M. (1981). Recent sediment influx and erosional processes in a Welsh upland lake catchment based on magnetic susceptibility measurements. *Quaternary Research* **16**, 356–372.

Deevey, E.S. (1944). Pollen analysis and Mexican archaeology: an attempt to apply the method. *American Antiquity* **10**, 135–149.

Deevey, E.S., Rice, D.S., Rice, P.M., Vaughan, H.H., Brenner, M., and Flannery, M.S. (1979). Mayan urbanism: impact on a tropical karst environment. *Science* **206**, 298–306.

Denevan, W.M. (1992). The pristine myth: the landscape of the Americas in 1492, pp. 369–385 in Butzer, K. (ed.) The Americas before and after 1492: current geographical research. *Annals of the Association of American Geographers* **82**, 369–385.

Garcia-Cook, A. (1986). El control de la erosion en la Tlaxcala: un problema secular *Erdkunde,* Band **40**, 251–262.

Gerhard, P. (1982). *The Northern Frontier of New Spain.* Princeton University Press.

Glick, T.F. (1979). *Islamic and Christian Spain in the Early Middle Ages.* Princeton University Press.

Gorenstein, S. and Pollard, H.P. (1983). *The Tarascan Civilization: A Late Prehispanic Cultural System.* Vanderbilt University. Publications in Anthropology. **28**. Nashville, Tennessee.

Guzman Avila, J.N. (1982). *Michoacan y la inversion extranjera 1880–1911,* Universidad de Michoacan, Morelia.

Halstead, P. (1989). The economy has a natural surplus: economic stability and social change among early farming communities of Thessaly, Greece, pp. 68–80 in P. Halstead, and I. O'Shea (eds) *Bad year economics: cultural repsonses to risk and uncertainty.* New Directions in Archaeology. Cambridge: Cambridge University Press.

Harris, O. (1995). "The coming of the white people". Reflections on the mythologisation of history in Latin America. *Bulletin of Latin American Research.* **14**, 9–24.

Le Roy Ladurie, F. (1980). *Montaillou: the promised land of error.* New York.

Lewthwaite, J (1986). The transition to food production: a Mediterranean perspective, pp. 53–66 in Zvelebil, M. (ed.) *Hunters in Transition.* Cambridge: Cambridge University Press.

Melville, K.A. (1990). Environmental and social change in the Valle del Mezqital, Mexico, 1521–1600. *Comparative Studies in Society and History,* **32**, 24–53.

Melville, K.A. (1994). *A plague of sheep: environmental consequences of the Conquest of Mexico.* Cambridge Univ. Press.

Metcalfe, S.E. (1987). Historical data and climatic change in Mexico – a review. *Geographical Journal* **153**, 211–222.

Metcalfe, S.E., Street-Perrott, F.A., O'Hara, S.L., Hales, P.E. and Perrott, R.A. (1994). The palaeolimnological record of environmental change: examples from the arid frontier of Mesoamerica, pp. 131–147 in Millington, A.C. and Pye, K. (eds.) *Environmental Change in Drylands: Biogeographical and Geomorphological Perspectives.*

Metcalfe, S.E., Street-Perrott, F.A.., Brown, R.B., Hales, P.E., Perrott, R.A., and Steininger, F.M. (1989). Late Holocene human impact on lake basins in Central Mexico. *Geoarchaeology* **4**, 119–141.

Miller, S. (1994). Wheat production in Europe and America: Mexican problems in comparative perspective. *Agricultural History* **68**, 17–34.

Newson, L.A (1994). Indian population patterns in Colonial Spanish America. *Latin American Research Review,* 41–74.

Niederberger, C. (1987). Palaeo-paysages et archaeologie pre-urbaine du Bassin du Mexico. *Études Mesoamericaines* **11**, Centre d'Etudes Mexicaines et Centramericaines (2 volumes).

O'Hara, S.L. (1991). *Late Holocene Environmental Change in the Basin of Patzcuaro, Michoacan, Mexico.* Unpublished D.Phil Thesis. University of Oxford.

O'Hara, S.L (1993). Hsitorical evidence of fluctuations in the level of Lake Patzcuaro, Michoacan, Mexico over the past 600 years. *Geographical Journal* **159**, 51–62.

O'Hara, S.L., Street-Perrott, F.A.and Burt, T.P. (1993). Accelerated

soil erosion around a Mexican highland lake caused by prehispanic agriculture. *Nature* **362**, 48–51.

O'Hara, S.L., Metcalfe, S.E. and Street-Perrott, F.A (1994). On the arid margin: the relationship between climate, humans and the environment. A review of evidence from the Highlands of Central Mexico. *Chemosphere* **29**, 965–981.

O'Hara, S.L. and Metcalfe, S.E (1995). Reconstructing the climate of Mexico from Historical Records. *Holocene* **5**, 485–490.

O'Hara, S.L. and Metcalfe, S.E. (in press). Late Holocene environmental change in west central Mexico:evidence from the Basins of Patzcuaro and Zacapu, in Redman, C.L. (ed) *Prehistoric Human Impact on the Environment: A Global Perspective.*

Pagden, A (1994). *European Encounters With the New World.* Yale University Press.

Paredes, C.M (ed.) (1995). *Y por mi visto: mandamientos, ordenenzas, licencias y otras disposiciones virreinales sobre Michacan en el siglo XVI.* Centro de Investigaciones y Estudios Superiores en Antropologia Social. Mexico.

Pollard, H.P. (1994). Prehistoric archaeology, ethnohistory and soil erosion: a debate over modern agricultural sustainability. *Bulletin of Culture and Agriculture Group* no. **49**, 16–20.

Ramirez, R.M. (1988). *Monumentos y arquitectura de Patzcuaro,* Tomo I, Morelia, Mexico.

Roberts, L. (1989). Disease and death in the New World. *Science,* **246**, 1245–1247.

Sale, K. (1990). *The Conquest of Paradise: Christopher Colombus and the Columbial Legacy.* New York: Alfred A.Knopf

Sears, P.B and Clisby, K.H. (1955). Palynology in southern North America IV. Pleistocene climate in Mexico. *Bulletin of the Geological Society of America* **66**, 1–530.

Shelter, S. (1991). Three faces of Eden, pp. 225–247 in Viola, H.J. and Margolis, C. (eds) *Seeds of Change: a Quincentennial Commemoration.* Washington, Smithsonian Institute.

van Andel, T.H. and Zangger, E. and Demitrack, S. (1990). Land use and soil erosion in prehistoric Greece. *Journal of Field Archaeology* **17**, 379–396.

Villasenor y Sanchez, J.A. (1748). *Theatro Americano. Descripcion general de los reinos y provincias de la Neuva Espana y sus jurisdicciones.* 2 vols. Mexico.

Wallen, C.C. (1955). Some characteristics of precipitation in Mexico. *Geofisica Annaler* **37**, 51–85.

Watts, W.A. and Bradbury, J.P. (1982). Paleoecological studies at Lake Patzcuaro on the west central Mexican plateau and at Chalco in the Basin of Mexico. *Quaternary Research* **17**, 56–70

Williams, B.J. (1972). Tepetate in the Valley of Mexico. *Annals of the Association of American Geographers* **62**, 618–626.

Williams, B.J. (1989). Contact period rural overpopulation in the Basin of Mexico: carrying capacity models tested with documentary data. *American Antiquity* **54**, 715–73.

Wilson, R. (1995). Shifting frontiers: historical transformations of identities in Latin America. *Bulletin of Latin American Research* **14**, 1–7.

Zeitlin, J.F. (1989). Ranchers and Indians on the Southern Isthnus of Tehuantepec: economic change and indigenous survival in colonial Mexico. *Hispanic American Historical Review* **69**, 23–61.

11. Reconstructing the Ethnobotany of a Depleted Flora: Food Plant Availability in the Murchison Basin, Western Australia, Prior to European Arrival

R. Esmée Webb

The Murchison Basin lies in the semi-arid zone of Western Australia. Its poor soils and unpredictable winter rainfall support mulga (*Acacia aneura*) scrub. This flora has been so denuded by over 100 years of pastoralism that it is difficult now to imagine that the region ever supported a viable gatherer-hunter population. However, archaeological research has shown that Aborigines used rockshelters in this region more than similar localities in other parts of WA that might seem more suited to human occupation. Moreover, reconsideration of the little ethnographic data available suggests that the Murchison Aborigines were more numerous prior to European arrival than anthropologists initially assumed. Therefore, an attempt is made here to assess the prehistoric viability of the Murchison Basin. Food plant abundance might explain why the Murchison Basin was used so (comparatively) 'intensively' in prehistory. This analysis was complicated because none of the known archaeological sites has yielded any micro- or macrofossil plant remains. Moreover, few ethnobotanic data are available. The social and economic life of the Murchison Aborigines collapsed long before anthropologists began to record traditional knowledge in this region. Therefore, food plant availability in the Murchison Basin prior to the introduction of pastoralism has been assessed here by comparing the extant flora with data about Aboriginal plant use from adjacent or analogous physiographic regions. Some additional data were gleaned from the memoirs of the first pastoralists to settle in the region. It is hoped in future to verify some of these data with the co-operation of those older Aborigines who remember what bushfoods used to be eaten, when they were collected and how they were prepared.

Keywords: Ethnobotany, semi-arid zone, Murchison Aborigines, Western Australia.

'Show 'em a bit of desert with one dead tree in it, next minute they've found a three-course meal with fruit and nuts to follow'. Terry Pratchett describing the Aboriginal inhabitants of the mysterious Discworld continent XXXX in *Interesting Times* (1994, 270).

THE SETTING

The area discussed lies between 115° and 117°30′ E and 26°30′ and 28°30′ S (Figure 11.1). It is known colloquially as the Murchison Basin, although it also includes the Greenough River system. Most of the region is now divided into pastoral leases and very sparsely populated. It has well-defined natural and cultural boundaries. It comprises the territory of the Wajarri-speaking people, who now prefer to be called Yamaji. At contact, they were socially distinct from their coastal neighbours who did not share with them the Western Desert male initiation practices of circumcision and subincision (Radcliffe-Brown 1912; 1930a; Bates 1913; 1966; White 1985).

The Murchison River flows over the western part of the Yilgarn craton (Figure 11.2). This huge expanse of Archaean rock, which terminates at the Darling Fault, is

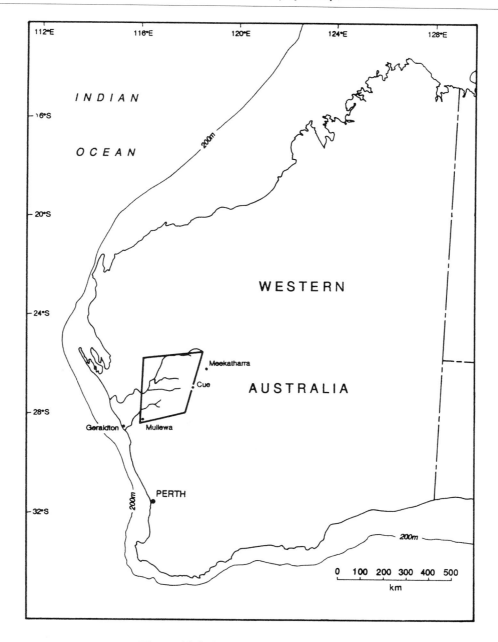

Figure 11.1: Location of the study area.

tectonically stable and has not been glaciated since the Permian. Hence, it preserves an ancient denuded landscape across which relict rivers now flow in incoherent drainages due to the lack of topographic relief (Myers & Hocking 1988). The deeply weathered shield rocks are directly overlain by unconsolidated Cainozoic deposits. The introduction of pastoralism in the 1860s had a devastating effect on this ancient landscape because its soils are nutrient-poor, very fragile and highly susceptible to erosion and degradation. As well as denuding mature vegetation, sheep crop the ground so closely that they kill off new growth, while their hooves compact the ground surface making it difficult for new seedlings to sprout. Hence, it is

not surprising that the Murchison Basin is now severely devegetated, by comparison with the dense bush described by the first Europeans to explore the region (Austin 1855, 49–57; Gregory & Gregory 1884, 18–49).

Rain falls mainly in winter in the Murchison Basin (Figure 11.3). The rivers then flow, although some of the deeper depressions in their beds hold potable water through even the longest droughts. However, average rainfall figures are quite misleading in the Australian semi-arid zone due to the high inter-annual and intra-annual variance in precipitation (Figure 11.4). Droughts are common, while 'good' rains only fall about every 7–10 years (Gentilli 1959; 1993). No palaeoclimatic data are

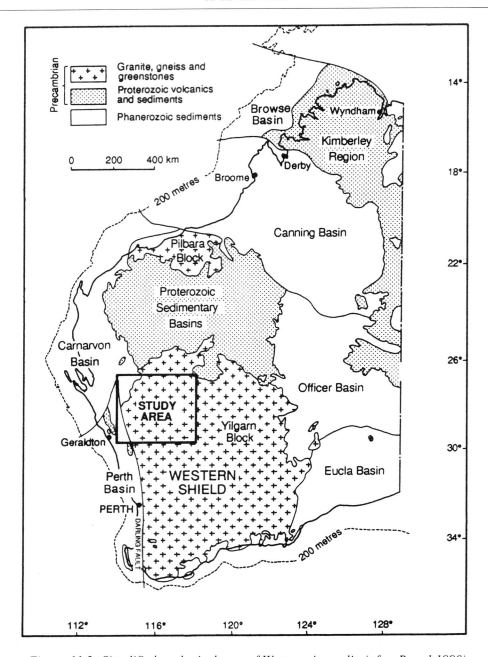

Figure 11.2: Simplified geological map of Western Australia (after Beard 1990).

available for the Murchison Basin, but what little is known about other parts of Western Australia suggests that conditions closely similar to the present day were probably established throughout the state about 6000 BP (Brown 1983; Wasson *et al.* 1991), when the Indian Ocean stabilised at its present level.

There is now a marked climatic gradient across the Murchison Basin, from southwest to northeast. As rainfall decreases and continentality increases, the vegetation becomes increasingly sparse and drought-tolerant. The biogeographic significance of the Mulga-Eucalyptus Line that divides the xerophytic floras of the Eremaean

Botanical Province from the drought-sensitive floras of the South-West Botanical Province has long been recognised (Diels 1906). It crosses the southwestern corner of the study area (Figure 11.5), passing close to Mullewa. This small town, located 100km inland from Geraldton and 500km north of Perth, marks the northeastern limit of cereal cultivation in Western Australia.

The vegetation of the Murchison region of the Eremaean Province has been described by Beard (1976; 1990), Pate and Dixon (1982), Mitchell and Wilcox (1988) and Cranfield (1990). The canopy comprises small trees, often in mallee form and tall shrubs of which mulga

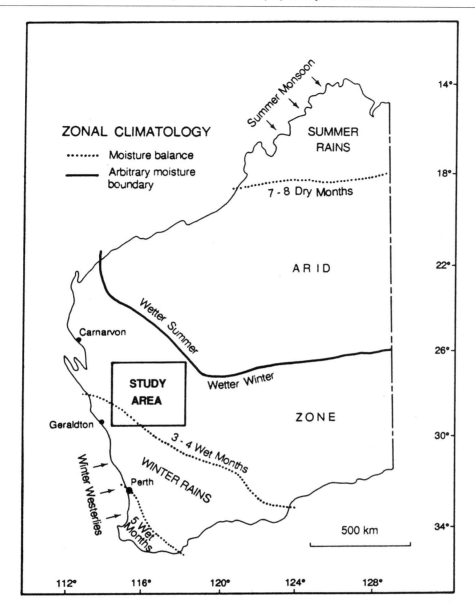

Figure 11.3: Present climatology of Western Australia (after Jarvis 1986).

(*Acacia aneura*) is the most abundant, although many other species of *Acacia* are also present. Some species of *Eucalyptus* and sheoak (*Allocasuarina*) form gallery woodland along active drainage lines. The understorey shrubs include many species of poverty bush (*Eremophila*) and *Cassia*. The ground layer comprises both perennial and ephemeral herbs and grasses (chiefly *Ptilotus, Helipterum, Danthonia, Eragrostis* and *Eriachne*). During years of low rainfall the annual grasses (eg *Aristida*) and ephemeral herbs (eg *Helipterum* and some species of *Ptilotus*), may not appear. Succulent halophytes such as Saltbush (*Atriplex*), Bluebush (*Maireana*) and Samphire (*Halosarcia*) grow in the beds of the many saline lakes.

Plants that require better soils and greater moisture, such as most species of *Banksia, Eucalyptus, Grevillea,*

Hakea and *Melaleuca*, are found only in the Southwestern Province (Beard 1976; 1990). The more drought-tolerant species of some of these genera can be found in the Eremaean Province.

THE PROBLEM

Although some archaeological research had been undertaken in the Murchison Basin prior to my fieldwork, little was known about the prehistoric pattern of Aboriginal usage of the region because few of the known sites had been dated radiometrically. Walga Rock appeared to have been first occupied about 10,000 BP, while people began to use the bank of the Murchison River at Billibilong

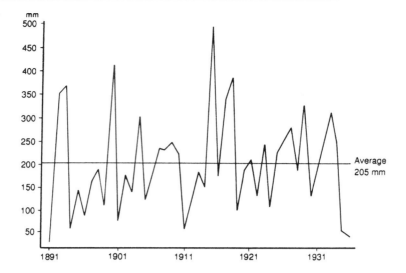

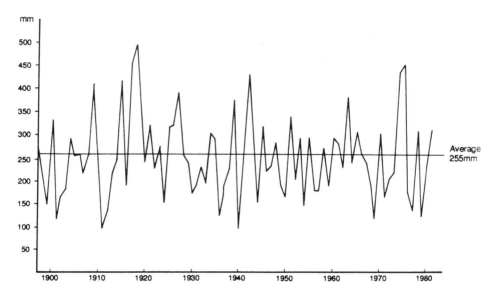

Figure 11.4: Rainfall records from Boolardy pastoral station (top) for 1891–1935 and from Yalgoo township (bottom) for 1898–1981. The two localities are only 200km apart, but even so their peak rainfall years do not always coincide.

Spring by at least 6000 BP (Bordes *et al.* 1983). Both sites appear to have continued in use until European contact. The rockshelters I investigated at Billibilong I, Madoonga, Meeberrie, Mullewa, Twin Peaks and Wurarga (Figure 11.6) proved to have been first occupied rather later, after 3500 BP (Webb n.d.). They also continued in use until contact. These data suggest that, as the Aboriginal population increased in number over time, more localities were used simultaneously.

Furthermore, when the number of artefacts recovered from shelters in the Murchison Basin is compared with similar data for sites in other regions of Western Australia, it is clear that not only did the pattern of artefact discard over time vary greatly from region to region, but that *on average* far more artefacts were discarded in each

rockshelter in the Murchison Basin than in similar sites elsewhere in the state (Figure 11.7). While it is likely that changes over time in flaking technology affected artefact production and discard rates, as would differences in the 'flakability' of the different raw materials used in different regions and/or differences in the types of activities carried out at different localities, it is also likely that differences in the millennial artefact discard rate on the scale seen in this figure reflect differences in the degree to which people used different regions, which in turn reflect the numbers of people involved.

The territory of any given Aboriginal group was finite. Therefore, if their population increased, more parts of their territory would have to be used more frequently by greater numbers of people, until its carrying capacity was

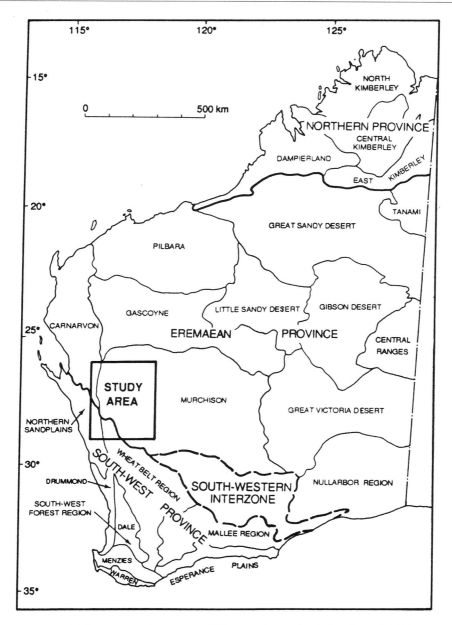

Figure 11.5: Botanical regions of Western Australia (after Beard 1990).

reached. On the other hand, the higher the carrying capacity of a given region, the greater the number of people it could support. Thus, the most parsimonious explanation for the inter-regional differences in usage seen in Figure 11.7 is that the pre-contact carrying capacity of the Murchison Basin was sufficiently high that the region could support a more numerous population than most other regions of Western Australia, some of which might now seem more suited to human occupation. This finding caused me to reassess my assumptions about the prehistoric carrying capacity of the Murchison Basin and the available estimates of Yamaji numbers pre-contact.

As mapped by Tindale (1974), Wajarri territory comprises one of the larger language areas in Australia (Figure 11.8). Initially, I assumed this was because the carrying capacity of the region was low, due mainly to my Euro-centric assessment of the present day environment. Like many other parts of Australia, the natural vegetation of the Murchison Basin is now so denuded and the endemic fauna so decimated by more than a century of pastoralism that it does not appear to be capable of supporting a numerous population of gatherer-hunters on a year-round basis. Moreover, both Radcliffe-Brown (1930b) and Tindale (1974) estimated Yamaji numbers at contact at the very low density of less than 2 people per 100km², although both also thought they were comparatively numerous, because their territory was large.

These population estimates clearly conflicted with

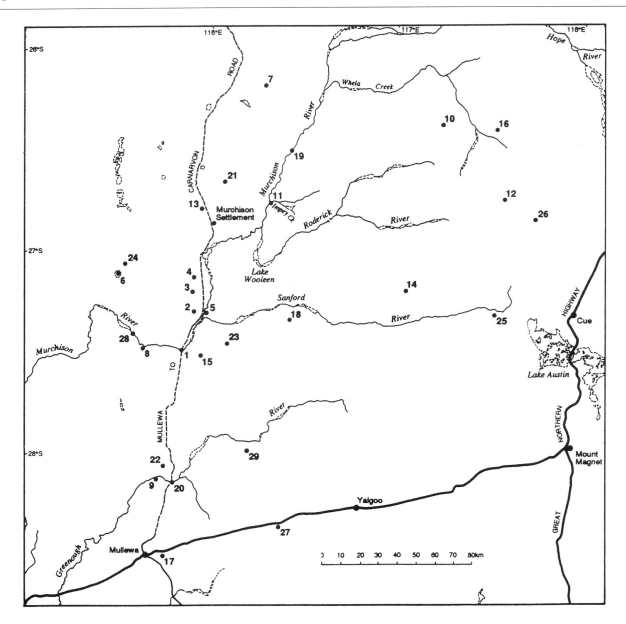

Figure 11.6: Location of known archaeological sites in the Murchison Basin. Places mentioned in the text are: 2. Billibilong I, 6. Billilly Claypan, 12. Madoonga, 13. Meeberrie, 17. Mullewa, 21. Quailbadoo Claypan, 23. Twin Peaks, 25. Walga Rock, 27. Wurarga, 29. Yuin.

Figure 11.7. Therefore, I made a new estimate, based on the numbers of Aborigines encountered by ET Hooley at different points along the Murchison River between 13 and 23 June 1866 (Sharp 1985, 89–98). I concluded that the pre-contact population could have been as numerous as 4–7 people per 100km² (Webb 1995). Similar densities have been calculated for the Nyungar of the Swan coastal plain by Hallam (1986). They suggest that Wajarri territory was large because the Yamaji were indeed numerous, corroborating Figure 11.7 and reinforcing the need to reassess the carrying capacity of the Murchison Basin.

Little ethnobotanic information was available on which

to base such a reassessment. *Ethnobotany* is understood here, *pace* Ford (1979), to be the *interpretation* of botanical remains as dietary and/or environmental data, rather than their mere taxonomic identification. Few of the archaeological localities investigated in this region have yielded any botanic data. Grindstones and pounders were found on the dunes bordering Quailbadoo (Pearce 1979) and Billilly claypans (Bordes *et al.* 1980; 1983). While these artefacts were not necessarily used to grind flour for damper, Tindale (1977) said that the Yamaji "were the southwestern-most people to extensively exploit grass seeds and wet-grind them for the making of forms of

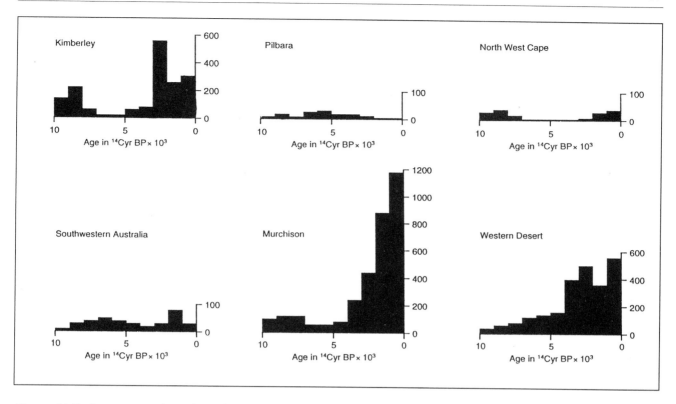

Figure 11.7: Average number of artefacts discarded in successive millennia on each site in those regions of Western Australia for which such data could be calculated.

bread". If seeds were wet-milled, processing would probably have occurred at claypans because they are one of the few reliable seasonal sources of freshwater in the Murchison Basin, apart from the rivers which are now saline. Depending on the ambient temperature, claypans can hold water for several months after rain.

Although the sediment in the known rockshelters has yet to be investigated for pollen, it is unlikely to be preserved because the deposits are highly acidic, friable and loosely-packed (Webb 1992; n.d.). No grinding material has been found in any of these rockshelters, either. Its absence may be explained by the scarcity of water in the immediate vicinity of most shelters in the Murchison Basin. Although *Acacia* seeds could be dry ground anywhere, it would hardly have been practical to attempt to wet-mill seeds in rockshelters without locally available water. On the other hand, I found quandong nuts (*Santalum acuminatum*) and *Acacia* seeds in the shelters I investigated. Although both plants were favoured Aboriginal food resources, it is possible that these finds were allochthonous to the layers from which they apparently came and, hence, their presence may not have been the result of human activity. The quandongs were found in the unconsolidated detritus on the shelter floors and possibly came from emu droppings (Leyland, pers. comm.), while the *Acacia* seeds could have fallen into the testpits from the floor surface during the course of excavation.

One other source of botanical information remains to be explored. Nests made almost certainly by the Lesser Stick-nest Rat (*Leporillus apicalis*) were found in Wurarga. Like the Packrat (*Neotoma* spp.), *L. apicalis* made its nests from urine-soaked plant material collected in the immediate vicinity of its home. Its nests can, therefore, provide a detailed picture of the local vegetation (Pearson & Dodson 1993). *L. apicalis* is now extinct on the mainland of Western Australia, hence the nests in Wurarga are likely to furnish evidence of the composition of the surrounding flora prior to European arrival. I hope to test that hypothesis in the future.

Not only has the Murchison Basin yielded few archaeobotanic data, but little ethnographic information is available from which the prehistoric economy of the Yamaji might be reconstructed, either. European pastoralists began to settle this region within two decades of its initial exploration in the 1850s. By the 1870s, when Frank Wittenoom arrived, the region was already divided into a series of discrete, often fenced, sheep stations 'owned' by Europeans. The effect of these enclosures on the Yamaji was catastrophic. The sheep ate the plants on which they also relied for food, while the pastoralists fenced off the water supplies they had traditionally used and demanded their labour as stockhands in return for food when starvation drove them to group around European homesteads. As a result, Yamaji society disintegrated rapidly

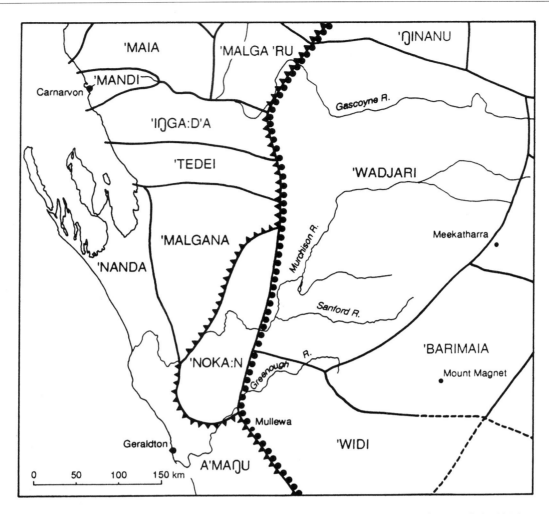

Figure 11.8: Linguistic and cultural boundaries in the Murchison Basin (after Tindale 1974).

(Fink 1960; Berndt & Berndt 1980). This process of acculturation was well underway by the time Forrest (1877, 160–7) and Giles (1889, 264–280) trekked through the Murchison in the 1870s. Hence, when anthropologists began to study Aboriginal hunting and food-gathering practices at the beginning of this century, they ignored the Murchison because the Yamaji had long ceased to pursue such economies. Therefore, no ethnobotanical research has yet been undertaken in this region, which is perceived as retaining relatively little relevant information. I hope that what follows will show that perception to be incorrect.

RECONSTRUCTING A DEPLETED FLORA: PLANT FOOD AVAILABILITY IN THE MURCHISON BASIN

So much traditional knowledge has been lost in this region that the chief aim of the research discussed here was simply to establish what food plants *ought* to have been available in the Murchison Basin prior to the introduction of

pastoralism and, hence, to estimate whether the region would have been able to support the numerous Aboriginal population my research suggested had lived there in prehistory. The lack of strictly ethnographic information about what plant foods the Yamaji ate, forced me to turn to the anecdotal and botanical sources described below.

First, I searched the memoirs of Europeans who visited and/or settled in Western Australia and/or the semi-arid zone for descriptions of Aboriginal plant use (Grey 1841; Austin 1855; Oldfield 1865; Maiden 1889). Of these anecdotal sources, only Wittenoom's (n.d.) memoirs proved really informative. He recorded some of the plant foods available in the Murchison Basin when he reached the district in 1874. Where the Wajarri name he gave can be related to a known plant (see appendix for sources), its scientific name has been added.

"In a good season the natives live very much on seeds and roots. The women collect seeds in large quantities, the coorarra [*Acacia tetragonophylla*] being the favourite; there is also the bogooda (*A. linophylla*) which in good seasons bears heavily a very hard seed, also the jam (mungarda, [*A.*

acuminata]), a flat leafed mulga (thurdoong) and others. These seeds are cracked fine on a granite stone in which by long use a deep groove is worn; they are hammered on one stone with another; as often as not they eat the meal, but sometimes make it into a ball a roast it. When eating coorarra, the natives smell horribly. In the sandy thickets there are trees with a light coloured leaf that, about August, have quantities of sweet gum. It has a pleasant taste and does not stick like gum. It is called 'pimba' [*A. ligulata*]. The natives used to collect this and ngow's [mallee fowl] eggs in the same country and about the same time. On the mulga trees, after good summer rain, a light coloured creeper grows very quickly and bears an oblong shaped fruit, full of seeds; when this is young, it is delicious, and when old the outside shell is roasted. It is called cogoola [*Leichhardtia australis*]. On the Murchison flooded flats and some other creeks, another creeper grows up mostly dead trees, with a nice leaf and a flower like a convolvulus [possibly *Ipomoea* spp.]. At the root, which is never immediately under the vine grows a large yam. The natives tap the ground with the wannas (sticks) and in this way find the yam. They dig out a round hole, perhaps a foot deep, quite away from the creeper. I have seen these holes so thick where there has been a large camp of natives that it would be dangerous to ride a horse through them. On other flooded places one might think herds of pigs had been rooting up the ground; this was caused by the natives, chiefly women, digging 'ngalgoo' [*Cyperus bulbosa*] which is a berry like a small rushy onion, but no oniony taste. They are the root of a small rushy looking plant and grow in large quantities, and in the season the women generally carry quantities in their 'wandoos', this being a kangaroo skin folded so as to contain their sundries (which are numerous) and carried on their backs, with leg parts of the skin tied under their chin. It is wonderful the loads they carry, and often a child on top of all. In good seasons, the natives in their wild state lived well; the vegetable food was very varied: there is a small plant with a root like a carrot, wild cress, junga and yallar, very succulent and known to 't'othersiders' [people from eastern Australia] as Parakeelia [*Calandrinia polyandra*]. This stuff they more often throw on the ashes than eat green. It would take a lot of thinking to detail all the native food that was abundant in good seasons in the old days. I expect most of it is still to be got, but what natives there are now are too well fed on stations to bother about it".

Some further local information is available. Tindale (1974, 144–5) noted that 'in a plant called by them *'bulibuli'* which grows at the edges of some claypans, [the Yamaji] had discovered a seed that could be gathered and stored for [at least 6] months in kangaroo skin bags or containers'. *Bulibuli* is thought to be *Tecticornia arborea*. Bordes *et al.* (1983, 20–4) found this halophytic chenopod growing at Billilly Claypan. It is eaten by Aborigines in the Eastern Goldfields, who call it *'kurumi'* (Dix & Lofgren 1974). A number of other locally available food plants were identified for Meagher (1974) by an Aboriginal woman then living in Mingenew, about 75km due south of Mullewa. Although they are not mentioned in the botanical surveys referred to above (Beard 1976; 1990; Pate & Dixon 1982; Mitchell & Wilcox 1988; Cranfield 1990), these plants

have been included in the appendix because they are known to grow between Mullewa and Wurarga (Leyland, pers. comm.). Finally, Nixon and Lefroy (1988, 85) listed the obvious bushfoods that European station children learned about from their Yamaji playmates: 'berries, fruit, the 'bimba' gum [probably *Acacia ligulata* (Leyland, pers. comm.)], from broken branches and sucking the juices from the flowers of the 'poverty' bush [*Eremophila* spp.]'. Although it has not yet been possible to verify whether Yamaji practice conformed to the details of food preparation and consumption cited in the appendix, it is probably safe to assume that specific food plants were prepared and consumed in closely similar fashions wherever they were eaten. It is also possible that other plants native to the Murchison Basin, but not listed in the appendix, were used by the Yamaji, possibly in ways not previously recorded, because they are known to have unique medicinal uses for some plants. The Land Council requested that details of such local usages not be published at present. However, I hope to document them in future with the assistance of knowledgeable Yamaji.

Second, with the assistance of Estelle Leyland, a botanist with specialised knowledge of the Murchison flora, I tabulated what plants probably grew in the region prior to the introduction of pastoralism (Webb n.d.), based on the botanical surveys of the extant vegetation mentioned above and the wider literature on the plants of Western and Central Australia (Jessop 1981; George 1984; Green 1985; Griffith 1985). Beard (1976) argued that no major species have completely disappeared from the Eremaean flora since European arrival, neither has the regional climate changed significantly in the last 10,000 years (Colhoun 1991; Wasson & Donnelly 1991). Therefore, I assumed that the species now growing in the region were probably available for Aboriginal use in prehistory.

Finally, the archaeological and ethnographic literature was searched to compile a list of those plants known to have been exploited by other Aborigines as food sources and/or medicinally, that could also be shown to grow in the Murchison Basin. Details of plant usage recorded among Western Desert or Nyungar people (Meagher 1974; Tindale 1974; 1977; Gould 1981; Pate & Dixon 1982; O'Connell *et al.* 1983; Veth & Walsh 1988; Cane 1989) were preferred over data collected from regions such as tropical northern Australia that have very different environments from the Murchison Basin. The plants identified, details of their usage (where known) and supporting documentary references are given in the appendix. Plants were usually only included if they corresponded in both genus and species with those known to have been exploited elsewhere. It cannot be assumed that, just because one species of a given genus is edible, other species are. The variety of edible and poisonous species included in the Solanaceae well illustrate that point (Peterson 1977). Plant genera were only included in the appendix when the sources searched either failed to differentiate the species exploited, or listed such a range

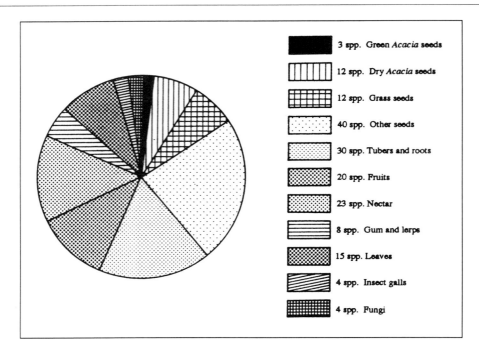

Figure 11.9: Numbers and types of plant species growing in the Murchison Basin and exploited by Aborigines in other parts of Australia as food.

of species that, although the species known in the Murchison Basin was not named, it was likely that it could have been used for the same purpose. The wider literature on Aboriginal food gathering practices was also searched for supporting data (Gould 1969; 1991; Hallam 1977; Meagher & Ride 1979; Hayden 1981; O'Connell & Hawkes 1981; Pate 1986; Veth 1987; 1993; Vinnicombe 1987; Walsh 1987, 1990). Finally, sources discussing the collection, preparation for consumption and storage of plant foods by Aborigines throughout Australia were consulted to gain an overall picture of prehistoric food gathering practices.

PLANTS USED

In Figure 11.9, the plants listed in the appendix have been divided into groups according to the types of food they provide. This figure illustrates Wittenoom's (n.d.) comment that the Yamaji 'live very much on seeds and roots', although it possibly over-emphasises the importance of seeds in their diet because all 30 species of *Grevillea* and *Hakea* known to grow in the Murchison Basin have been included. They all produce edible seeds. If those genera are omitted, then Figure 11.9 suggests that 21% of the known food plants provide seeds, 23% provide edible roots, 15% provide fruits, 24% provide sugars and 12% provide 'leaves'. Roots, seeds and fruits comprise over half of the known plant resources. They can be considered dietary staples, while the 'leaves' would have provided variety, vitamins and trace elements not otherwise

available. These data suggest that the Yamaji could easily have maintained a balanced plant food diet, prior to the introduction of pastoralism.

Figure 11.9 also shows how important *Acacia* seeds were in the Yamaji diet. In all probability the seeds of all species were eaten (Leyland, pers. comm.). However, only those species have been included here that are known both to grow in the Murchison Basin and to have been used by Aborigines elsewhere in Australia. Although the seeds of some species were eaten green during the spring, when they would have been rich in vitamins as well as carbohydrate and protein, most were left until summer to ripen, when they were shelled and ground into flour to make damper. The seeds of at least 12 grass species could also have been eaten. Tindale (1974, 110) believed that the Yamaji stored grass seeds. One of his informants claimed that the Yamaji "had an advantage over [other] people because they placed great reliance on grass seed food, whereas other people lived only on the hammered seeds of shrubs [probably *Acacia* spp.], did not use the process of wet milling of grass seed and thus often went hungry" (*ibid.*, 102). Smith (1986; 1989) thought that Aborigines not only began to process seeds fairly soon after they entered central Australia, but that seed processing was essential to their survival in the desert. On the other hand, Cane (1987; 1989) investigated the energetics of processing seeds to make damper and concluded that the costs are sufficiently high compared with the benefits gained from consumption that seeds would never have formed a dietary staple.

The importance of tubers in the Yamaji diet is illustrated

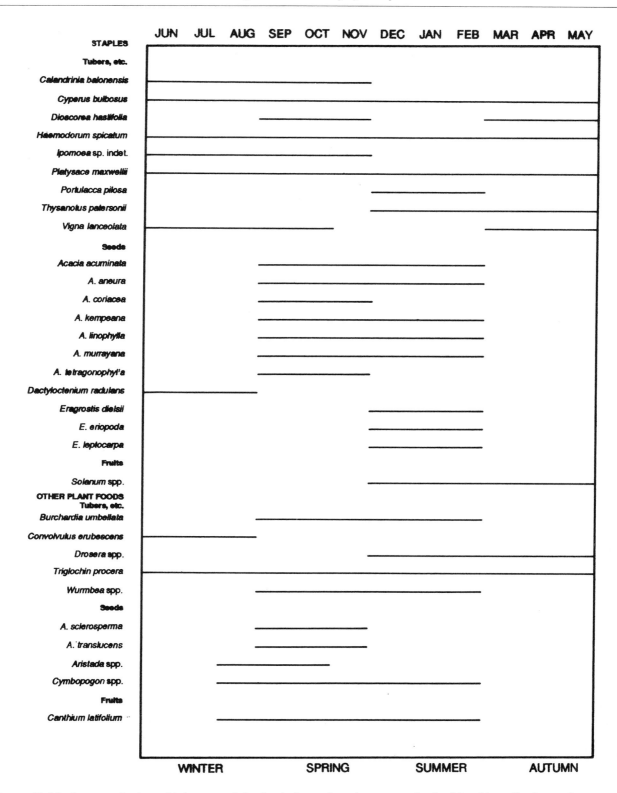

Figure 11.10: Seasons during which some of the food plants thought to grow in the Murchison Basin are known to be available.

by Austin (1855, 55). He found "stony slopes full of holes made by [the Aborigines] in digging up some root they eat, and that must be very plentiful, and a favourite food" when exploring the Murchison Basin. Also, Wittenoom (n.d.) remembered the Yamaji eating 'a large yam', probably a species of *Ipomoea* (Leyland, pers. comm.).

Tubers yield more calories when ingested than seeds for less energy expended in their collection (Gould 1969; 1991; Hallam 1986; O'Connell & Hawkes 1981; Gott 1982; Brand & Cherikoff 1985; Pate 1986; Veth & Walsh 1988; Cane 1987; 1989; Jones & Meehan 1989). Moreover, many tubers can be and were eaten raw during collection. Most can also be roasted. In total, about 30 tuberous plants native to the Murchison Basin have been identified that were eaten by Aborigines elsewhere in Australia. Many of them were Nyungar staples (Meagher 1974).

Gould (1981) particularly emphasised the importance of fruits in Aboriginal diet. Not only are they highly nutritious and easy to collect but they can be dried and stored. He cited considerable evidence that Central and Western Desert people both collected fallen, desiccated *Solanum* and *Santalum* fruits in order to store them and also processed fresh fruits, by removing the flesh from the kernel and impaling it on twigs. These fruit-kebabs were stored against future lean times when the flesh would be re-hydrated and eaten. There is no ethnographic evidence that the Yamaji followed this practice, however it is quite likely that if they had known about it or thought of it for themselves they would have kept such storable food as a protection against recurrent periods of drought-induced low plant productivity. Lerps, a sugary secretion analogous to maple syrup, could also have been collected and rolled into 'gum balls' for future consumption. Some Aborigines still use gum balls as 'travelling tucker' when undertaking long trips because they are easily reconstituted with water (Leyland, pers. comm.).

Given the currently-denuded state of the vegetation it is impossible to estimate realistically the frequency with which different food plants might have been found in the Murchison Basin before the introduction of pastoralism. Therefore, the energy costs that the Yamaji might have expended while gathering plant foods cannot now be assessed. Moreover, the nutritional value of most of the plants listed in the appendix is unknown. Nonetheless, the range and diversity of the food plants identified by this study as potentially available for human consumption in the Murchison Basin supports the picture painted in Figure 11.7. It suggests that the Yamaji probably were numerous prior to European arrival because their territory was capable of supporting a large number of people, although its intrinsic carrying capacity can only be estimated in the broadest possible terms.

RESOURCE SCHEDULING

Rather more information can be deduced from the appendix about the seasons during which some of the staple food plants could be exploited (Figure 11.10). For example, 12 of the seed-bearing species were available during spring and 10 in summer. None was available during the autumn or winter months. However, if Tindale is right that the Yamaji stored seeds for up to six months, they could clearly have relied throughout the year on seed flour damper, there were so many species from which to choose. Most of the tuberous plants could also be exploited throughout the year, although digging for some of them in summer would be difficult because no vegetative traces remain above the ground, which is then also very hard (Hallam, pers. comm.). Of the species identified, 10 are available in spring, nine in summer, eight in autumn and seven in winter. There is no evidence that Aborigines ever stored tubers against times of hardship. Indeed, it would be counterproductive to do so. They can best be stored by leaving them in the ground. Fruits would, of course, only be available in late summer and autumn. However, fruit-kebabs could have been stored and hence been available out of season.

Thus, a variety of staple plant foods would have been available throughout the year, reinforcing Wittenoom's (n.d.) comment that the "natives in their wild state, lived well".

I see the following pattern of seasonal exploitation of the available resources in Figure 10. During spring and summer plant foods would have been widely available throughout the Murchison Basin, but supplies of fresh water would have been diminishing. The easy availability of plant foods would have enabled the Yamaji to focus on the 'best' waterholes. On the other hand, during autumn and winter, when fresh water would have been easier to obtain, only plants with underground storage organs would have been widely available. However, game might well have been more plentiful at that time, allowing people to focus on their watering holes. There is some anecdotal evidence to support this pattern. Austin (1855, 48–56) found evidence that, during the winter previous to his expedition, sizeable Aboriginal groups having camped by the rivers where they had trapped and eaten emu and kangaroo. Hooley (Sharp 1985, 86–98) also met large groups of Aborigines camped by the Murchison River in the winter. This seasonal pattern of territorial exploitation is similar to that seen amongst Western Desert peoples (Gould 1969; 1981; 1991; Peterson 1978; O'Connell *et al.* 1983). It would have ensured that water and food resources were not over-exploited, and that most parts fo the Murchison Basin were occupied during most of the year, deterring people from other social groups from entering the region.

CONCLUSIONS

Two main conclusions can be drawn from this study. First, it has shown yet again that judicious use of botanical surveys and ethnographic accounts can yield a satisfying amount of ethnobotanical data for a previously unstudied area whose extant vegetation is severely depleted. However, both the seasons at which staple foods are available in the Murchison Basin and the ways in which the Yamaji used different plants still need to be established. I hope to begin this verification process shortly in consultation with some of the older Yamaji people who remember what bushfoods they ate as children, when they were available and how they were processed. If it proves feasible, that study will be one of the few carried out in the Australian semi-arid zone.

Second, it has shown that the Murchison Basin supports a wide variety of food plants. Prior to the introduction of pastoralism they should have been sufficiently abundant to have provided adequate resources to nourish a numerous Aboriginal population. This finding corroborates my archaeological researches. Hence, I conclude that Wajarri territory was large not because its carrying capacity was low, but because the Yamaji were sufficiently numerous prior to European arrival to be able to maintain a large territory.

Acknowledgements

I thank the conference organisers for allowing me to present this paper verbally and subsequently to publish it, although its topic and regional references lay far outside the range of most of the other presentations.

I thank Estelle Leyland for sharing her specialist knowledge of the Murchinson flora with me. She contributed greatly to the compilation of the appendix by carefully checking the data I collated, while adding much additional unpublished information from her own research.

I thank Guy Foster (UWA) and Justin Jacyno (RHUL) for drawing the figures.

The clarity of the final version of this text is due, at least in part, to critical comments made by Jill Thompson and an anonymous referee. Any remaining infelicities or inaccuracies are my responsibility.

REFERENCES

Austin, R. (1855). *Journal of an expedition sent by the government to explore the interior of Western Australia north and east of the settled districts for extensive tracts of fertile land available for pastoral and agricultural purposes*. Perth: Government Printer.

Bates, D. (1913). *Social Organisation of some Western Australian Tribes*. Melbourne: Australian and New Zealand Association for the Advancement of Science Report **14**.

Bates, D. (1966). *The Passing of the Aborigines: a Lifetime Spent Among the Natives of Australia* (2nd ed.). London: Murray.

Bates, D. (1985).. (Ed. I. White) *The Native Tribes of Western Australia* (diaries and papers of Daisy Bates). Canberra: National Library of Australia.

Beard, J.S. (1976). *The Vegetation of the Murchison Region*. Perth: Western Australian Vegetational Survey sheet **6**, University of Western Australia Press.

Beard, J.S. (1990). *Plant life of Western Australia*. Kenthurst, NSW: Kangaroo Press.

Berndt, R.M. and Berndt, C.H. (eds.) (1980). *Aborigines of the West*. Perth: University of Western Australia Press.

Bindon, P. (1996). *Useful Bush Plants*. Western Australia Museum.

Bird, C.F.M. and Beeck, C. (1988). Traditional plant foods in the southwest of Western Australia: the evidence from salvage ethnography, pp. 113–122 in Meehan, B. and Jones, R. (eds.) *Archaeology with Ethnography: an Australian perspective*. Canberra: Prehistory Department, Research School of Pacific Studies, Australian National University.

Bordes, F., Dortch, C.E., Thibault, Cl., Raynal, J-P. and Bindon, P. (1983). Walga Rock and Billibilong Spring: two archaeological sequences from the Murchison Basin, Western Australia. *Australian Archaeology* **17**, 1–26.

Brand, J.C. and Cherikoff, V. (1985). Australian Aboriginal bushfoods: the nutritional composition of plants from arid and semi-arid areas. *Australian Aboriginal Studies* **1985/2**, 38–46.

Brown, R.G. (1983). Sea level history over the past 15,000 years along the Western Australian coastline, pp. 29–36 in Hopley, D. (ed.) *Australian sea levels in the last 15,000 years: a review*. Townsville: Geography Department Occasional Paper **3**, James Cook University Press.

Cane, S.B. (1987). Australian Aboriginal subsistence in the Western Desert. *Human Ecology* **15**, 391–434.

Cane, S.B. (1989). Australian Aboriginal seed grinding and its archaeological record: a case study from the Western Desert, pp. 99–119 in Harris, D.R. and Hillman, G.C. (eds.) In: *Foraging and Farming*. London: Unwin-Hyman.

Colhoun, E.A. (1991). *Climate During the Last Glacial Maximum in Australia and New Guinea*. Wollongong: Australia and New Zealand Geomorphological Group Special Publication **2**, Geography Department, University of Wollongong.

Cranfield, R.J. (1990). List of vascular plants recorded from the Murchison Catchment Survey area 1985–1988. *Kingia* **1**, 327–347.

Crawford, I.M. (1982). *Traditional Aboriginal Plant Resources in the Kalumburu Area: Aspects in Ethno-economics*. Perth: Western Australian Museum.

Cribb, A.B. and Cribb, J.W. (1974). *Wild Food in Australia*. Sydney: Collins.

Cribb, A.B. and Cribb, J.W. (1981). *Wild Medicine in Australia*. Sydney: Collins.

Dewar, R.E. (1984). Environmental productivity, population regulation and carrying capacity. *American Anthropologist* **86**, 601–614.

Diels, L. (1906). *Die Vegetation der Erde, vii: die Pflanzenwelt von West Australien*. Leipzig: Englemann.

Dix, W.C. and Lofgren, M.E. (1974). *Kurumi: possible Aboriginal incipient agriculture associated with a stone arrangement. Records of the Western Australian Museum* **3**, 73–7.

Fink, R.A. (1960). *Changing Status and Cultural Identity of Western Australian Aborigines*. Ann Arbor, Michigan: Uni. Microfilms.

Ford, R.I. (1979). Palaeoethnobotany in American Archaeology. *Advances in Archaeological Method and Theory* **2**, 285–336.

Forrest, J. (1875). *Journal of the proceedings of the Western Australian exploring expedition through the centre of Australia, from Champion Bay on the west coast, to the overland telegraph line between Adelaide and Port Darwin*. Perth: Government Printer.

Gentilli, J. (1959). *Weather and Climate in Western Australia*. Perth: Western Australian Government Tourist and Publicity Bureau.

Gentilli, J. (1993). Floods in the desert – heavy rains in the dry regions of Western Australia. *The Western Australian Naturalist* **19**, 201–218.

George, A.S. (1984). *Proteaceae of Western Australia*. Kenthurst, NSW: Kangaroo Press.

Giles, W.E.P. (1889). *Australia twice traversed: the romance of exploration, being a narrative compiled from the journals of five exploring expeditions into and through central South*

Australia and Western Australia from 1872 to 1876. London: Low, Marston, Searle and Rivington.

Goddard, C. and Kalotas, A. (eds.) (1985). *Puṉu: Yankunytjatjara plant use.* Singapore: Australian Institute for Aboriginal Development (Angus and Robertson).

Golson, J. (1971). Australian Aboriginal food plants: some ecological and culture-historical implications, pp. 196–238 in Mulvaney, D.J. and Golson, J. (eds.) *Aboriginal man and environments in Australia* Canberra: Australian National University Press.

Gott, B. (1982). Ecology of root use by the Aborigines of southern Australia. *Archaeology in Oceania* **17**, 59–67.

Gould, R.A. (1969). Subsistence behaviour among the Western Desert Aborigines of Australia. *Oceania* **39**, 253–275.

Gould, R.A. (1981). Comparative ecology of food-sharing in Australia and northwest California, pp. 422–454 in Harding, R.S.O. and Teleki, G. (eds.) *Omnivorous Primates* New York: Columbia University Press.

Gould, R.A. (1991). Arid-land foraging as seen from Australia: adaptive models and behavioral traits. *Oceania* **62**, 12–33.

Green, J.W. (1985). *Census of the Vascular Plants of Western Australia.* Perth: Western Australian Herbarium, Department of Agriculture.

Gregory, A.C. and Gregory, F.T. (1884). *Journals of Australian explorations.* Brisbane: Beal.

Grey, G. (1841). *Journals of two expeditions of discovery in Northwest and Western Australia during the years 1837, 38 and 39* (2 vols). London: Boone.

Griffith, K. (1985). *A Field Guide to the Larger Fungi.* Hong Kong: Amsel Ltd.

Hallam, S.J. (1977). Population and resource usage on the western littoral. *Memoirs of the Victorian Archaeological Survey* **25A/2**, 16–36.

Hallam, S.J. (1986). Yams, alluvium and 'villages' on the west coastal plain, pp. 116–132 in Ward, G.K. (ed.) *Archaeology at ANZAAS 1984.* Canberra: Canberra Archaeological Society.

Hallam, S.J. (1989). Plant usage and management in southwest Australian societies, pp. 136–150 in Harris, D.R. and Hillman, G. (eds.) *Foraging and Farming* London: Unwin-Hyman.

Hayden, B. (1981). Subsistence and ecological adaptations of modern hunter/gatherers, pp. 422–454 in Harding, R.S.O and Teleki, G. (eds.) *Omnivorous Primates.* Columbia Univ. Press.

Isaacs, J. (1987). *Bush food: Aboriginal food and herbal medicine.* Willoughby, NWS: Weldon.

Jarvis, N. (ed.) (1986). *Western Australia: an Atlas of Human Endeavour* (2nd. ed.). Perth: Dept. of Land Administration.

Jessop, J.A. (ed.) (1981). *Flora of Central Australia.* Sydney: Reed.

Jones, R. and Meehan, B. (1989). Plant foods of the Gidjingali: ethnographic and archaeological perspectives from northern Australia on tuber and seed exploitation, pp. 120–135 in Harris, D.R. and Hillman, G.C. (eds.) *Foraging and Farming.* London: Unwin-Hyman.

Kamminga, J. (1988). Wood artefacts: a checklist of plant species utilised by Australian Aborigines. *Australian Aboriginal Studies* **1988/2**, 26–56.

Latz, P.K. (1995). *Bushfires and Bushtucker: Aboriginal Plant Use in Central Australia.* Alice Springs: IAD Press.

Lawrence, R. (1968). *Aboriginal Habitat and Economy.* Canberra: Department of Geography Occasional Paper **6**, Australian National University.

Low, T. (1989). *Bush Tucker: Australia's Wild Food Harvest.* North Ryde, NSW: Angus and Robertson.

Low, T. (1990). *Bush Medicine.* North Ryde, NSW: Collins / Angus and Robertson.

Maiden, J.H. (1889). *The Useful Native Plants of Australia.* London: Trübner and Co.

Meagher, S.J. (1974). The food resources of the Aborigines of the southwest of Western Australia. *Records of the Western Australian Museum* **3**, 14–65.

Meagher, S.J. and Ride, W.D.L. (1979). Use of natural resources by the Aborigines of southwestern Australia, pp. 66–80 in Berndt, R.M. and Berndt, C.H. (eds.) *Aborigines of the West.* Perth: University of Western University Press.

Melville, G.F. (1947). An investigation of the drought pastures of the Murchison districy of Western Australia. *Journal of the Department of Agriculture of Western Australia* **24**, 1–29.

Mitchell, A.A. and Wilcox, D.G. (1988). *Plants of the Arid Shrublands of Western Australia.* Perth: University of Western Australia Press.

Myers, J.S. and Hocking, R.M. (1988). *Geological Map of Western Australia Explanatory Notes.* Perth: Geological Survey of Western Australia.

Nixon, M. and Lefroy, R.F.B. (1988). *Road to the Murchison: an Illustrated History of the District and its People.* Murchison, WA: Shire Office.

O'Connell, J.F. and Hawkes, K. (1981). Alyawara plant use and optimal foraging theory, pp. 99–125 in Winterhalder, B. and Smith, E.A. (eds.) *Hunter-gatherer Foraging Strategies* Chicago: University of Chicago Press.

O'Connell, J.F., Latz, P.K. and Barnett, P. (1983). Traditional and modern plant use among the Alyawara of central Australia. *Economic Botany* **37**, 80–109.

Oldfield, A. (1865). On the Aborigines of Australia. *Transactions of the Ethnographical Society of London* (N.S) **3**, 215–298.

Palmer, A. (1985). *Yalgoo.* Fremantle: Lap Industries.

Pate, F.D. (1986). The effects of drought on Ngatatjara plant use: an evaluation of optimal foraging theory. *Human Ecology* **14**, 95–115.

Pate, J.S. and Dixon, K.W. (1982). *Tuberous, Cormous and Bulbous plants.* Perth: University of Western Australia Press.

Pearce, R.H. (1979). *Analysis of some Western Australian Small Tool assemblages.* Perth: Unpublished MA thesis, University of Western Australia.

Pearson, S. and Dodson, J.R. (1993). Sticknest rat middens as sources of palaeoecological data in Australian deserts. *Quaternary Research* **39**, 347–354.

Peterson, N. (1977). Aboriginal uses of Australian Solenaceae, pp. 171–188 in Hawkes, J.G., Lester, R.N. and Skelding, A.D. (eds.) *The Biology and Taxonomy of the Solanaceae* London: Linnean Society Symposium Series **7**.

Radcliffe-Brown, A.R. (1912). The distribution of native tribes in part of Western Australia. *Man* **12**, 143–6.

Radcliffe-Brown, A.R. (1930a). The social organization of Australian tribes. *Oceania* **1**, 34–63, 206–246.

Radcliffe-Brown, A.R. (1930b). Former numbers and distribution of Australian Aborigines. *Official Yearbook of the Commonwealth of Australia* **23**, 687–696.

Scott, M.P. (1973). Some Aboriginal food plants of the Ashburton district, Western Australia. *The Western Australian Naturalist* **12**, 94–6.

Sharp, E.I. (1985). *E.T. Hooley Pioneer Bushman.* Perth: Lamb.

Simpson, N., Jones, B. and Marmion, D. 1992 *Wajarri Wangga.* Yamaji Language Centre, Geraldton, WA.

Smith, M.A. (1986). The antiquity of seed grinding in central Australia. *Archaeology in Oceania* **21**, 29–39.

Smith, M.A. (1989). Seed gathering in inland Australia: current evidence from seed-grinders on the antiquity of the ethnohistorical pattern of exploitation, pp. 305–317 in Harris, D.R. and Hillman, G.C. (eds.) *Foraging and Farming.* Unwin-Hyman.

Smith, M.V. and Kalotas, A.C. (1985). Bardi plants: an annotated list of plants and their use by Bardi Aborigines of Dampierland, in northwestern Australia. *Records of the Western Australian Museum* **12**, 317–359.

Stafford-Smith, D.M. and Pickup, G. (1990). Pattern and production in arid lands. *Proceedings of the Ecological Society of Australia* **16**, 195–200.

Strahan, R. (ed.) (1983). *The Australian Museum Complete Book of Australian Mammals*. Sydney: Angus and Robertson.

Tindale, N.B. (1974). *Aboriginal tribes of Australia*. Berkeley / Los Angeles: University of California Press.

Tindale, N.B. (1977). Adaptive significance of the Panara or grass seed culture of Australia, pp. 345–349 in Wright, R.V.S. (ed.). *Stone tools as Cultural Markers*. Canberra: Australian Institute of Aboriginal Studies.

Veth, P.M. (1987). Martujarra prehistory: variation in arid zone adaptations. *Australian Archaeology* **25**, 102–111.

Veth, P.M. (1993). *Islands in the interior*. Ann Arbor: International Monographs in Prehistory **3**, University of Michigan.

Veth, P.M. and Walsh, F.J. (1988). The concept of 'staple' plant foods in the Western Desert region of Western Australia. *Australian Aboriginal Studies* **1988/2**, 19–25.

Vinnicombe, P. (1987). *Dampier Archaeological Project*. Perth: Department of Aboriginal Sites, Western Australian Museum.

Walsh, F.J. (1987). The influence of spatial and temporal distribution of plant food resources on traditional Martujarra subsistence strategies. *Australian Archaeology* **25**, 88–101.

Walsh, F.J. (1990). An ecological study of traditional Aboriginal use of 'country': Martu in the Great and Little Sandy Deserts, Western Australia. *Proceedings of the Ecological Society of Australia* **16**, 23–37.

Wasson, R.J. and Donnelly, T.H. (1991). *Palaeoclimatic Reconstructions for the Last 30,000 Years in Australia – a Contribution to Prediction of Future Climate*. Canberra: Technical Memorandum **91/3**, Division of Water Resources, CSIRO.

Wasson, R.J., Fleming, P.M. and Donnelly, T.H. (1991). *Palaeoclimate of Australia at 6000 Years BP*. Canberra: Technical Memorandum **91/8**, Division of Water Resources, CSIRO.

Watson, P. (1983). *This Precious Foliage: a Study of the Aboriginal Psychoactive Drug pituri*. Sydney: Oceania monograph **26**, University of Sydney.

Webb, R.E. (1992). Sand traps for the unwary – problems in the interpretation of sedimentological analyses. *Queensland Archaeological Research* **9**, 43–9.

Webb, R.E. (n.d.). *Aboriginal adaptations to an uncertain environment: a re-examination of the prehistory of the Murchison Basin, Western Australia, in its continental context*. Perth: Unpublished PhD thesis, University of Western Australia (in preparation).

White, I. (ed.) (1985). *The Native Tribes of Western Australia* (diaries and papers of Daisy Bates). Canberra: National Library of Australia.

Wittenoom, F.F.B. (n.d). *Memoirs of the Murchison Pastoral and Goldfields Areas*. Geraldton, WA: MSS reprinted by the Geraldton Historical Society

Appendix: Scientific and common names of those native plants and fungi whose natural distributions include the Murchison Basin, that are known to have been used by Aborigines elsewhere in Australia and are presumed, therefore, to have been used by the Yamaji. Information on the part of the plant exploited and how it was used were taken from the cited sources. Plants marked * were 'staples', used extensively by Western Desert and/or Nyungar people. Wajarri names recorded at Boolardy pastoral station are given where known (Simpson *et al.* 1992).

*Acacia acuminata (Raspberry Jam / *mungarda*)	seeds ground into flour for damper, available in spring / summer, gum edible wood used for spears, clubs, etc.	Meagher 1974:61 Bindon 1996:5 Bird & Beeck 1988:118
*A. aneura (Mulga / *yalurr*)	seeds roasted & ground for damper, also ground & eaten uncooked, available spring / summer gum & lerps highly prized flowers eaten raw or soaked as drink insect galls edible, edible grubs live in roots moth larvae in branches, honeyants beneath roots also water obtainable from roots bark decoction or pills ingested, 'tobacco', paste made from gum, ash & bark for wounds increase ceremonies ensure supplies important wood source, used for shields, spear blades, clubs, boomerangs, woomeras, churingas, didgeridoos, throwing / digging sticks, etc.	Scott 1973:94 O'Connell *et al.* 1983:95-6, 98 Cane 1989:102 Veth 1993:72 Veth & Walsh 1988:25 Latz 1995:88-91 Bindon 1996:7 Isaacs 1987:231
*A. coriacea (Wiry Wattle)	large seeds ground for flour when dry, soaked & eaten raw when green, available in spring potable decoction made from seed & 'cap' (*sic*) dried seeds strung into necklaces 'milk' drunk, ash used with pituri wood used for boomerangs, spears, etc.	Isaacs 1987:217 Cane 1989:102 Lazt 1995:93-4 Bindon 1996:9 Kamminga 1988:34
A. grasbyi (Minnieritchie)	seeds roasted & ground for flour available in spring / summer wood used for spear points, clubs & boomerangs	Bindon 1996:15
*A. kempeana (Wanderrie Wattle)	seeds roasted & ground for flour available in spring / summer gum & lerps edible, either raw or soaked flowers eaten raw or soaked as drink important source of edible grubs live in roots leaves chewed or infusion drunk medicinally inner bark has medicinal value wood used for spear points and throwers especially when mulga not available	O'Connell *et al.* 1983:86-93, 96 Isaacs 1987:217, 231 Kamminga 1988:36 Veth & Walsh 1988:25 Latz 1995:102-4 Bindon 1996:18
*A. ligulata (Umbrella Bush / *bimba*)	seeds roasted & ground for damper, also eaten green pods brittle, so seeds difficult to gather *bimba* (gum) highly prized flowers eaten raw or soaked as drink edible grubs live in roots bark infusion for coughs, dizziness & 'nerves' also for 'smoking out' sickness, can cause hairloss	O'Connell *et al.* 1983:86-93, 96 Veth & Walsh 1988:25 Latz 1995:105 Leyland (pers.comm.) Bindon 1996:19 Isaacs 1987:231
*A. linophylla (Bush Bean / *bagurda*)	seeds roasted & ground for flour also steamed & eaten when young & green available in spring / summer	Bindon 1996:20
*A. murrayana (Sandplain Wattle)	seeds soaked &/or roasted & ground for flour can also be eaten raw, available in spring / summer seeds ground green as a substitute for coffee gum edible, edible grubs live in roots	Lawrence 1968:80-1 O'Connell *et al.* 1983:86-93 Latz 1995:110 Bindon 1996:24
A. pruinocarpa (Gidgee)	seeds roasted & ground for flour, difficult to extract, so used rarely, available in summer	Isaacs 1987:231 Veth & Walsh 1988:25

	sweet gum highly prized, lerps edible	Leyland (pers.comm.)
	flowers eaten raw or soaked as drink	Kamminga 1988:37
	to 'smoke out blood' from mother and baby	Latz 1995:114-5
	ash used with pituri, green bark chewed with resin	
	wood used for boomerangs, etc.	
	roots important source of spear wood	
A. ramulosa (Wanyu?)	seeds roasted & ground for damper	Latz 1995:115
A. sclerosperma (no common name recorded)	dry seeds edible, available in spring gum edible, flowers eaten raw or soaked as drink	Veth & Walsh 1988:25 Leyland (pers.comm.)
*A. tetragonophylla (Curara)	seeds roasted & ground for flour, also eaten green pleasant, nutty flavour, available in spring edible grubs live in roots bark / roots infused for coughs tannin in bark also stuns fish wood used for boomerangs, spears, throwers, etc.	Golson 1971:212; Latz 1995:119; Bindon 1996:28 O'Connell *et al*. 1983:95-6 Cribb & Cribb 1981:18 Isaacs 1987:231 Kamminga 1988:38
A. translucens (Red Sand Wattle)	dry seeds & insect galls edible, available in spring leaves & twigs mashed in water as wash for skin sores & headaches	Veth & Walsh 1988:25 Bindon 1996:29
*A. victoriae (Prickly Acacia / *waliputa*)	seeds roasted & ground into flour for damper also eaten green - an emergency food gum edible edible grubs live in roots & trunk dry seeds strung as necklaces wood used for knife handles, spear blades	Scott 1973:94 Isaacs 1987:217 Latz 1995:121 O'Connell *et al*. 1983:95-6 Bindon 1996:31 Kamminga 1988:38
A. xiphophylla (Snakewood)	ash used with pituri gum & seeds edible prized for carving boomerangs, digerdoos & spearshafts	Leyland (pers. comm.) Bindon 1996:32
Achyranthes aspera (Chaff Flower)	diuretic, plant crushed & steeped probable origin of Maiden's comments	Low 1990:40
Agaricus spp. (mushrooms)	both *A. arvensis* & *A. campestris* eaten raw	Griffiths 1985:18
Allocasuarina spp. (desert oaks)	cone sucked to relieve thirst roots & trunks can be tapped for water seeds pounded into flour, also eaten green ash used with pituri wood used for clubs, spears, etc. children make necklaces from leaves	Bird & Beeck 1988:118 Latz 1995:123 Leyland (pers. comm.)
Alyxia buxifolia (Dysentery Bush)	decoction used for diarrhoea	Leyland (pers. comm.)
*Amyema spp. (mistletoes)	berries of both *A. fitzgeraldii* & *A. preissii* favourite childrens' food, very sticky, grow on *Acacia* & *Senna*	Meagher 1974:27, 63 Latz 1995:125-7 Bindon 1996:37
Aristida spp. (wire grasses)	seeds edible, usually collected around ants' nests available in early spring	Golson 1971:213 Latz 1995:128
Arthropodium spp. (chocolate lilies)	small tubers, probably eaten raw	Leyland (pers. comm.)
*Astroloma serratifolium (Prickly Cranberry)	berries edible when soft	Meagher 1974:60 Bindon 1996:44
Atriplex muelleri (Mueller's Saltbush)	succulent leaves steamed and eaten	Low 1989:129
A. nummularia (Old Man Saltbush)	flowers semi-annually, leaves boiled twice as potherb lots of seeds ground for damper leaf decoction for sores, burns & wounds	Isaacs 1987:218 Bindon 1996:45
A. vesicaria (Bladder Saltbush)	leaves steamed boiled twice as potherb seeds ground for damper	Bindon 1996:45

Banksia spp. (banksias)	nectar sucked from flowers of 3 species known in Murchison (*Banksia ashbyi, B. attenuata* & *B. prionotes*), also soaked to make sweet drinks	Meagher 1974:59 Bindon 1996:49
Boerhavia diffusa (Tar Vine)	roots eaten raw or lightly roasted Hawkmoth caterpllars eaten after storing 2-3 days to remove stomach contents, yandied & cooked then keep well	Latz 1995:130-1 Bindon 1996:55
*Brachychiton gregorii (Kurrajong / *gaya*)	young roots probably roasted & debarked important source of water a fallback food, available when little else roasted seeds edible, collected at water holes from crows' droppings or burnt to avoid irritating fur on pod, flowers eaten raw, gum is <u>not</u> edible large grubs found in flowers eaten wood used for carrying vessels, shields, etc. but can split, bast can be used as string	Pate & Dixon 1982:220 Isaacs 1987:218-9 Latz 1995:133-4 Bindon 1996:57 Leyland (pers.comm.) Crawford 1982:34 Kamminga 1988:39
Brachysema aphyllum (Leafless Brachysema)	nectar sucked from flowers	Meagher 1974: 27, 63 Bindon 1996:59
Burchardtia umbellata (Milkmaids)	tubers eaten raw or cooked in ashes available spring / summer	Bindon 1996:61
Bursaria spinosa (Blackthorn)	nectar sucked from flowers also soaked to make sweet drink contains aesculin, no use recorded wood used for clubs	Isaacs 1987:219 Leyland (pers. comm.) Low 1990:212 Kamminga 1988:39
*Calandrinia spp. (parakeelyas)	roots edible, raw, cooked in ashes or boiled available in winter / spring seeds ground for flour, eaten raw or cooked flowers eaten leaves eaten as thirst quencher whole plant roasted & eaten	Smith & Kalotas 1985:342 Latz 1995:134-5 Brand & Cherikoff 1985:42 Latz 1995:134-5 Scott 1973:96 Isaacs 1987:219
Callistemon spp. (bottlebrushes)	nectar sucked from flowers	Isaacs 1987:219
Callitris columellaris (Cypress Pine)	leaves & twigs boiled for colds, steam inhaled used for 'smoking' babies, not for cooking, taints food leaves crushed & soaked for wash or mixed with fat as an ointment resin mixed with dung/ash used as adhesive, wood sometimes used for implements	Isaacs 1987:232 Latz 1995:135-6 Bindon 1996:63
Calytrix spp. (fringed myrtles)	crushed leaves soaked as antiseptic	Leyland (pers. comm.)
Canthium latifolium (Wild Currant)	sweet fruits are favoured food, only available in good seasons, stewed then skins & seeds discarded dry berries can be rehydrated, if eaten raw can cause lips to bleed, available in spring / summer wood used for boomerangs	Lawrence 1968:78 Veth 1993:72 Bindon 1996:68 Latz 1995:136-7
*Carpobrotus spp. (pigfaces)	fruit edible raw, and young leaves also eaten leaves steamed or roasted leaf juice rubbed on burns, scalds and stings also for rheumatism & muscular aches	Bindon 1996:76 Low 1990:172, 229
Clematicissus angustissima (Bush Grapes / Adjeco)	large tubers roasted fruits eaten juice used as anti-irritant	Leyland (pers. comm.) Golson 1971:216 Isaccs 1987:203
Cleome viscosa (Tickweed)	crushed leaves applied as headache poultice& for rheumatism, also soaked to make wash for colds & swellings, crushed leaf vapour inhaled as decongestant	Low 1990:13, 152, 185, 226-7 Bindon 1996:84
Codonocarpus cotinifolius (Desert Poplar)	sappy roots edible, leaves are narcotic, also make 'tea' edible grubs live in roots & trunk, viscera poisonous leaves & buds chewed for toothache, foliage 'sweats'	Cribb & Cribb 1974:138 Latz 1995:133-4 Bindon 1996:86

	to yield water, has cooling effect, powder used for aches and pains, 'special' tree at Mullewa	Leyland (pers. comm.)
Convolvulus erubescens (Bindweed)	roasted and pounded, available in winter leaves can be steamed & eaten as a stop gap food decoction used for stomach aches	Pate & Dixon 1982:220 Latz 1995:151
Crotolaria cunninghamii (Birdflower)	leaf decoction used as eyewash & for earache bark used for sandals & rope	Latz 1995:153 Bindon 1996:92
Cymbopogon spp. (lemon scented grasses)	seeds edible, available in spring / summer leaves chewed as decongestant for colds, also made into aromatic salve, used as eyewash, scent inhaled for chest illness, can induce nightmares if wash is drunk!	Leyland (pers. comm.) O'Connell *et al.* 1983:96 Latz 1995:156 Bindon 1996:94-5
*Cyperus spp. (sedges / *ngarlga*)	roots eaten raw or roasted, taste sweet & mutty important food source because plentiful available all year round	Scott 1973:95; Veth 1993: 72; Latz 1995:158-9; Bindon 1996:97
*Dactyloctenium radulans (Button Grass)	sought after food source, grows along rivers after rain seeds ground for flour, collected from around ants' nests available in winter	Scott 1973:94; Cane 1989: 102; Veth 1993:72; Latz 1995:160; Bindon 1996:98
Dianella revoluta (Spreading Flax Lily)	white tender bases of leaves eaten raw, or pounded & roasted on hot rocks, fruit eaten raw leaf fibres are strong & silky	Leyland (pers. comm.) Bindon 1996:99
*Dioscorea hastifolia (Nanicole)	tubers roasted and pounded, very prolific staple also eaten raw, available in spring / autumn fruit eaten when green, valued because crisp	Meagher 1974:26, 54 Hallam 1986, 1989b Bindon 1996:101
Dodonaea viscosa (Hop Bush)	root decoction for snakebite, wounds & toothache fruits infused for 'beer', leaves chewed for toothache, also to 'smoke' babies wood used for boomerangs, digging & walking sticks spears & throwers	Cribb & Cribb 1974:171; 1981:27, 50, 166; Isaacs 1987:234; Bindon 1996:104 Smith & Kalotas 1985:342 Kamminga 1988:41
Drosera spp. (sun dews)	small stem tubers eaten raw or cooked available in summer / autumn	Pate & Dixon 1982:221
Dryandra spp. (dryandras)	flowers sucked for nectar or soaked to make sweet drinks	Bindon 1996:106-7
Duboisia hopwoodii (Pituri)	leaves & twigs contain nicotine alkaloids, used as chewing tobacco & intoxicant, extensively traded as 'currency', used as anasthetic to stun game, especially emus, at waterholes, poisonous to European stock	Watson 1983; Isaacs 1987: 235; Low 1990:195-9 Latz 1995:163-4 Bindon 1996:108
Dysphania rhadinostachya (Crumweed)	important food source because high in protein whole plant scorched to release seeds, threshed winnowed, seeds crushed with water, cooked in coals to make sweet damper, available late in year leaf decoction for colds & headaches ground into powder, mixed with fat, as ointment	Latz 1995:164-5 Bindon 1996:104

Low 1990:109 |
*Enchylaena tomentosa (Ruby Saltbush)	leaves edible, fruits delicious, taste like pomegranate children's food chiefly leaves are anti-scorbutic fruit have antiseptic juice, can alsobe used as dye	O'Connell *et al.* 1983:93-5 Latz 1995:166-7 Cribb & Cribb 1974:30, 106 Bindon 1996:111
Enneapogon spp. (neverfail grasses)	seeds edible	Golson 1971:218
*Eragrostis dielsii (Mulka Grass)	staple food, seed ground with water for damper common in saline areas, available in summer loaves keep well & are highly nutritious	Lawrence 1968:81 O'Connell *et al.* 1983:86-93 Latz 1995:168-70
*E. eriopoda (Wire Wanderrie Grass)	very abundant seeds collected by ants, ground with water for damper, available in summer paste made from seeds has medicinal uses	Cane 1989:102; Veth 1993: 72; Latz 1995:168-70; Bindon 1996:112
*E. leptocarpa (Woollybutt Grass)	staple food, seeds ground with water for damper all species Eriopoda grow densely in mulga available in summer	O'Connell *et al.* 1983:86-93 Latz 1995:168-70

Eremophila spp. (poverty bushes)	nectar is sucked from the flowers of 5 of 11 spp. known in Murchison (*E. freelingii, E. latrobei, E. leucophylla, E. longifolia & E. maculata*), flowers & leaves can also be eaten, although the flowers of *E. maculata* may be poisonous (cyanide), succulent fruit of *E. longifolia* edible, but usually eaten by emu, not people, edible caterpillars live on leaves of *E. longifolia*, treated like those found on *Boerhavia*. seeds can be mashed in water to make sweet black drink, Europeans used as a tea substitute	Golson 1971:219 Brand & Cherikoff 1985:43 Isaacs 1987:235 Veth & Walsh 1988:25 Latz 1995:175-8 Bindon 1996:113-6
	6 of 11 spp. known in Murchison used medicinally (*E. alternifolia, E. duttonii, E. freelingii, E. gilesii, E. latrobei & E. longifolia*), leaves dried, infused, inhaled for deep pleasant dreams, or drunk for colds, coughs, diarrhoea, headaches, insomnia, eyewash, scabies, toothache, rheumatism, etc., made into aromatic analgesic salves for boils, etc., used in ceremonies & for 'smoking' babies, lining graves, etc., medicines can be stored, Europeans used as a tea substitute flowers used as decoration, resin from *E. fraseri* used as cement in artefact manufacture	Cribb & Cribb 1981:29, 50 O'Connell *et al.* 1983:96 Low 1990:97, 99
Eriachne spp. (false wanderrie grasses)	seeds edible	Golson 1971:219
Erodium cygnorum (Crowsfoot)	roots very small, edible when cooked seeds eaten when other food scarce	Cribb & Cribb 1974:160 Golson 1971:219 Latz 1995:179
Eucalyptus camaldulensis (River Red Gum / *urilba*)	bark from young roots edible, cooked & pounded into flour, seeds edible lerps & nectar highly prized because very sweet & starchy, good source of carbohydrate witchetty grubs live under bark & in roots boiled sap is strong disinfectant, gum or heartwood infusion for diarrhoea, gum paste for wounds & bleeding, steamed leaves for colds & fevers leaf tip decoction drunk for coughs & colds, ash used with pituri, sap used as anticeptic, but oil *not* used as inhalant /insect repellant by Aborigines, wood used for clubs and carrying vessels also bark, but less durable, for toy weapons flowers as necklaces	Cribb & Cribb 1981:71-2 Cane 1989:102 O'Connell *et al.* 1983:96 Latz 1995:182-4 Veth & Walsh 1988:25 Isaacs 1987:235 Bindon 1996:119 Kamminga 1988:43
E. dichromophloia (Bloodwood)	kino / gum boiled in sweetend water as nectar for toothache, coughs & colds, also used as tonic / disinfectant, insect galls are edible	Isaacs 1987:235 Bindon 1996:121
E. loxophleba (York Gum)	bark of young roots edible, cooked & pounded into flour, gum edible, chewed with roots, flowers sucked & soaked for sugar, wood used for spears roots chewed for medicinal purposes	Meagher 1974:56 Bindon 1996:126 Bird & Beeck 1988:118
E. oleosa (Water Mallee)	roots can be tapped for water wood used for clubs, digging sticks, spears carrying dishes	Isaacs 1987:223 Kamminga 1988:45 Bindon 1996:127
E. terminalis (Bloodwood)	parasitic insect produces large 'bush cocoanut' galls or 'apples' on the ends of branches, soft parts are a special favourite, flowers sucked & soaked for sweetness wood used to make ceremonial artefacts, kino is deep red, used as a varnish or finish	Bindon 1996:132
Eulalia spp. (grasses)	seeds edible available in spring / summer	Leyland (pers. comm.)
Euphorbia australis (Caustic Weed)	milky sap from crushed plant used for skin sores & cancers	Bindon 1996:135

Euphorbia drummondii (Balsam)	sap rubbed on breasts to increase lactation decoction as wash / drink for skin complaints sap is irritant, not to be drunk, keep away from eyes	Latz 1995:195 Bindon 1996:136
Evolvus alsinoides (Speedwell)	used as a substitute for pituri	Low 1990:197 Leyland (pers. comm.)
Exocarpus aphyllus (Leafless Ballart)	decoction of mashed stems for colds & to wash sores, chest poultice for 'wasting diseases', babies 'smoked' to strengthen them	Bindon 1996:137 Leyland (pers. comm.)
Exocarpus sparteus (Broom Ballart)	great quantities of fruit collected seasonally, by shaking bushes onto spread skins, tastes slightly acidic, like currants, Europeans used for jam	Bindon 1996:138
Frankenia spp. (samphires)	flowers and young leaves eaten	Leyland (pers. comm.)
Gastrolobium laytonii (Kiteleaf Poison)	used sparingly as pain-killing narcotic poisonous if ingested	Low 1990:192
Grevillea spp. (bottlebrushes)	seeds of all 15 spp. known in the Murchison edible flowers sucked for nectar, or soaked to make sweet drinks	Leyland (pers. comm.)
Grevillea juncifolia (Honeysuckle Oak)	fibrous bark soaked for wash, bark ash used as dressing for burns, sores, wounds & skin complaints	Latz 1995:201 Leyland (pers. comm.)
G. stenobotrya (Sand Dune Grevillea)	ash used with pituri, decoction used as medicinal wash also fumes inhaled seedpods used as rattles	Latz 1995:202
G. striata (Beefwood)	charcoal ingested, ash used with pituri solution & dried sap used dressings for wounds / burns itchy grub nests soaked in milk, good for burns kino used in artefact manufacture as water soluble cement / gum, slabs split from trunks to make shields & woomeras, blazed as survey points by Europeans	Cribb & Cribb 1981:36 Isaacs 1987:236 Latz 1995:202-3 Bindon 1996:150 Cribb & Cribb 1974:103
Gyrostemon ramulosus (no common name recorded)	soft wood easily carved, now for ornaments	Latz 1995:205
*Haemodorum paniculatum (Bloodroot)	red bulb, sweet & juicy, tastes 'hot' if eaten raw also eaten roasted, can cause dysentery	Meagher 1974:27, 60 Hallam 1986, 1989b
*H. spicatum (Bloodroot)	bulbs usually roasted in ashes, very 'hot' taste if eaten raw, available all year round leaf bases roasted, pounded with termite nest & eaten used to sure dysentery	Meagher 1974:27, 54-9 Pate & Dixon 1982:221 Bindon 1996:154
Hakea spp. (bottlebrushes)	seeds of all 14 spp. known in the Murchison can be eaten either raw or cooked nectar sucked from flowers, also soaked to make sweet, slightly alcoholic, drinks wood used for boomerangs	Meggitt 1957:143 Latz 1995:206-10 Bindon 1996:157 Kamminga 1988:48
H. subaerea (Corkwood)	burnt bark & ash used for burns & sore nipples	Leyland (pers. comm.)
Helichrysum apiculatum (everlasting composite)	crushed roots eaten to remove worms	Low 1990:185
*Ipomoea muelleri (Poison Morning Glory / *gulya*?)	large tubers roasted in ashes, highly prized food available in winter / spring high moisture content, useful in summer but food value quite low seeds edible leaves used for burns, itches, stings & headaches	Scott 1973:95 O'Connell *et al*. 1983:84-5 Latz 1995:214-7 Golson 1971:222 Leyland (pers. comm.)
Isotoma petraea (Rock Isotome)	sap is highly toxic, bitter & irritant to eyes, but crushed leaves used as poultices, also plant dried, pounded with *A. aneura* bark & used for colds or as substitute / booster for pituri	Low 1990:17, 192 Latz 1995:218 Bindon 1996:163

Leichhardtia australis (Wild Pear / *gagurla*)	roots roasted and pounded, also eaten raw only used as last resort honey sucked from flowers, also eaten raw fruit taste like young peas, also eaten roasted older leaves are steamed & eaten young leaves eaten raw ground seeds are allegedly used as a contraceptive	O'Connell *et al.* 1983:84-5, 93-5 Golson 1971:222 Brand & Cherikoff 1985:43 Latz 1995:224-5 Bindon 1996:165
Lepidium spp. (peppercresses)	drought-evading genus, leaves & stems steamed & eaten, available when there is little else	Lawrence 1968:83
Lobelia spp. (lobelias)	crushed leaves induce vomitting found at Tallering Peak	Low 1990:177 Leyland (pers. comm.)
Lomandra spp. (mat rushes)	leaves used as bandages	Low 1990:185
Lycium australe (Water Bush)	fruit eaten, leaves contain water	Leyland (pers. comm.)
Lycoperdon spp. (puffballs)	young plants eaten	Griffiths 1985:58
Lysiana cassuarinae (Mistletoe)	fruit eaten, parasitic on *Acacia* spp.	Latz 1995:125-6 Bindon 1966:171
Marsilea drummondii (Nardoo)	aquatic, sporocarps ground into flour, made into paste with water & eaten raw	Bindon 1966:174
Melaleuca spp. (paperbark trees / *ngundilbi*)	leaves crushed & inhaled for colds, catarrh wash for sores, etc., flexible bark as bandages also blankets & splints wood used for children's spears	Isaacs 1987:237 Latz 1995:226-7 Leyland (pers. comm.) Kamminga 1988:49
Myrtacaea (bottle brushes & heaths)	flowers of most species soaked for sweet drinks nectar plentiful in heaths, flowers shaken to collect dew, 11 genera known in Murchison	Leyland (pers. comm.)
Nicotiana excelsior (Bush Tobacco)	chewed or smoked as tobacco	Latz 1995:232
Nuytsia floribunda (Christmas Tree)	suckers peeled and eaten raw, tastes like sugar candy soft wood is used for shields	Low 1989:110-1 Bindon 1996:186
Orchidacea (orchids)	tubers & roots *not* eaten when flowering, firing increases productivity, eaten cooked or raw	Bird & Beeck 1988:116
Pimelea microcephala (Shrubby Rice Flower)	sweet fruit edible bark infusion used to treat venereal disease decoction drunk for throat / chest complaints inner bark fibre used for string	Cribb & Cribb 1974:75 Low 1990:182 Latz 1995:245 Bindon 1996:199
Pisolithus tinctorious (Puffball)	eaten raw when young, or cooked when old	Latz 1995:245
Pittosporum phylliraeoides (Native Willow)	very bitter seeds, only used if nothing else available, ground into flour for damper, gum edible decoctions of leaves for colds, seeds ground into paste for bruises, compress of warm leaves helps lactation, fruit highly astringent, very bitter red seeds are poisonous wood used for shields, bark used for sheaths, wallets, trays, etc.	Bindon 1996:200 Cribb & Cribb 1974:185 Isaacs 1987:226, 238 Latz 1995:246 Leyland (pers. comm.) Kamminga 1988:50
Pityrodia spp. (foxgloves)	for headaches, colds, wounds & diarrhoea	Leyland (pers. comm.)
Platysace maxwellii (yam)	roots eaten raw or roasted, edible all year round contain moisture, so eaten to quench thirst	Meagher 1974:26, 57 Bindon 1996:203
Plectrachne melvillei (Spinifex Grass)	seeds edible, but only used in emergency resin used as all-purpose adhesive	Bindon (pers. comm.) Latz 1995:288-93
Polyporus mylittae (Blackfellow's Bread)	eaten raw when soft & white	Griffiths 1985:56

Portulaca pilosa (Pigweed)	roots roasted in hot sand, available in ?summer seeds edible, leaves eaten raw and cooked leaves eaten whole as a cooling diuretic, antiscorbutic prevents or cures scurvy (Vitamin C deficiency), also used as 'blood cleanser'	Pate & Dixon 1982:220 Lawrence 1968:82 Golson 1971:226-7 Low 1989:151; 1990:71, 147 Bindon 1996:206
Prasophyllum spp. (leek orchids)	'wild potato' bulb roasted & eaten	Meagher 1974:27, 63 Bindon 1996:208
Prostanthera magnifica (Mintbush)	leaves very strongly scented, crushed & inhaled for colds & 'flu, also boiled as general purpose 'wash' dried leaves put in waterholes to stun birds, especially emu - dangerous to humans so poisoned water is marked	Bindob 1996:209 Leyland (pers. comm.)
Pterocaulon sphacelatum (Ragwort)	dried plant ground to powder & inhaled for colds & sore throats or as decongestant, fresh flowers or twigs placed in nasal septum for same purposes, wash made for cuts & sores, also used as a pituri substitute,	Low 1990:109, 152, 191 Bindon 1996:214
Ptilotus obovatus (Cotton Bush)	edible grubs live in roots flower heads used as body decorations, also as tinder	Latz 1995:256 Bindon 1996:216
Rhagodia nutans (Bush Spinach)	young leaves steamed & eaten	Leyland (pers. comm.)
Salsola kali (Roly Poly)	insect galls edible, but plant rare in the Murchison Basin edible grubs live in roots, after plant is dead acts as a diuretic	Veth & Walsh 1988:25 Leyland (pers. comm.) Latz 1995:258 Cribb & Cribb 1981:162
Santalum acuminatum (Quandong / *warlgu*)	fruit flesh & kernels edible, collected from emu drop- pings, flesh can be dried & stored, high in vitamin C reconstituted by grinding into paste with water roasted kernals high in protein water can be tapped from trunk wood used for bowls, etc.	Meagher 1974:62, 92; Gould 1981:51, 208 Latz 1995:259-60 Bindon 1996:219 Kamminga 1988:51
S. spicatum (Sandalwood / *walarra*)	fruit flesh & kernels edible nuts crushed for oil used as liniment on joints leaves pounded to treat gonorrhoea oil used to polish spears	Meagher 1974:61 Bindon 1996:220 Leyland (pers. comm.) Bird & Beeck 1988:118
Sarcostemma australe (Caustic Bush)	'bush bandaid', milk used as coagulant on wounds also for scabies & itchy spres, best gathered after rain, infusion of whole plant used similarly, rubbedon breasts for lactation, smoke for arthritis, etc. adhesive for feathers	Latz 1995:262 Bindon 1996:223 Leyland (pers. comm.)
Scaevola spinescens (Currant Bush / *gubaru*)	fruit edible raw root infusion for stomach aches & urinary infections decoction for boils & rashes, fumes inhaled for colds boiled to strong liquid, use with care <u>only in Murchison</u> used as cancer preventive	Cribb & Cribb 1974:75; 1981:42, 207 Isaacs 1987:239 Bindon 1996: 224 Leyland (pers. comm.)
Senna spp. (cassias)	edible grubs live in roots of all 3 spp. known in the Murchison (*S. nemophila*, *S. artemesioides* & *S.* *pleurocarpa*), their leaves, roots & flowers are purg- ative, boiled leaves also make medicinal wash for fevers, ingestion not recommended leaves made into shelters, leaves & flowers used for decoration	O'Connell *et al.* 1983:95-6 Latz 1995:264-6 Cribb & Cribb 1981:61-3 Bindon 1996:225
Solanum spp. (wild tomatoes / *gamburarra*)	bitter-sweet juicy fruit of 3 spp. known in Murchison (*S. ellipticum*, *S. esuriale* & *S. orbiculatum*) are edible raw, <u>when completely ripe</u> (yellow), when dry can be rehydrated, available in summer / autumn	Isaacs 1987:228 Latz 1995:276-9 Bindon 1996:232, 234
Solanum lasiophyllum (Flannel Bush)	root decoction makes poultice for swelled legs	Isaacs 1987:239
Sporobocus spp. (grasses)	seeds edible	Leyland (pers. comm.)

Stemodia spp. (blue rods)	tobacco substitute, also crushed for headaches & colds, put in nose, slept on, especially by babies	Goddard & Kalotas 1985:138 Low 1990:106, 226
Streptoglossa odora (Stinking Daisy)	crushed to relive headaches, colds & chest complaints	Low 1990:109 Latz 1995:281
Stylobasium spathulatum (Pebble Bush)	seeds highly nutritious, ground into flour for damper dried beans strung as necklaces	Veth & Walsh 1988:25 Latz 1995:282 O'Connell *et al.* 1983:98
Swainsonia formosus (Sturt's Desert Pea)	seeds are allegedly edible Western Desert people use flowers as decorations	Bindon 1996:239
Tecticornia arborea (Kurumi / *buli buli*)	halophyte, seeds ground into flour for damper, collected from claypans as they dry out & seeds fall, grindstones usually found nearby found at Billilly Claypan	Dix & Lofgren 1974 Tindale 1974:110 Bindon 1996:243 Bordes *et al.* 1983:24
Thryptomene maisonneuvii (Tea Tree)	dew collected on & honey sucked from flowers	Latz 1995:285
Thysanotus patersonii (Fringed Violet)	tuber probably eaten raw available in summer / autumn high water content, squeezed or sucked out vine and leaves roasted, eaten with roots of *E. loxophleba*	Meagher 1974: 26, 61 Pate & Dixon 1982:220 Latz 1995:286 Bindon 1996:251
Trichodesma zeylanicum (Northern Bluebell)	crushed for wounds, decoction as diuretic cure for snakebite, smoked as tobacco?	Low 1990:39, 41, 190-2 Bindon 1996:255
Triglochin procera (Arrow Grass)	roots roasted, available all year round	Pate & Dixon 1982:221
Triodia basedowii (Hard Spinifex)	seeds edible, but only used as a stop gap resin used as all-purpose adhesive important fire vector	Veth & Walsh 1988:25 O'Connell *et al.* 1983:96 Latz 1995:288-93
Vigna lanceolata (native yam)	good food source, tubers roasted, pounded and eaten, available autumn / spring	Veth 1993:72; Latz 1995: 296-7; Bindon 1996:262
Wurmbea spp. (early nancies)	small corms of 3 sp. known in Murchison usually eaten raw, available in spring / summer	Pate & Dixon 1982:221 Leyland (pers. comm.)

12. Blitzkrieg or Sitzkrieg: The Extinction of Endemic Faunas in Mediterranean Island Prehistory

Mark Patton

Since the time of Darwin, it has been widely recognised that island ecosystems can serve as "laboratories" for the study of more general evolutionary and ecological processes. More recently, this idea has been taken up by archaeologists in attempting to understand processes of socio-cultural, as well as ecological change. This paper will use examples from the prehistory of the Mediterranean islands to explore the relationships between human communities and wild mammals, looking in particular at the circumstances surrounding the extinction of four species: *Phanourios minutus* and *Elephas cypriotes* on Cyprus, *Prolagus sardus* on Sardinia and Corsica, and *Myotragus balearicus* on the Balearic Islands. Although the extinction of these species appears to have been caused at least in part by humans, it will be argued that the processes leading to extinction were fundamentally different in each case. These processes will be examined in the light of Diamond's (1989) distinction between "Blitzkrieg" and "Sitzkrieg" extinctions. It will be argued that, whilst *Phanourios minutus* and *Elephas cypriotes* became extinct as a result of rapid overkill by humans ("Blitzkrieg"), *Prolagus* and *Myotragus* became extinct as a result of habitat destruction and competition from domestic animals ("Sitzkrieg"). These different trajectories may reflect differences both in the mode of human exploitation of the environment, and in the reproductive biologies of the species concerned.

Keywords: Extinction, island biogeography, endemic species.

THE ISLAND LABORATORY

Since the time of Darwin, it has been widely recognised that island ecosystems can play an important role as "laboratories" for the study of more general ecological and evolutionary processes. In looking at the flora and fauna of the Pacific Islands, Darwin (1968[1859]) identified several recurrent features of island ecosystems. Firstly he noted that the number of species of all kinds which inhabit oceanic islands was relatively small: New Zealand, he observed, had only 960 species of flowering plant, whilst the remote island of Ascension originally possessed less than half a dozen. Secondly, he noted that, whilst species are few in number in an island context, the proportion of endemic kinds (i.e. those found nowhere else in the world) is often very high. Darwin noted, however, that these species, although unique to their particular islands (for example the Galapagos), are closely related to those on other islands and adjacent mainlands, suggesting divergent evolution from a common ancestor. Finally, he noted that certain types of animal (land mammals, frogs, toads, reptiles) were completely absent from the true oceanic islands, despite the fact that these ecosystems could support such species, as shown by the survival of species introduced by humans.

The theme of islands as laboratories for the study of evolution was further developed by A.R. Wallace (1880), and latterly by MacArthur and Wilson (1963; 1967). The Theory of Island Biogeography of MacArthur and Wilson

(1967) represents an attempt to define and quantify the factors involved in the colonisation of islands by animal and plant species, the survival or extinction of those species and their subsequent evolutionary development. Their approach was founded partly on Neo-Darwinian evolutionary biology, and partly on the more recent science of ecology. Like Darwin, they were not concerned with islands for their own sake, but with the possibilities which islands offered for the study of more general evolutionary and ecological processes. Specifically, they argued that islands provide a good model for ecosystems more generally, since most ecosystems (woods, streams, dunes, marshes etc) which support a particular range of species, exist as "islands" surrounded by very different environments, potentially as hostile to those species as the sea is to terrestrial animals and plants.

Fundamental to MacArthur and Wilson's model is the concept of "Species Equilibrium". Since an island's resources can only support a limited range of species, there will tend to be an equilibrium between the arrival of new species and the extinction of those already there. Thus species may come and go, but the number of species remains approximately the same. We would therefore expect the human colonisation of an island (or, by analogy, a continental area) to be followed by the extinction of some of the native species. The Island Biogeography model has been criticised by some ecologists (cf Berry 1979; Williamson 1981) on the grounds that it fails to take sufficient account of the biology of individual species. More recently the whole paradigm of equilibrium ecology (on which the model is based) has been called into question (de Angelis & Waterhouse 1987; Schaffer 1985). The model, however, remains influential in archaeology (cf Cherry 1990) and, as such, provides a convenient starting point for any discussion of interactions between prehistoric humans and island ecosystems.

In attempting to understand the mechanisms of human induced extinctions, two types of explanation have been developed (Marshall 1989). The first relies on the concept of "overkill", as developed by Wallace (1911) and elaborated by Martin (1967; 1973). Overkill models postulate direct human predation as the cause of a species' extinction, with predation occuring at a faster rate than the reproduction of the victim species. "Blitzkrieg" (Martin 1973) is defined as a "special case of overkill" in which extinction is particularly rapid: in archaeological terms this leads, as Guilday (1989) has argued, to a dearth of kill sites:

> "The swifter the job was done, the narrower the archaeological window, therefore the fewer the sites that might be expected to record the event." (Guilday 1989).

Marshall (1989) also distinguishes between "Direct Blitzkrieg", in which human hunting is the sole cause of extinction, and "Associated Blitzkrieg", in which hunting by humans caused the extinction of species already stressed by environmental change.

Diamond (1989) has proposed an alternative "Sitzkrieg" model, in which extinction occurs more gradually, as a result of more complex processes, including habitat destruction and the introduction of non-native species, some of which compete with endemic species for resources, and some of which act as vectors of disease. There may be a distinction to be drawn here between hunter-gatherer and farming populations, since extinctions on the "Sitzkrieg" model are more likely to occur in the context of agricultural activities, involving large scale clearance and the introduction of domestic livestock. Following Diamond's (1989) "Sitzkrieg" model, therefore, we might expect to see evidence for a long period of coexistence between hunter-gatherers and certain wild species, followed by the rapid extinction of those species after the transition to food production.

The prehistory of the Mediterranean islands offers a number of case-studies which may help us to test these contrasting models of human-induced extinction, and to understand in more detail the nature of the relationships between humans and non-domestic animals. Four endemic species are of particular interest. Pygmy Hippo (*Phanourios minutus*) and Elephant (*Elephas cypriotes*) on Cyprus have been known about for some time (Bate 1903; Forsyth-Major 1902), but until recently there was no evidence for the predation of these species by humans. This has been overturned by recent excavations at the site of Akrotiri Aetokremnos (Simmons 1991), where bones of these animals were found in association with worked flints, suggesting predation by human hunter-gatherers. The Post-Glacial fauna of Sardinia and Corsica includes an endemic "rabbit-rat", *Prolagus sardus*. Evidence from the Corbeddu Cave (Sondaar *et al.* 1984) on Sardinia suggests human predation of this animal at *ca.* 11000 bp, though claims of earlier exploitation remain controversial (Cherry 1992). On the Balearic island of Mallorca, the remains of an endemic caprine, *Myotragus balearicus*, have been identified. Evidence from the caves of Son Muleta and Son Matge (Waldren 1982) show that this animal was definitely exploited by prehistoric human communities, and the evidence from Son Matge in particular suggests that it may have been coralled. All of these species eventually became extinct, probably due to the activities of human groups, but the extinction of the Cypriot pygmy hippo and elephant seems to have been far more rapid than that of the other two species. A detailed study of the fate of these species may provide important clues to the nature of the relationships between humans and wild mammal populations.

PYGMY HIPPO AND ELEPHANT

The pygmy hippo and elephant of Cyprus are in many respects typical of endemic island megafauna. As in other instances (cf Lister 1989), it is likely that ecological limitation, combined with the absence of large predators, placed a selective advantage on dwarfism in an island context. Within the Mediterranean context, Cyprus is only one of a number of islands to have produced evidence for dwarfing of these species: remains of pygmy elephant have been found on Sardinia, Sicily and Malta (Guilday 1989), and on a number of Aegean islands including Crete (Dermitzakis & Sondaar 1978; Bachmayer *et al.* 1976), whilst remains of pygmy hippo have been recorded on Sicily and Malta (Guilday 1989). The particular interest of the Cypriot evidence lies in the association of pygmy elephant and hippo remains with evidence for human activity.

The rock shelter of Akrotiri Aetokremnos (Site E) has produced large quantities of pygmy hippo and elephant remains (Simmons 1991), from two distinct horizons, separated by a sterile layer. The lower of these two layers produced a series of radiocarbon dates, ranging from 11,200 ± 500 BP (UCL-194) to 10,560 ± 90 BP (Beta-40382/ETH-7160), whilst the dates from the upper layer vary between 10,485 ± 80 BP (Beta-41406/ETH-7160) and 9490 ± 120 BP (TX-5833A). The remains are associated with lithic material, dominated by thumbnail scrapers, microliths and burins. The quantity of animal bone from this site suggests intensive human predation of pygmy elephant and hippo. These species seem to have become extinct at a relatively early stage in the Holocene: no pygmy elephant or hippo bones have been recovered from the Early Neolithic sites of Kalavassos-Tenta (Todd 1987) or Khirokitia (Davies 1984; 1989). A single metacarpal of a pygmy hippo was found on the Early Neolithic site of Cape Andreas Kastros (Davies 1989), and a single longbone was found on the contemporary site of Akanthou Arkosyko (Reese 1989) but, as Davies (1989) suggests, these may well have been collected by Neolithic people long after the death of the animals themselves. It seems likely, therefore, that these species became extinct as a result of direct human predation, before the establishment of an agricultural economy, or the introduction of domestic livestock to Cyprus. The radiocarbon dates from Kalavassos-Tenta (the earliest dated Neolithic site on Cyprus) suggest that this phase began at least a millennium after the final phase of activity at Akrotiri Aetokremnos. The lithic assemblage from Akrotiri Aetokremnos is fundamentally different from the Neolithic assemblages, for example from Kalavassos-Tenta or Khirokitia, and there is no archaeological evidence to suggest any form of continuity between the phase represented at Akrotiri Aetokremnos and the Cypriot Early Neolithic. On present evidence, therefore, it seems likely that the original human population either left Cyprus or itself became extinct, and that the island was reoccupied at the beginning of the Neolithic. The extinction of pygmy elephant and hippo in Cyprus would appear to be a classic example of "Blitzkrieg", with extinction occuring within little more than a millenium of initial human contact. Hunter-gatherer groups are unlikely to have had much impact in terms of habitat destruction, and there is no evidence to suggest that they brought any other plant or animal species with

them to Cyprus. It is more likely that the hippo and elephant were simply unable to reproduce themselves fast enough to replace the animals killed by humans. These small and probably slow moving animals would be relatively easy to hunt and kill, and the evidence from Akrotiri Aetokremnos suggests fairly intensive exploitation. Hippo and elephant are also relatively slow to reproduce: they have long periods of gestation and maternal dependence, and generally give birth to single young. These island endemics evolved in an environment in which predators did not exist, and were unable to survive the onslaught of hunting by humans. More recent cases of extinction, such as the dodo of Mauritius and the moa of New Zealand attest to the vulnerability of naive island species to human predation. Describing the impact of Polynesian colonists (and of the dogs and rats which they introduced) on the native fauna of New Zealand, King (1984) states that:

> "Nothing in its evolutionary history had prepared [the native fauna] for such an attack, and it was this pathetic vulnerability, more then any particular ruthlesness on the part of the invaders, that made the impact so inescapable".

These words might as easily have been written about the impact of human predation on the pygmy elephant and hippopotamus of Cyprus.

It remains unclear whether, in Marshall's (1989) terms, the extinction of pygmy elephant and hippopotamus in Cyprus represents an example of "direct" or "associated" Blitzkrieg. These extinctions do seem to have occured shortly after the climatic changes of the Pleistocene/ Holocene transition, which may in themselves have placed these species under significant stress. It is also necessary to consider the circumstances under which pygmy elephant and hippopotamus became extinct on Sardinia, Sicily, Malta and the Aegean islands, since in these instances there is no evidence for human predation. It seems clear that at least some of these species survived the climatic changes of the late glacial period: at Charkadio on Tilos remains of pygmy elephant were found in a context which provided radiocarbon dates of 4390 ± 600 BP and 7090 ± 680 BP (Bachmayer *et al.* 1976). It should also be remembered that a paucity of evidence is a condition of the "Blitzkrieg" model and that, to quote Martin (1989):

> "...on other Mediterranean islands, as in America, the absence of extinct fauna in an archaeological context should not be held against the possibility of sudden prehistoric overkill."

Prolagus sardus

Prolagus sardus, the so-called "rabbit-rat" of Sardinia and Corsica, seems to have existed alongside humans for far longer than the pygmy hippo and elephant of Cyprus. Evidence for early human predation of this species has been claimed at the Corbeddu Cave in Sardinia. Sondaar *et al.* (1984) have claimed that some of the bones from the lowest level (Level 3) of the site exhibit butchery marks, and also that the age distribution of the remains suggests human exploitation. The radiocarbon dates from this layer suggest a date range between 14,560 and 13,450 bp (Sondaar *et al.* 1984). Most scholars are sceptical of the claims of human intervention in the assemblage from this layer (cf Cherry 1992), which has produced no artefacts or human remains. The overlying layer (Level 2) also produced large quantities of *Prolagus* remains, associated with a series of radiocarbon dates, ranging from 11,040 ± 130 bp (UtC-250) to 7860 ± 130 bp (UtC-301). The extent to which humans were responsible for this assemblage is also open to question, since the assemblage has not been adequately published. Whilst some scholars have questioned the claim by Sondaar *et al.* (1984) that the remains were associated with artefacts (E. Webb pers. comm.), human remains were recovered from Level 2, demonstrating the coexistence of humans and *Prolagus* on Sardinia from an early stage in the Holocene. Irrespective of the specific taphonomic problems of the Corbeddu assemblage, it would be astonishing if human hunter-gatherers, present on Sardinia from *ca.* 11,000 bp, did not exploit *Prolagus*. There is independent evidence for the exploitation of *Prolagus* by human hunter gatherers from pre-Neolithic horizons at Araguina-Sennola and Strette, Corsica (Vigne 1987; Vigne *et al.* 1981), the latter associated with a radiocarbon date of 9140 ± 300 bp (LY-2837). *Prolagus* seems to have survived, at least on Corsica, until the Iron Age, though its numbers seem to have declined significantly from Middle Neolithic times onward: it accounts for 27% of the faunal assemblage from the Early Neolithic horizon (Layer 17) at Araguina-Sennola in Corsica, but only 0.6% of the assemblage from the Middle Neolithic horizons (Layers 14–16) on the same site (Vigne 1987). The species is mentioned by Polybius in the 3rd Century BC (Vigne 1988), and *Prolagus* bones were found in association with an iron nail at Teppa di Lupino, Corsica (Tobien 1935). *Prolagus* is absent, however, from layers dating to the 1st Century AD at Scaffa-Piano, Corsica, suggesting that the species became extinct on the main island of Corsica between the 2nd Century BC and the 2nd Century AD (Vigne 1988). On the isolated islet of Tavarola, however, the species seems to have survived into the 18th Century AD (Cetti 1777). *Prolagus*, therefore, seems to have survived human exploitation for a period of around 10,000 years. This may in part be a function of its reproductive biology: *Prolagus* was a relative of the rabbit, and is likely to have reproduced itself at a much faster rate than pygmy elephant or hippo. *Prolagus* seems not to have been exterminated by direct human predation: it became extinct only after the transition to agriculture, perhaps as a result of habitat destruction, competition from domestic animals or diseases carried by those animals. In fact the decline of *Prolagus* seems to coincide with a significant intensification of agricultural production (Vigne 1988): palynological evidence from Corsica (Reille 1977; Renault-Miskovsky 1969) suggests

a marked intensification in the Late Neolithic on the coast, and at the beginning of the Iron Age in the interior. This intensification is also evident from the faunal remains (Vigne 1987): although domestic pigs and caprines were introduced to Sardinia and Corsica in the Early Neolithic, cattle were not introduced until the Middle Neolithic. Lewthwaite (1985) has developed a model according to which the Early Neolithic economy of Corsica was based largely upon the exploitation of *Prolagus* and marine resources, with small-scale herding of sheep, goat and pig representing a relatively minor diversification of the resource base. The true "commitment to agriculture", in Lewthwaite's model, comes at a later stage. The faunal evidence outlined by Vigne (1987), whilst offering broad support to many aspects of Lewthwaite's model, suggests a rather more complex set of processes. The dramatic decline in the significance of hunted resources, from 100% of the faunal assemblage in the Pre-Neolithic horizon at Araguina-Sennola, to 2–4% in the Cardial horizons at Basi and Strette, suggests a radical change in economic strategy rather than a simple diversification of the resource base. During the Epi-Cardial and Middle Neolithic phases on Corsica, it is only at Araguina-Sennola that we see evidence for hunting as a significant element of the economy. Vigne (1987) has drawn attention to the anomalous nature of this assemblage, and suggests that Araguina served as a late winter and spring hunting camp: the cultural layers are separated by sterile lenses, suggesting intermittant occupation, and the assemblage also includes remains of migratory birds which are most likely to have been present in late winter. This Early Neolithic transformation (which did not bring about the immediate extinction of *Prolagus*) must surely be seen as evidence for a major economic intensification in which hunting, previously an all-year activity and the mainstay of the economy, became a seasonal and supplementary activity. Given the long time period covered by the Pre-Neolithic in Sardinia and Corsica, and the apparent stability of both human communities and natural resources during this period, it seems hardly likely that this sudden transformation was forced on human communities by the limitations of the island ecosystem. It would perhaps be more plausible to suggest that intensification was related to increasing social complexity, and that new strategies were adopted in order to meet increasing social demands for surplus production. The Middle Neolithic transformation, which involved the adoption of cereal cultivation, the introduction of domestic cattle and perhaps also the exploitation of secondary products (the age structure of the caprine population in Middle Neolithic deposits at Araguina-Sennola suggests the rearing of these animals for milk production) can be seen as evidence for a further intensification. This transformation is likely to have involved clearance on a far greater scale than is evident in the Early Neolithic record, and it is in this context that the gradual extinction of *Prolagus* should be understood. *Prolagus* therefore presents us with a classic example of a "Sitzkrieg" extinction, in marked contrast to that of the pygmy hippo and elephant of Cyprus.

Myotragus balearicus

On the Balearic island of Mallorca, remains of an extinct endemic caprine, *Myotragus balearicus*, have been identified. This species seems to have been present on the island for between 6 and 8 million years prior to the arrival of human communities, and Juniper (1984) has suggested that the presence of *Myotragus*, in the absence of significant predators, would have had a marked effect on the natural vegetation of the island, with tree-cover being effectively confined to inaccessible slopes, and the vegetation cover being dominated by heavily armed and poisonous plants, such as the endemic *Astragalus balearicus*, *Sonthus spinosus* and *Centaurea balearica*. Human communities arrived in Mallorca at a relatively late stage. Waldren (1982) has identified an "Early Settlement Phase" on the basis of evidence from the caves of Son Muleta and Son Matge. This phase is apparently aceramic, and is characterised by the absence of introduced domestic animals. The cave of Son Matge has produced the most significant evidence, including a bed of *Myotragus* coprolites. This deposit is up to 125cm in thickness, and has abrupt edges, suggesting that the animals were deliberately coralled. Butchered bones were associated with the deposit, suggesting that animals were occasionally slaughtered in the cave, and the existence of a number of artificially trimmed horns provides further evidence for the deliberate management of herds. The *Myotragus* coprolite bed has produced two radiocarbon dates, of 6680 ± 120 bp (QL-29) and 5820 ± 360 bp (SCIC-176). Butchered *Myotragus* remains were also found in kitchen middens overlying the coprolite beds, and these deposits have produced radiocarbon dates of 5750 ± 115 bp (I-5516) and 4650 ± 120 bp (QL-988). Whilst the deposits of the Early Settlement Phase have produced neither pottery nor the remains of introduced domestic animals, the radiocarbon dates from Son Matge suggest a chronological overlap with Neolithic cultures in the Western Mediterranean, and the evidence for coralling suggests that these settlers were at least familiar with techniques of animal husbandry. Clutton-Brock (1984) goes so far as to suggest that the abundance of *Myotragus* may account for the fact that the earliest settlers did not introduce domestic animals. The islands may have been discovered as a result of fishing expeditions, and may have been settled precisely because of the abundance of an endemic species which, having presumably little fear of humans, could easily be herded and coralled. The earliest evidence for introduced domestic animals on the Balearic Islands is from the "Neolithic Early Ceramic Phase" at Son Matge. This horizon has produced radiocarbon dates of 4650 ± 120 bp (QL-988) and 4093 ± 392 bp (BM-1408). Within the hearth deposits associated with this horizon were found bones of domestic goat, pig, cattle

and *Myotragus*. The associated pottery has been compared by Waldren (1982) to material from Middle and Late Neolithic sites in South-Eastern Iberia, such as Tabernus, Abrigio de Ambrosio and Cueva de l'Or. *Myotragus* seems to have become extinct shortly after the beginning of this phase: the latest dated remains are from the deposit which also produced a radiocarbon date of 4093 ± 392 bp. The Early Ceramic Phase also sees the appearance of open-air settlements, as at Ferrandell-Oleza. The faunal assemblage from this site is dominated by caprines, but bones of pig, cattle and dog are also present. Whilst Clutton-Brock (1984) suggests an increasing reliance on domestic animals as *Myotragus* was hunted to extinction, the long period of coexistence between *Myotragus* and human communities (a minimum of 2500–3000 years), together with the absence of any evidence for the gradual introduction of livestock, suggests that the decline of *Myotragus* is more likely to have been a consequence, rather than a cause, of the introduction of other domestic livestock. As on Corsica and Sardinia, the evidence suggests that island communities initially adapted mainland strategies to the local environment (animal husbandry techniques applied to *Myotragus*, for example), but that later intensification, perhaps for social reasons, lead to the adoption of the full Neolithic package, to the detriment of endemic species. Once again, therefore, we seem to be dealing with "Sitzkrieg", rather than "Blitzkrieg" extinction.

CONCLUSION: THE EXTINCTION OF ENDEMIC FAUNAS AND THE ISLAND BIOGEOGRAPHY MODEL

The evidence from the Mediterranean islands corroborates Diamond's (1989) suggestion that human-induced extinctions can occur as a result of at least two distinct sets of processes: "Blitzkrieg", in which extinction occurs through direct human predation, and "Sitzkrieg", in which extinction occurs more gradually, and as a result of a more complex series of human/animal interactions, including the destruction of habitat and competition between endemic species and introduced domesticates. The process by which a species becomes extinct in the context of human activities depends upon a range of factors, some natural and some cultural. The reproductive biology of the victim species is clearly one factor, which may explain why *Prolagus* and *Myotragus* survived long periods of human predation, whilst the Cypriot pygmy hippo and elephant did not. In cultural terms, "Blitzkrieg" extinctions are most likely to be caused by hunter-gatherer groups, whereas "Sitzkrieg" extinctions are more likely to be caused by food-producing communities, whose effect on the ecosystem and natural landscape is generally far greater. In many cases, as with both *Prolagus* and *Myotragus*, "Sitzkrieg" extinctions occur after a long period of coexistence with human communities, and these extinctions may be associated with significant phases of economic intensification. It is not possible, therefore, to separate the question of human/animal relations from that of social relations within the human communities concerned: a change in the social formation of those communities may involve increasing demands for surplus production, and these demands in turn may place pressure on the natural environment in a number of ways, potentially leading to the extinction of some animal and plant species. These processes, like the evolutionary processes observed by Darwin (1968[1859]), are by no means unique to islands, but the insular environment, with a range of unique species, provides a laboratory for their study.

In the light of the evidence from the Mediterranean islands, it may be necessary to modify in certain respects the "Theory of Island Biogeography", as outlined by MacArthur & Wilson (1967). Their approach has been widely adopted by archaeologists over the past decade (cf Cherry 1990; Terrell 1986), and is therefore of considerable interest to us. The Island Biogeography model involves a series of assumptions, some of which may have to be questioned or modified. This is not wholly surprising from an archaeological perspective, since the model was not formulated with human communities in mind.

The first of these assumptions is that insular environments are fundamentally environments of ecological "poverty" (Lack 1976), characterised by reduced biodiversity, to which human communities, like other species, have to adapt. In the case of human communities, this "poverty" depends partly upon the extent to which coastal resources were exploited, since the diversity of these will not be affected by insularity. It is also true, however, that from a resource point of view, the relatively small number of species in an island ecosystem does not necessarily imply a low biomass, and may be off-set by the abundance of animals of specific endemic species: on Sardinia/Corsica, Mallorca and Cyprus, the existence of such species gave rise to specific human adaptations. These islands must have appeared to human settlers as environments of plenty, and it is surely no coincidence that these were the only Mediterranean islands to be occupied by human communities which did not possess domestic livestock. In the case of Mallorca, it seems clear that the earliest settlers came from a parent population which did have domestic animals: the fact that they did not, in the initial stages, import livestock to the Balearic Islands, is probably due to the abundance of endemic *Myotragus*. Having evolved in an environment without predators, endemic species are likely to have had little fear of humans, and would thus be relatively easy to hunt or, in the case of *Myotragus*, to herd. From the ecological point of view, therefore, island environments may have advantages as well as disadvantages for human communities.

The Island Biogeography model also involves the concept of "Species Equilibrium", according to which the colonisation of an island by a new species (including humans) is likely to be balanced by the extinction of species already there. As we have seen, however, the

impact of hunter-gatherer communities on the ecology of the Mediterranean islands seems in most cases to have been relatively limited. On Sardinia & Corsica, human communities coexisted with *Prolagus* for around 10,000 years, and perhaps for much longer, whilst on the Balearic Islands, human communities coexisted with *Myotragus* for around 3000 years. The exception to this pattern is Cyprus, where pygmy elephant and hippo do seem to have been wiped out by human hunting in little more than a millennium, probably as a result of their inability either to reproduce themselves fast enough to replace the victims of human predation (as in the case of *Prolagus*) or to adapt behaviourally by entering into a mutualistic relationship with humans (as in the case of *Myotragus*). If the impact of hunter-gatherer communities on Mediterranean island ecosystems was limited, however, the same cannot be said of agricultural communities. Neolithic colonists brought domestic animals to the Mediterranean islands, which competed with endemic species for grazing & browsing, and may also brought diseases to which these species had no immunity. The natural vegetation was cleared for cultivation and pasture, destroying the habitat of native species. It is in this context that "Sitzkrieg" extinctions occur. In one sense, this pattern actually conforms to MacArthur & Wilsons' (1967) model of "Species Equilibrium": it could be argued that island ecosystems such as Sardinia/Corsica and the Balearic Islands could accomodate one further species (humans), but could not accomodate the full package of new plant and animal species which arrived as part of the transition to food production. In another sense, however, it demonstrates the inadequacy of the Island Biogeography model in relation to human communities: the effect of human colonists on an island ecosystem depends not only upon their biology, but also on a range of cultural factors. The transition to fully developed food production on Sardinia/ Corsica, and on the Balearic Islands, should probably not be seen as an environmental adaptation (there is no evidence to suggest that the previous food procurement strategies were unstable) but as a cultural strategy, permitting the production of an increased food surplus, perhaps in order to fulfill social demands. For human communities, therefore, ecology and culture are inextricably bound up together. As Meillassoux (1964) writes:

"The action of the environment is not unilateral since, by their actions, people produce a transformation in nature, which then becomes the object of some new human action."

This point is particularly well illustrated by the prehistory of the Mediterranean islands. Looking at the prehistory of the Mediterranean Islands as a whole, it is interesting to note that there are three major phases of island colonisation, each of which can be related to a phase of economic intensification (Figure 12.1): the first is in the 6th Millennium cal BC, coinciding with the initial adoption of the Neolithic package, the second is in the 4th and 3rd Millennia cal BC, which can perhaps be related to

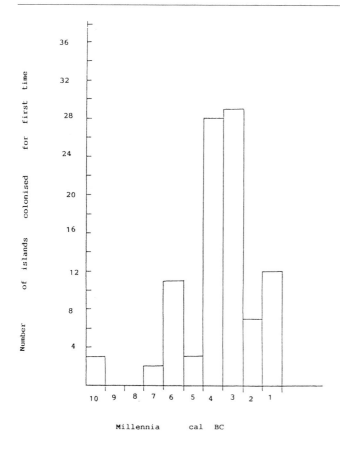

Figure 12.1: Patterns of colonisation in the Mediterranean islands. Based on Cherry (1990) with additions.

the "Secondary Products Revolution" (Sherratt 1979), and the third is in the 1st Millennium cal BC, coinciding with the emergence of Classical civilisations. The extinction of *Myotragus* occured within the second of these phases of intensification, whilst the decline of *Prolagus* began in the second phase and resulted in extinction in the third. The extinction of pygmy elephant and hippo on Cyprus occured in the context of an earlier (but much less dramatic) phase of island colonisation, which coincides with the onset of post-glacial conditions. More detailed studies of other species might be expected to reveal similar correlations, and on the basis of such studies, we may perhaps begin to understand and theorise the relationships between cultural and environmental change in Mediterranean prehistory.

Acknowledgements

I am grateful to Esmée Webb and to Keith Dobney for their constructive comments on an earlier version of this text.

REFERENCES

Bachmayer, F., Symeonidis, N., Seeman, R. and Zapfe, H. (1976). Die Ausgrabungen in der Zwerfelefantenhole Charkadio auf den Insel Tilos. *Ann. Naturhistor. Mus. Wien* **80**, 113–144.

Bate, D.M.A. (1903). Discovery of a pigmy elephant in the Pleistocene of Cyprus. *Proceedings of the Royal Society of London* **71**, 498–500.

Berry, R.J. (1979). The outer Hebrides: where genes and geography meet. *Proceedings of the Royal Society of Edinburgh* **77**, 21–43.

Cetti, F. (1777). *Appendice alla Storia Naturale dei Quadrupedi di Sardegna.* Sassari, Private Publication.

Cherry, J.F. (1990). The first colonisation of the Mediterranean Islands: A review of recent research. *Journal of Mediterranean Archaeology* **3**, 145–221.

Cherry, J.F. (1992). Palaeolithic Sardinians? Some questions of evidence and method, pp. 43–56 in Tykot, R.H. and Andrews, T.K. (eds.) *Sardinia in the Mediterranean: A Footprint in the Sea.* Sheffield: Academic Press.

Clutton-Brock, J. (1984). Preliminary report on the animal remains from Ferrandell- Oleza, with comments on the extinction of Myotragus balearicus, and on the introduction of domestic livestock to Mallorca, pp. 99–118 in Waldren, W.H., Chapman, R., Lewthwaite, J. & Kennard, R-C. (eds.) *The Deya Conference of Prehistory. Early Settlement in the West Mediterranean Islands and the Peripheral Areas.* Oxford: BAR (International Series) S229.

Darwin, C. (1968). [1859] *The Origin of Species by Means of Natural Selection, or the Preservation of Favoured Races in the Struggle for Life.* Oxford: Oxford University Press.

Davies, S.J.M. (1984). Khirokitia and its mammal remains: A Neolithic Noah's Ark, pp. 147–162 in Le Brun (ed).

Davies, S.J.M. (1989). Some more animal remains from the aceramic Neolithic of Cyprus, pp. 189–22 in Le Brun (ed).

de Angelis, D.L. and Waterhouse, J.C. (1987). Equilibrium and non-equilibrium concepts in ecological models. *Ecological Monographs* **57**, 1–21.

Dermitzakis, M.D. and Sondaar, P-Y. (1978). The importance of fossil mammals in reconstructing palaeogeography, with special reference to the Pleistocene aegean archipelago. *Annales Géologiques des Pays Hélleniques* **29**, 808–840.

Diamond, J.M. (1989). Quaternary megafaunal extinctions: variations on a theme by Paganini. *Journal of Archaeological Science* **16**, 167–175.

Forsyth-Major, C.J. (1902). On the pygmy hippopotamus from the Pleistocene of Cyprus. *Proceedings of the Zoological Society of London* **2(i)** 238–9; 2 (ii) 107–112.

Guilday, J.E. (1989). Pleistocene extinctions and environmental change: A case study of the Appalachians, pp. 250–258 in Martin and Klein (eds).

Juniper, B.E. (1984). The natural flora of Mallorca, Myotragus and its possible effects and the coming of man to the Balearics, pp. 145–163 in Waldren, W.H., Chapman, R., Lewthwaite, J. & Kennard, R-C. (eds.) *The Deya Conference of Prehistory. Early Settlement in the Mediterranean Islands and the Peripheral Areas.* Oxford: BAR (International Series) S229.

King, C. (1984). *Immigrant Killers: Introduced Predators and the Conservation of Birds in New Zealand.* Oxford University Press.

Lack, D. (1976). *Island Biology illustrated by the Land Birds of Jamaica.* Oxford: Blackwell.

Le Brun, A. (ed) (1984). *Fouilles Récentes à Khirokitia (Chypre), 1977–1981.* Paris: Editions Récherche sur les Civilisations, ADPF.

Le Brun, A. (ed) (1989). *Fouilles Récentes à Khirokitia (Chypre), 1983–1986.* Paris: Editions Rècherche sur les Civilisations, ADPF.

Lewthwaite, J. (1985). From precocity to involution: the Neolithic of Corsica in its west mediterranean context. *Oxford Journal of Archaeology* **4**, 47–68.

Lister, A.M. (1989). Rapid dwarfing of red deer on Jersey in the last interglacial. *Nature* **342**, 539–542.

MacArthur, R.H. and Wilson, E.O. (1963). An equilibrium theory of insular zoogeography. *Evolution* **17**, 373–387.

MacArthur, R.H. and Wilson, E.O. (1967). *The Theory of Island Biogeography*. Princeton: Princeton University Press.

Marshall, L.G. (1989). Who killed cock robin? An investigation of the extinction controversy, pp 785–806 in Martin and Klein (eds).

Martin, P.S. (1967). Prehistoric overkill, pp. 75–120 in Martin and Wright (eds).

Martin, P.S. (1973). The discovery of America. *Science* **179**, 969–974.

Martin, P.S. (1989). Prehistoric overkill: the global model, pp. 354–403 in Martin and Klein (eds).

Martin, P.S. and Klein, R.G. (eds) (1989). *Quaternary Extinctions: A Prehistoric Revolution*. Tucson: University of Arizona Press.

Martin, P.S. and Wright, H.E. (eds) (1967). *Pleistocene Extinctions: The Search for a Cause*. New Haven: Yale University Press.

Meillassoux, C. (1964). *Anthropologie Economique des Gouro de Cote d'Ivoire*. Den Haag: Mouton.

Reese, D. (1989). Tracking the extinct pygmy hippopotamus of Cyprus. *Field Museum of Natural History Bulletin* **60**, 22–29.

Reille, M. (1977). Quelques aspects de l'activité, humaine en corse durant le subatlantique et ses conséquances sur la végétation, pp. 329–342 in Univ, P and Curie, M. (eds) *Approche Ecologique à l'Homme Fossile*. Paris: Editions AFEQ.

Renault-Miskovsky, J. (1969). Etude des pollens de l'Abri d'Araguinna-Sennola. *Livret-Guide de l'Excursion C17 (Corse) du VIIIè Congrès de l'INQUA*. Paris: CNRS, 44–51.

Schaffer, W.M. (1985). Order and chaos in ecological systems. *Ecology* **66**, 93–106.

Sherratt, A.G. (1979). Plough and pastoralism: aspects of the secondary products revolution, pp. 261–305 in Hodder, I., Hammond, N. and Isaac, G. (eds.) *Patterns in the Past*. Cambridge: Cambridge University Press.

Simmons, A.H. (1991). Humans, island colonisation and Pleistocene extinctions in the Mediterranean: The view from Akrotiri Aetokremnos, Cyprus. *Antiquity* **65**, 857–69.

Sondaar, P.Y., DeBoer, P.L., Sanges, M., Kotsakis, T. and Esu, D. (1984). First report on a Palaeolithic culture in Sardinia, pp. 29–59 in Waldren, W.H., Chapman, R., Lewthwaite, J. and Kennard, R-C (eds.) *The Deya Conference of Prehistory. Early Settlement in the West Mediterranean Islands and the Peripheral Areas*. Oxford: BAR (International Series) S229.

Terrell, J. (1986). *Prehistory in the Pacific Islands*. Cambridge: Cambridge University Press.

Tobien, H. (1935). Über die pleistozanen und postpleistozanen *Prolagusformen* Korsikas und Sardiniens. *Ber. Naturf. Gens.z.Freiburg i Br.* **34**, 253–344. Todd, I.A. (1987). *Vasilikos Valley Project 6: Excavations at Kalavassos Tenta*. Goteborg: Paul Astroms Forlag.

Todd, I.A. (1987). *Vasilikos Valley Project 6: Excavations at Kalavassos Tenta*. Goteborg: Paul Astroms Forlag.

Vigne, J.D. (1987). L'exploitation des ressources alimentaires carnées en Corse du VII au IVe Millènaire, pp. 193–199 in Guilaine, J., Courtin, J., Roudil, J-L., and Vernet, J-L. (eds.) *Premières Communautés Paysannes en Méditeranée Occidentale*. Paris: CNRS.

Vigne, J.D. (1988). *Les Mammifères Post-Glaçaires de Corse: Etude Archéozoologique*. Paris: XXVIè Supplément à Gallia Préhistoire.

Vigne, J.D., Marinval-Vigne, M.C., de Lanfranchi, F. and Weiss, M-C. (1981). Consommation du 'lapin-rat' (Prolagus sardus Wagner) au Néolithique ancien Méditerannéen. Abri d'Araguina-Sennola (Bonifaccio, Corse). *Bulletin de la Société Préhistorique Française* **78**, 222–4.

Wallace, A.R. (1880). *Island Life, or the Phenomena and Causes of Insular Faunas and Floras, including a Revision and Attempted Solution of the Problem of Geological Climates*. London: Macmillan.

Wallace, A.R. (1911). *The World of Life*. New York: Moffat.

Waldren, W.H. (1982). *Balearic Prehistoric Ecology and Culture*. Oxford: BAR. (International Series) S149.

Williamson, M. (1981). *Island Populations*. Oxford University Press.

13. Estimating the Rate of Paleoindian Expansion into South America

James Steele, Clive Gamble and Tim Sluckin

The parts which humans played in the extinctions of Late Pleistocene megafauna of the Americas will remain poorly understood so long as debate persists concerning the existence of culturally-adapted populations in the Americas for tens of millennia prior to the observed extinction peaks. In this paper, we discuss the implications of radiocarbon calibration for dating the first Americans. We demonstrate that while there remain many valid questions about the quality of the radiocarbon database, the spatial structure of 'agreed' Paleoindian dates from South America nonetheless suggests that that continent was colonised by people dispersing from North America at about the time of first appearance of Clovis sites in the north. Models of megafauna extinctions which take account of a human role may need to be adapted to conform with models of Paleoindian range expansion characterised by high mobility, low population densities, and low to moderate population growth rates.

Keywords: Clovis, extinctions, megafauna, Monte Verde, Paleoindian, radiocarbon.

INTRODUCTION

Catastrophic human impact on the endemic fauna of the Americas at the end of the Pleistocene has been inferred from the coincidence of the first appearance of humans in the Americas with the extinction of at least eight genera of North American megafauna (*Camelops*, *Equus*, *Mammut*, *Mammuthus*, *Northrotheriops*, *Palaeolama*, *Smilodon* and *Tapirus* – Grayson 1991), and of elements of the South American megafauna (including *Equus* and *Mammut* – Politis *et al*. 1995). Multifactorial explanations of these extinctions are now favoured which take account of background variation in origination and extinction rates, of paleoenvironmental evidence of terminal Pleistocene climate and habitat changes, and of direct and indirect human impact. The role of human predation and habitat disruption has, however, been obscured by debate on the possible presence of humans in the Americas for many millennia prior to their earliest clear archaeological visi-

bility. A strong will persists in many quarters to see the ancestors of modern American Indians as having existed in their homelands for tens of thousands of years prior to Clovis, leading a life which was both ecologically and archaeologically 'transparent upon the landscape'.

For those who resist this tendency, simulation modelling of the expansion of human foragers into the Americas at the end of the Pleistocene has played an important part in the explanation of early phases of the Paleoindian archaeological record (e.g. Mosimann & Martin 1975; Whittington & Dyke 1984; Belovsky 1988; Steele *et al*. 1996). One reason for this is that the archaeology suggests there was an extraordinarily rapid expansion process with no direct parallels in the ethnographic or historical records. Formal modelling tools have proved invaluable aids to thinking about the dynamics of such sustained momentum (Meltzer 1995).

Unfortunately the value of formal models of Paleoindian range expansion has often been compromised by uncertainties about archaeological dating of first occurrences of humans in different parts of the Americas. Such information is needed to 'calibrate' these formal models. This situation is now changing, with the publication of tables of radiocarbon dates for early material with reliable cultural associations in northeast Siberia (Kuzmin 1994a, b), in the Clovis area of North America (Haynes *et al.* 1984; Haynes 1987; 1992; 1993), and in South America (Whitley & Dorn 1993). In this paper, we summarise and analyse this data in order to be able to construct formal models which better approximate the temporal and spatial dynamics of the actual range expansion process.

LATE PLEISTOCENE ARCHAEOLOGY OF NORTH-EASTERN SIBERIA AND BERINGIA

In northeast Siberia, the Verkhoyansk Range (glaciated from 25,000 to 14,000 BP) appears to have blocked human expansion during the Pleistocene, perhaps because it represented an important environmental boundary in terms of temperature and moisture differences (Hoffecker *et al.* 1993). Kuzmin's compilation of radiocarbon dates for northeast Siberia indicates that humans were present in Yakutia and in the Kamchatka peninsula by the late Upper Paleolithic (Yakutia: Berelekh, ^{14}C dates extending back to 13,420 BP; Kamchatka: layer 7 of Ushki 1, ^{14}C dates extending back to 13,000–14,000 BP, Kuzmin 1994a). There are still no secure dates from this early period from Chukotka, where late glacial ice may have been quite extensive (Velichko 1995, 106), but current excavations at El'akchan may soon change that (Hoffecker *et al.* 1993, 259).

A land-bridge connected northeast Siberia to Alaska through most of oxygen isotope stage-three (from about 60,000 BP), lasting until 11,000–10,000 BP (Hoffecker *et al.* 1993, 46). In eastern Beringia, Paleoindian sites with lanceolate points have been dated to 11,360 ± 70 BP (average of two dates from the oldest hearth, Mesa site, Kunz and Reanier 1994) and 11,315 ± 90 BP (average of four dates from Component 1, Walker Road Site, Nenana Valley, Powers & Hoffecker 1989).

An ice-free corridor between the Cordilleran and Laurentide ice sheets appears to have opened up between 13,000 and 12,000 BP (Lundqvist & Saarnisto 1995), and while the possibility of a Western migration route along the Pacific coast should not be discounted, this corridor remains the most likely entry route into the lands south of the ice sheets (Ives *et al.* n.d.).

South of the ice-sheets from the Clovis culture area of North America, Haynes compiled dates with good cultural associations from 10 sites that he believed revealed "a remarkably tight constraint on Clovis to three centuries between 11,200 and 10,900 bp." (1992, 364; but see below). Meadowcroft rock shelter in Pennsylvania is an unexplained earlier outlier: Adovasio *et al.* (1990) state

that the six deepest dates with unequivocal cultural associations average to 13,955 – 14,555 BP, although there is a possibility that we are overaging the cultural deposits at Meadowcroft if there is coal in this material (Tankersley *et al.* 1990). Pre-12,000 BP dates from South America remain controversial (cf. Lynch 1990; Whitley & Dorn 1993; and see below).

CALIBRATION BEYOND THE DENDRO CURVE

The recent appearance of a preliminary extension of the radiocarbon calibration curve to about 18,400 BP (Bard *et al.* 1990, 1993, cf. Stuiver & Reimer 1993) has enabled researchers to make a first approximation of the ages of terminal Pleistocene sites and events in sidereal years (see e.g. Tushingham & Peltier 1993; Lowell & Teller 1994 for Quaternary geography; Whitley & Dorn 1993; Street *et al.* 1994; Batt & Pollard 1995 for Palaeolithic archaeology). Calibration by ^{230}Th-^{234}U dating of marine corals has indicated that ^{14}C dates from the late glacial are systematically younger than their absolute ages, and need to be corrected by up to 2,000 years to derive the age of a sample in sidereal years (Bard *et al.* 1993; Edwards *et al.* 1993). This correction has been challenged by some workers on the basis of discrepant varve calibrations (e.g. Bjorck *et al.* 1995). Hajdas *et al.* (1995), however, found that the Lake Holzmaar (Germany) varve chronology indicated an offset of *ca.* 1, 400 years between the ^{14}C age and the calendar age of samples from 12,600 BP (radiocarbon years), while the varve sequences at Holzmaar appear also to have lost several hundred years of the Younger Dryas event – at Holzmaar (Hajdas *et al.* 1995) the YD is dated to 11,940 – 11,490 cal BP, whereas at Lake Gosciaz it is varve-dated to the range 12,400 – *ca.*11550 cal BP, matching the ice core dates of *ca.* 12,700 – *ca.* 11,550 and better matching the ^{230}Th-^{234}U coral dates of *ca.* 13,220 – *ca.* 11,560 cal BP (Street *et al.* 1994, 15). This implies that the offset for pre-YD ^{14}C dates from Lake Holzmaar should be substantially greater than 1,400 years. The finding that ^{14}C dates get systematically younger than their absolute ages in the late glacial would, of course, be supported by evidence of increased levels of atmospheric ^{14}C in the late glacial, and this has now been reported by Goslar *et al.* (1995). Bard *et al.* (1993) note that their observation of the discrepancies between ^{230}Th-^{234}U dates and ^{14}C dates on the Barbados corals has been paralleled by observations of similar discrepancies in the 30,000–10,000 BP ^{14}C period when comparing ^{14}C with K-Ar and TL dates, and also with ^{230}Th-^{234}U dates from speleothems. It therefore seems to us to be realistic to proceed with preliminary calibration of late glacial radiocarbon dates using the coral data, in spite of residual disagreements between the coral and some (but not all) of the varve series.

CALIBRATING CLOVIS AND ITS PRECURSORS

Calibration of the eastern Beringian sites mentioned earlier, using the ^{230}Th-^{234}U-based calibration scheme derived by Stuiver and Reimer (1993) from the Bahamian coral (Bard *et al.* 1993), suggests that they were occupied as early as 13,270 cal BP (Mesa Site, two sigma range 13,490–13,100) and 13,220 cal BP (Component 1, Walker Road site, Nenana Valley, two-sigma range 13,470–13,020). Averaging the probability distributions for these two sites using CALIB 3.03 gives a date of 13,250 cal BP for the occupation of eastern Beringia (two-sigma range 13,460–13,080). Throughout this paper, calibrated dates have been rounded to the nearest ten year interval.

South of the ice sheets, Batt and Pollard (1995) have suggested that a tight three-century clustering for the calibrated ^{14}C dates from the Clovis sites listed by Haynes *et al.* (1984) only results if they are *averaged* on the assumption that they all sample a single 'event horizon' – and this is statistically improbable. If the averaged dates from each Clovis site are *summed* as samples from an underlying probability distribution, then the prediction is that calibrated dates from these sites all lie within the range (at the two-sigma confidence level) of 13,990–12,140 cal BP- a range of 1,850 years rather than 300. Repeating this analysis with the revised summary Clovis radiocarbon date set given in Taylor *et al.* (1996), and summing the probability distributions across these site averages using CALIB 3.03 (Stuiver & Reimer 1993), gives a calibrated date range for Clovis of 13,520–12,800 cal BP (to the one-sigma confidence level) or of 13,910–12,230 cal BP (to the two-sigma confidence level) – a range slightly smaller than that calculated by Batt and Pollard (1995) using Haynes' earlier (1984) dataset, but still greater than the 300–^{14}C year interval previously favoured by Haynes himself (in fact, Haynes now recognizes a 700–year range as the best estimate for Clovis, 11,700–1,000 BP – Haynes, pers. comm. 1996). Of course, it is possible that a Bayesian analysis of these Clovis dates which took account of ^{14}C dates for the underlying and overlying sediments bracketing the cultural layers could improve the precision of these estimates (cf. Buck *et al.* 1994).

The eastern Beringian sites therefore date from the early part of the possible range for Clovis, and might (arguably) be interpreted as northern precursors. This calibrated date range for Clovis correlates quite closely with the end of the late glacial 'Bolling-Allerød' interstadial, and the beginning of the Younger Dryas cooling event – the estimated sidereal date range for the Younger Dryas in the North Atlantic region is 12,700–11,500 cal BP in Europe (Street *et al.* 1994, 15), and about 12,600–11,000 cal BP in North America (Lowell & Teller 1994, 801) – although Stuiver *et al.* (1991, 5) suggest that "the full-fledged YD episode lasted from about 12,100 to 11,300 cal yr BP." Haynes had earlier proposed that Clovis was a terminal Pleistocene (late Younger Dryas) event-horizon, preceding the Early Holocene increase in precipitation (Haynes 1991; 1993) – but with the calibrated range for Clovis, *at the two-sigma interval*, now calculated at 13,910–12,230 cal BP this appears to be untenable. The end of Clovis seems more likely to correspond globally to the *inception* of the full-fledged North Atlantic YD event. Of course, it remains plausible that the later part of the Clovis period was associated with a transient climatic reversal – for example, perhaps there was a westward extension of the effects of the Killarney Oscillation, a lower-amplitude cooling episode detected in eastern North America and AMS ^{14}C dated to the period 11,290–10,960 BP (Levesque *et al.* 1993; 1994).

We should note a caution at this point: the calibration procedure in CALIB 3.03, which uses an inferred atmospheric spline fitted on the basis of the coral data, assumes a marine reservoir correction of -400 years as a constant (Stuiver & Reimer 1993), whereas recent work suggests that for the Younger Dryas a North Atlantic marine reservoir correction of -700 to -800 may be necessary (Bard *et al.* 1994). This discrepancy in the calibration procedure is likely to have had the effect of artificially 'ageing' at any rate the *younger* Clovis sites by up to 400 calendar years, and thus artificially truncating the younger end of the estimated date range for Clovis. Recent work by Goslar *et al.* (1995) also confirms that much of the Younger Dryas represents a ^{14}C plateau, and that conventional radiocarbon dates in approximately the 9,800–10,500 BP range may therefore sample a much wider range of sidereal years. Increased standard errors will almost certainly therefore be a concomitant of calibration of dates from the younger ends of the ranges for Early Paleoindian remains from North America and perhaps also from South America.

REANALYSIS OF THE SOUTH AMERICAN DATASET

Clovis has usually been assumed to be the cultural ancestor of the earliest Paleoindian cultures in South America. However, Whitley and Dorn (1993) have compiled a table of ^{14}C-dated South American Paleoindian sites which are 'accepted' by the majority of archaeologists, and excluding "a number of highly controversial sites and phases" (*ibid.*, 629). They calibrated these dates using the inferred atmospheric spline in CALIB 3 (Stuiver & Reimer 1993), and compared the date distribution with estimates of the effective distances of the sites from the southern limit of the Clovis area. Accepting Haynes' earlier proposal that Clovis was tightly constrained to the 11,200–10,900 BP interval (and that the date for an earliest Clovis progenitor for South American Paleoindian cultures must therefore be 13,110 cal BP), they found that it was improbable in the extreme that the late glacial human presence in South America could be traced to a Clovis ancestry.

We believe that this South American dataset merits

Table 13.1: Results of weighted least-squares regression analysis of the relationships between dates and distance from El Paso. Equations are of the form Y = a + bX. Weights used were the reciprocal of the squared standard deviation (for uncalibrated dates) or of the square of half the one-sigma range (for calibrated dates). The table shows two sets of results, with Monte Verde 2 – the principal outlier – either included or excluded. * = model significant at 95% level, ** = model significant at 99% level.

Y	X	a (s.e.)	b (s.e.)	p	r^2
All sites					
BP	geodesic	11856 ±542	-0.16 ±0.07	0.10 n.s.	0.11
cal BP	geodesic	13666 ±484	-0.10 ±0.06	0.13 n.s.	0.08
BP	road map	11712 ±588	-0.06 ±0.05	0.27 n.s.	0.02
cal BP	road map	13543 ±530	-0.05 ±0.05	0.30 n.s.	0.01
Excluding MV 2					
BP	geodesic	11967 ±343	-0.15 ±0.04	0.004**	0.41
cal BP	geodesic	13799 ±368	-0.13 ±0.05	0.02*	0.28
BP	road map	11923 ±389	-0.10 ±0.04	0.02*	0.32
cal BP	road map	13721 ±408	-0.08 ±0.04	0.05 n.s.	0.20

further analysis. Spatial analyses of radiocarbon dates that aim to detect age-gradients consistent with a directional diffusion or migration of the associated cultural traditions or their bearers are exemplified by Roper's (1976) trend-surface analysis of radiocarbon dates for the Central Plains tradition. In the present case, however, where far fewer dates from far fewer dated sites are available, a simpler method seems appropriate whereby space is reduced to a single dimension – distance from a hypothetical point of origin. An appropriate statistical technique for such analysis is weighted least-squares regression, since the distributions of variance in the calibrated dates and the distances compiled by Whitley and Dorn (1993: Table 1) do not violate the normality assumption (cf. Draper & Smith 1981, 108–117). We assume the distance variable to be error-free, and treat the conventional ^{14}C dates as the dependent variable. Radiocarbon dates (whether conventional or calibrated) are not point data, but we can treat them as such by treating the modal value of the probability distribution as a point datum, and weighting this datum inversely to the square of the standard deviation. With calibrated dates, of course, this procedure is extremely imperfect: where more than one modal value exists, they must be averaged, while the probability distribution of *calibrated* dates for a sample will rarely be normal. For the analysis attempted here, where calibrated dates are used we are obliged to treat the one-sigma calibrated date range as if it were normally distributed when constructing the table of weights.

The Appendix to this paper gives the dates used in our re-analysis, with their calibrations (derived using CALIB 3.03), and some additional information on the sites, their locations and the distances from the southern limit of the Clovis area as calculated by Great Circle routes (shortest distances assuming no effects of topography) and as

calculated by Whitley and Dorn from road atlases. We note in passing that while we have followed Whitley and Dorn, who measured their distances from a Clovis origin in El Paso (taken as the southern limit of the southwestern United States), points in the Clovis tradition have in fact been found as far south as Turrialba in Costa Rica, a site which has not yet been dated by the radiocarbon method but which is several thousand kilometres closer to any one of these South American early sites (Ranere & Cooke 1991, 238).

In some cases, we have amended the dates used or the calibrations made by Whitley and Dorn (and in one case we have substituted one more securely-dated site for another in the same cultural tradition), and the reasons for this are given in the notes to the Table. Wherever possible we have checked the information on each date with the laboratory which made the original measurement. We have added one site which was published after Whitley and Dorn's paper appeared (Monte Alegre, Roosevelt *et al.* 1996). In calibrating we have made a southern hemisphere correction (-40 ^{14}C years) for sites south of the equator, and as far as possible have corrected for δ^{13}C when this was not done by the radiocarbon laboratory. We have made no use of any error multipliers.

Table 13.1 gives the results of the weighted least-squares regression models for uncalibrated and calibrated dates against distance, for both Great Circle and road atlas distances. It is evident that the trend is for younger sites with distance southwards, for all combinations of date-type and distance estimator. This trend achieves significance at the 0.05 level for none of the combinations when all available sites are included, but does achieve significance for three of four combinations (the exception is calibrated dates plus road map distances) when Monte Verde 2 is excluded. This confirms the outlier status of

Monte Verde, although the date estimated here for the site is nonetheless consistent with an end-Pleistocene colonization. The great circle distance seems a somewhat more robust predictor of first colonization date than the road map distance: this does not mean that the Paleoindians *flew*, but implies that physical resistance due to topography was not the most important source of relative frictions on expansion. Probably habitat variation was more important here, and this is the subject of our further investigations (Glass, Steele & Wheatley, in press).

The intercept gives the best estimate of the time at which the expanding population passed El Paso, while the slope coefficient gives the relationship between increments in time and in distance. The intercept values for the calibrated dates cluster about 13,700 cal BP, with standard errors of the order of 400–500 cal years. This is at the old end of the two-sigma range for Clovis (see above), and implies that Paleoindian dispersal into South America was in parallel with, rather than consequent to, the establishment of Clovis occupation to the North. The slope coefficients range from -0.10 to -0.15 for the great circle distances, with standard errors of about 0.05. This implies an average rate of expansion 'as the crow flies' of 7 to 10km per year. For the road map distances, which are all substantially greater than these great circle distances, the slope coefficients range from -0.05 to -0.10, with standard errors of about 0.04, implying a rate of expansion 'over the ground' of 10 to 20 km per year. The latter velocities are likely to be more realistic *as averages*.

DISCUSSION

Whitley and Dorn's analysis of their data led them to argue that a 'Clovis-first' model of the colonization of South America was extremely implausible. As we have seen, however, and particularly after excluding Monte Verde as an outlier, the regression model suggests a decrease in age of 'accepted' early sites with distance southwards, while the intercepts lie within the two-sigma confidence interval for Clovis (when Clovis is treated statistically as a period rather than an event-horizon).

An indirect supporting argument for Whitley and Dorn's interpretation was the implausibility of the demographic assumptions about fertility and mobility made in some models of Paleoindian expansion, assumptions which are believed to be necessary to account for the observed rate of Paleoindian range expansion. But if these demographic assumptions are implausible, this does not invalidate the empirical finding of a north-south gradient in the dates. The dated evidence suggests, rather, that we need to look for an alternative model of the dynamics of late glacial Paleoindian range expansion. Belovsky (1988) has presented such a model, purporting to demonstrate that under plausible ecological assumptions an expansion rate identical to that predicted by the Martin and Budyko models, and leading to colonization of the southern end of

South America only 600 years after entry from the Central American isthmus, can be generated with maximum human population growth rate limited to 1.3% – the upper limit of the Haynes model (Haynes 1966), which Whitley and Dorn accepted as plausible. Other rapid colonization models include Beaton's 'Transient Explorer Strategy' (Beaton 1991). MtDNA evidence of a Wisconsin-age colonization of the Americas cited as corroboration by Whitley and Dorn (1993) is flawed by the use of questionable assumptions about the rate of evolution of mtDNA: other studies have yielded much more recent divergence dates of 15,000 BP or later (cf. Torroni *et al.* 1994 and discussion in Weiss 1994).

We would not suggest that our analysis is the last word on the subject. Clearly there is still a serious dearth of radiocarbon-dated sites from this period, and equally clearly too many of the existing sample of radiocarbon-dated sites need more radiocarbon measurements if we are to derive an accurate and precise estimate of their true age. Nonetheless, we would hope that future work on this problem will use our methodology as a baseline. At present, it remains our impression that the strongest case remains that for a late-last-glacial colonization of the Americas, and that the dates from South American sites are consistent with a range expansion derived from the earliest period of the Clovis culture in North America. If (as many workers now recognize) it is time to rethink the original *blitzkrieg* models of human impact on the endemic megafauna of the Americas at the end of the Pleistocene, then this debate should develop in tandem with a careful consideration of the quite separate archaeological issue of the *timing* of human arrival.

Acknowledgements

This work was prepared while one of us (JS) was the recipient of an NERC Research Fellowship. Thanks are due to the following for information, comments and/or suggestions during the development of this paper: Jonathan Adams, Gustavo Barrientos, Cathy Batt, Alex Bayliss, Gustavo Politis, Vance Haynes, Rupert Housley, Mark Pollard, Christine Prior, Stephen Shennan, and the staff of the various Radiocarbon Laboratories who so kindly and efficiently responded to our queries. They do not necessarily agree with our opinions expressed here. The editors and referees for this volume provided most helpful comments and guidance at the revision stage.

GENERAL NOTES
a   Lat/Long is approximate, and estimated, in cases enclosed in square brackets. Otherwise, exact as extracted from the literature.
b   Great circle distance (kms) from El Paso, located at 31° 46′ N, 106° 29′ W.
c   Shortest roadway distances (kms) from El Paso as calculated from road maps by Whitley and Dorn (1993, 647), who "take these as reasonable and conservative surrogate measures for

the shortest and most-feasible routes, assuming foreknowledge of the local environment on the part of the migrating population."

d　Uncalibrated radiocarbon dates. Dates marked '†' were corrected for δ¹³C by the dating lab, either by measurement or by applying a standard correction for the material; dates marked '‡' were reported as not corrected (or as unlikely to have been corrected) for δ¹³C by the lab, and have been adjusted during calibration by the standard correction for the material; while dates marked '°' are those of which we could get no further information, but which we assume were uncorrected and which we have therefore corrected during calibration for δ¹³C using the standard for the material (or by 25‰ where the material was unknown).

e　A southern hemisphere correction of -40 radiocarbon years was applied to sites south of the equator (Stuiver & Reimer 1993). This, of course, takes no account of variation through time in the effect of hemispheric circulation patterns on atmospheric carbon ratios: it is possible that this correction should only be applied to southern-hemisphere sites south of the tropics.

Dates in italics have been omitted from the analysis either because they were also omitted (with reasons given) by Whitley and Dorn (1993) (El Abra, Fell's Cave), or because they are statistical outliers in a sample (Monte Verde, Tres Arroyos).

NOTES ON INDIVIDUAL SITES

(where there is a discrepancy between radiocarbon data as stated in published sources and as stated in communications given to us in response to our queries by the original dating Laboratories, we have used the data given by the Labs).

1. Source: Correal Urrego (1981). Following Whitley and Dorn, we adopt the younger of the two dates (this was mistakenly recorded in Whitley and Dorn as 11,200). The two dates differ significantly at the 0.05 level, and thus cannot be averaged.
2. Source: Correal Urrego (1981).
3. Source: Temme (1982).
4. Source: Lynch et al. (1985)
5. Source: Rick (1981, 1987).
7. Source: Nunez et al. (1983). The two dates are statistically the same at the 95% level, and can thus be averaged. We use the average for calibration. (Whitley and Dorn mistakenly recorded the date for this site as 11,410).
8. Source: Guidon & Arnaud (1991).
9. Source: Montane (1968).
10. Source: Prous (1986a; b).
11. Source: Beltrao et al. (1986). 10,950 ± 1020 is a TL date. Whitley and Dorn mistakenly treated this as a ¹⁴C date and calibrated it in their table. In fact, the standardisation needed here involves *decreasing* the age of the sample – TL dates are dates BP, where 'the present' is the date the sample was measured, while ¹⁴C dates BP means 'before 1950'. We assumed the TL date was measured in 1980, and deducted 30 years to standardise it with the ¹⁴C data.
12. Source: Prous (1986a; b).
13. Source: Dillehay (1994). The six dates from layer MV-5 (excluding TX-3208, which is clearly an outlier and which Haynes (1992, 367) suggests may be due to burning old wood) are statistically the same at the 95% level, and can be averaged. With reference to the 13,565 date (TX-3208), the lab reports that "Quoting from the submitter's comments sent to us in 1984 after the dates were run: "Charcoal ... recovered ... in direct association with mastodon bone. When first recovered from limited excavations (Dillehay, Pino, Davis, Valastro, Varela, & Casamiquela 1972, 549), it was believed that this date might have been "an older charcoal fragment deposited

by the peat layer" or a fragment that applies to the human occupation. Extensive excavation performed in 1983 discovered that this fragment is part of a continuous scatter of small charcoal specks around a hearth. Although the sample can now be accepted as a cultural date, it is still 500 years earlier than dated cultural artifacts." The two dates on 'wooden artifacts' from the upper level of SCH-4 (TX-4437 and TX-5375) are also statistically the same at the 95% level, and can also separately be averaged. Here, we use the average of the averaged dates for these two levels to date the site, following Dincauze's principle (1991).

14. Source: Flegenheimer (1987). Whitley and Dorn mistakenly recorded this date as 10,691.
15. Source: Flegenheimer (1986). A recent date from the cultural level itself.
16. Source: G. Barrientos (pers. comm. 1995). Whitley and Dorn followed Lynch (1990) in 'averaging' the modal values of two dates from Los Toldos (8750 ± 480 and 12600 ± 600). In fact, these two dates are significantly different at the 0.05 level and thus cannot be averaged. We follow Politis (n.d.), who suggests that the older date from Los Toldos, measured in 1972 with a composite charcoal sample from the lower levels of the site, needs to be reassessed or discarded. Politis notes that a site with a similar industry to that from the lowest cultural levels at Los Toldos, Piedra Museo, has been proposed as possibly contemporary. Here, we have substituted the latter site (with its more secure date) for Los Toldos.
17. Source: Bird (1988).
18. Source: Massone (1983; 1991). We follow Whitley and Dorn (1993) in using the younger date from this site, but include the date list given by Massone (1991) (who believes that the Beta date is the most reliable).

REFERENCES

Bard, E., Arnold, M., Fairbanks, R.G. and Hamelin, B. (1993). ²³⁰Th-²³⁴U and ¹⁴C ages obtained by mass spectrometry on corals. *Radiocarbon* **35**, 191–199.

Bard, E., Arnold, M., Mangerud, J., Paterne, M., Labeyrie, L., Duprat, J., Melieres, M.A., Sonstergaard, E. and Duplessy, J.C. (1994). The North Atlantic atmosphere-sea surface C¹⁴ gradient during the Younger Dryas climatic event. *Earth and Planetary Science Letters* **126**, 275–287.

Batt, C.M. and Pollard, A.M. (1995). Radiocarbon calibration and the peopling of North America. Paper given to the American Chemistry Society, Archaeological Chemistry Symposium.

Beaton, J.M. (1991). Colonizing continents: some problems from Australia and the Americas, pp. 209–230 in Dillehay, T.D. and Meltzer, D.J. (eds.), *The First Americans: Search and Research*. Boca Raton, FL., CRC Press.

Belovsky, G.E. (1988). An optimal foraging-based model of hunter-gatherer population dynamics. *Journal of Anthropological Archaeology* **7**, 329–372.

Beltrão, M.C. de M.C., Enriquez, C.R., Danon, J., Zuleta, E. and Poupeau, G. (1986). Thermoluminescence dating of burnt cherts from the Alice Boer Site, Brasil, pp. 203–213 in Bryan, A.L. (ed.), *New Evidence for the Pleistocene Peopling of the Americas*. Orono, Maine: Center for the Study of the First Americans.

Bird, J.B. (1988). *Travels and Archaeology in South Chile*. J. Hyslop (ed.). Iowa City: University of Iowa Press.

Björck, S., Wohlfarth, B. and Possnert, G. (1995). ¹⁴C AMS measurements from the Late Weichselian part of the Swedish Time Scale. *Quaternary International* **27**, 11–18.

Buck, C.E., Litton, C.D. and Scott, E.M. (1994). Making the most of radiocarbon dating: some statistical considerations. *Antiquity* **68**, 252–263.

Correal Urrego, G. (1981). *Evidencias Culturales y Megafauna Pleistocenica en Colombia*. Publicacion de la Fundacion de Investigaciones Arqueologicas Nacional 12, Banco de la Republica, Bogota.

Dillehay, T.D. (1989). *Monte Verde: A Late Pleistocene Settlement in Chile, Volume 1: Palaeoenvironment and Site Context.* Washington, D.C.: Smithsonian Institution Press.

Dillehay, T.D. (1994). An overview of the research findings and cultural implications of the Late Pleistocene site of Monte Verde, Chile. *L'Anthropologie* **98**, 128–148.

Dincauze, D.F. (1991). Review of Dillehay (1989). *Journal of Field Archaeology* **18**, 116–119.

Draper, N. R. and Smith, H. (1981). *Applied Regression Analysis. Second Edition.* New York: John Wiley and Sons, Inc.

Edwards, R.L., Beck, J.W., Burr, G.S., Donahue, D.J., Chappell, J.M.A., Bloom, A.L., Drufel, E.R.M. and Taylor, F.W. (1993). A large drop in atmospheric $^{14}C/^{12}C$ and reduced melting in the Younger Dryas, documented with ^{230}Th ages of corals. *Science* **260**, 962–968.

Flegenheimer, N. (1986). Evidence of Paleoindian occupation in the Argentine pampas. Paper presented at the World Archaeological Congress, Southampton, England.

Flegenheimer, N. (1987). Recent research at localities Cerro la China y Cerro El Sombrero, Argentina. *Current Research in the Pleistocene* **4**, 148–149.

Glass, C., Steele, J. and Wheatley, D. (in press). Modelling human range expansion across a heterogeneous cost surface. *Proceedings CAA 97*, Birmingham.

Goslar, T., Kuc, T., Ralska-Jasiewiczowa, M., Rozanski, K., Arnold, M., Bard, E., van Geel, B., Pazdur, M.F., Szeroczynska, K., Wicik, B., Wieckowski, K. and Walanus, A. (1993). High-resolution lacustrine record of the Late Glacial/Holocene transition in Central Europe. *Quaternary Science Reviews* **12**, 287–294.

Goslar, T., Arnold, M., Bard, E., Kuc, T., Pazdur, M.F., Ralskajasiewiczowa, M., Rozanski, K., Tisnerat, N., Walanus, A., Wicik, B., Wieckowski, K. (1995). High-concentration of atmospheric C^{14} during the Younger Dryas cold episode. *Nature* **377**, 414–417.

Grayson, D.K. (1991). Late Pleistocene mammalian extinctions in North America: taxonomy, chronology and explanations. *Journal of World Prehistory* **5**, 193–231.

Guidon, N. and Arnaud, B. (1991). The chronology of the New World – 2 faces of one reality. *World Archaeology* **23**, 167–178.

Hajdas, I., Ivy-Ochs, S.D. and Bonani, G. (1995). Problems in the extension of the radiocarbon calibration curve (10–13 kyr BP). *Radiocarbon* **37**, 75–79.

Hajdas, I., Zolitschka, B., Ivy-Ochs, S., Beer, J., Bonani, G., Leroy, S.A.G., Negendank, J.W., Ramrath, M. and Suter, M. (1995). AMS radiocarbon dating of annually laminated sediments from Lake Holzmaar, Germany. *Quaternary Science Reviews* **14**, 137–143.

Haynes, C.V., Jr (1966). Elephant-hunting in North America. *Scientific American* **214[6]**, 104–112.

Haynes, C.V., Jr (1987) Clovis origin update. *The Kiva* 52, 83–93.

Haynes, C.V., Jr (1991). Geoarchaeological and paleohydrological evidence for a Clovis-age drought in North America and its bearing on extinction. *Quaternary Research* **35**, 438–450.

Haynes, C.V., Jr (1992). Contributions of radiocarbon dating to the geochronology of the peopling of the New World, pp. 355–374. in Taylor, R.E., Long, A. and Kra, R.S. (eds.) *Radiocarbon After Four Decades*. New York: Springer-Verlag.

Haynes, C.V., Jr (1993). Clovis-Folsom geochronology and climatic change, pp. 219–236 in Soffer, O. and Praslov, N.D. (eds.), *From Kostienki to Clovis: Upper Paleolithic-PaleoIndian Adaptations*. New York: Plenum Press.

Haynes, C.V., Jr, Donahue, D.J., Jull, A.J.T. and Zabel, T.H. (1984). Application of accelerator dating to fluted point Paleoindian sites. *Archaeology of Eastern North America* **12**, 184–191.

Hoffecker, J.F., Powers, W.R. and Goebel, T. (1993) The colonization of Beringia and the peopling of the New World. *Science* **259**, 46–53.

Ives, J.W., Beaudoin, A.B. and Magne, M.P.R. (n.d.). Evaluating the role of a western corridor in the peopling of the Americas. Draft dated December 1993, submitted to *Proceedings of the Circum-Pacific Prehistory Conference, Session 2A 'Routes into the New World', Seattle, 1989.*

Kunz, M.L. and Reanier, R.E. (1994). Paleoindians in Beringia: evidence from Arctic Alaska. *Science* **263**, 660–662.

Kuzmin, Y.V. (1994a). Prehistoric colonization of northeastern Siberia and migration to America: radiocarbon evidence. *Radiocarbon* **36**, 367–376.

Kuzmin, Y.V. (1994b). Natural environment and chronology of the Paleolithic in Eastern Siberia and the peopling of the New World. Paper given at the Third World Archaeological Congress, New Delhi, December 4–11 1994.

Levesque, A.J., Mayle, F.E., Walker, I.R., and Cwynar, L.C. (1993). The Amphi-Atlantic oscillation – a proposed late glacial climatic event. *Quaternary Science Reviews* **12**, 629–643.

Levesque, A.J., Cwynar, L.C. and Walker, I.R. (1994). A multiproxy investigation of late glacial climate and vegetation change at Pine Ridge Pond, southwest New Brunswick, Canada. *Quaternary Research* **42**, 316–327

Lowell, T.V. and Teller, J.T. (1994). Radiocarbon vs. calendar ages of major lateglacial hydrological events in North America. *Quaternary Science Reviews* **13**, 801–803.

Lundqvist, J. and Saarnisto, M. (1995). Summary of Project IGCP-253. *Quaternary International* **28**, 9–18.

Lynch, T.F. (1990). Glacial-age man in South America? A critical review. *American Antiquity* **55**, 12–36.

Lynch, T.F., Gillespie, R., Gowlett, J.A.J. and Hedges, R.E.M. (1985). Chronology of Guitarrero Cave. *Science* **229**, 864–867.

Massone, M. (1983). El poblamiento human aborigen de Tierra del Fuego. In *Culturas Indigenas de la Patagonia*, pp. 131–144. Madrid: Ediciones Cultura Hispánica.

Massone, M. (1991). El estudio de las cenizas volcanicas y su implicancia en la interpretacion de algunas registros arqueologicos de Chile austral. *Anales del Instituto de la Patagonia* **20**, 11–115.

Meltzer, D.J. (1995). Clocking the first Americans. *Annual Review of Anthropology* **24**, 21–45.

Montane, J. (1968). Paleo-Indian remains from Laguna de Tagua-Tagua, central Chile. *Science* **161**, 1137–1138.

Mosimann, J.E. and Martin, P.S. (1975). Simulating overkill by Paleoindians. *American Scientist* **63**, 304–313.

Núñez, L., Varela, J. and Casamiquela, R. (1983). *Ocupación Paleoindio en Quereo*. Antofagasta: Universidad del Norte.

Politis, G.G. (n.d.). A Review of Late Pleistocene Sites of Argentina. Ms.

Politis, G.G., Prado, J.L. and Beukens, R.P. (1995). The human impact in Pleistocene-Holocene extinctions in South America – the Pampean case., pp. 187–205 in E. Johnson, (ed.), *Ancient Peoples and Landscapes*, Lubbock, Texas: Museum of Texas Tech University.

Powers, W.R. and Hoffecker, J.F. (1989). Late Pleistocene settlement in the Nenana Valley, central Alaska. *American Antiquity* **54**, 263–287.

Prous, A. (1986a). L'archéologie au Brésil: 300 siècles d'occupation humaine. *L'Anthropologie* **90**, 257–306.

Prous, A. (1986b). Os mais antigos vestígios arqueológicos no Brasil Central (Estados de Minas Gerais, Goiás e Bahia), pp.

173–181 in Bryan, A.L. (ed.), *New Evidence for the Pleistocene Peopling of the Americas*. Orono, Maine: Center for the Study of the First Americans.

Ranere, A.J. and Cooke, R.G. (1991). Paleoindian occupation in the Central American tropics, pp. 237–253 in Bonnichsen, R. and Turnmire, K.L. (eds.), *Clovis: Origins and Adaptations*. Corvallis, Oregon: Centre for the Study of the First Americans.

Rick, J.W. (1980). *Prehistoric Hunters of the High Andes*. New York: Academic Press.

Rick, J.W. (1987). Dates as data – an examination of the Peruvian preceramic radiocarbon record. *American Antiquity* **52**, 55–73.

Roosevelt, A.C., Lima da Costa, M., Lopes Machado, C., Michab, M., Mercier, N., Valladas, H., Feathers, J., Barnett, W., Imazio da Silveira, M., Henderson, A., Sliva, J., Chernoff, B., Reese, D.S., Holman, J.A., Toth, N. and Schick, K. (1996). Paleoindian cave dwellers in the Amazon: the peopling of the Americas. *Science* **272**, 373–384.

Roper, D.C. (1976). A trend-surface analysis of Central Plains radiocarbon dates. *American Antiquity* **41**, 181–189.

Steele, J., Sluckin, T., Denholm, D. and Gamble, C.S. (1996). Simulating hunter-gatherer colonization of the Americas. *Analectica Praehistorica Leidensia* **28**, 223–227.

Street, M., Baales, M. and Weninger, B. (1994). Absolute chronologie des Späten Palaolithikums und des Frühmesolithikums im Nordlichen Rheinland. *Archäologisches Korrespondenzblatt* **24**, 1–20.

Stuiver, M., Braziunas, T.F., Becker, B. amd Kromer, B. (1991). Climatic, solar, oceanic and geomagnetic influences on Late-Glacial and Holocene atmospheric $^{14}C/^{12}C$ change. *Quaternary Research* **35**, 1–24.

Stuiver, M. and Reimer, P.J. (1993). Extended ^{14}C data base and revised CALIB 3.0 ^{14}C age calibration program. *Radiocarbon* **35**, 215–230.

Tayler, R.E., Haynes, C.V., Jr and Stuiver, M. (196). Clovis and Folsom age estimates: stratigraphic context and radiocarbon calibration. *Antiquity* **70**, 515–525.

Temme, M. (1982). Excavaciones en el sitio precerámico de Cubilán (Ecuador). *Miscelanea Antropologica Ecuatoriana* (Quito) **2**, 135–164.

Torroni, A., Neel, J.V., Barrantes, R., Schurr, T.G. and Wallace, DC. (1994). Mitochondrial DNA clock for the Amerinds and its implications for timing their entry into North America. *Proceedings of the National Academy of Sciences of the U.S.A.* **91**, 1158–1162.

Tushingham, A.M. and Peltier, W.R. (1993). Implications of the radiocarbon timescale for ice-sheet chronology and sea-level change. *Quaternary Research* **39**, 125–129.

Velichko, A. (1995). The Pleistocene termination in Northern Eurasia. *Quaternary International* **28**, 105–111.

Weiss, K.M. (1994). American origins. *Proceedings of the National Academy of Sciences of the U.S.A.* **91**, 833–835.

Whitley, D.S. and Dorn, R. (1993). New perspectives on the Clovis vs. Pre-Clovis controversy. *American Antiquity* **58**, 626–647.

Whittington, S.L. and Dyke, B. (1984). Simulating overkill: experiments with the Mosimann and Martin model, pp. 451–465 in Martin, P.S. and Klein, R.G. (eds.), *Quaternary Extinctions*. Tucson: University of Arizona Press.

APPENDIX

LIST OF DATES USED IN THIS ANALYSIS, AND ASSOCIATED INFORMATION

Site	Lat/Long[a]	Dist. (geodesic)[b]	Dist. (road map)[c]	^{14}C dates [d,e]	S.D.	Sample code and material	Cal yrs BP	Range to 1- & 2-sigma, Cal years BP
1. El Abra, Columbia	[5°1' N, 73°57' W]	4498	6,470	11210[†] 12400[†]	90 *160*	GrN-5941, peat GrN-5556, *organic deposit*	13117	13225–13018 13346–12918
2. Tibito, Columbia	[4°58' N, 73°59' W]	4513	6,470	11740[†]	110	GrN-9375, bone collagen	13685	13853–13534 14031–13396
3. Cubilan, Ecuador	[3°37' S, 79° 14' W]	4882	7,320	10500°	130	Ki-1640	12373	12539–12168 12686–11870
4. Guitarrero, Peru	9°12' S, 77°43' W	5493	8,480	10535[‡]	290	GX-1778, charcoal	12414	12722–11954 13003–11005
5. Pachamachay, Peru	11°7' S, 76°11' W	5763	8,990	11800°	930	UCLA-2118A, charcoal	13708	14947–12755 16330–11004
6. Monte Alegre, Brazil	1° 60' S, 54° 4' W	6679	[N/A]	11145[†] 11110[†] 10905[†] 10875[†] 11030	135 310 295 <u>295</u> 112	GX17413, seeds GX17406, seeds GX17407, seeds GX17414, seeds	12944	13065–12828 13189–12708
7. Quereo, Chile	[31°50' S, 71°18' W]	7990	11,720	11400° <u>11600°</u> 11441	155 <u>190</u> 132	N-2965, wood N-2966, wood	13353	13520–13205 13708–13067
8. Pedra Furada, Brazil	8°50' S, 42°33' W	8153	11,994	10400[‡]	180	GIF-5862, charcoal	12243	12481–11880 12677–11087
9. Tagua-Tagua, Chile	[34°18' S, 71°2' W]	8239	12,020	11380[‡]	320	GX-1205, charcoal	13248	13610–12930 14008–12616
10. Lapa do Boquete, Brazil	[15°29' S, 44°22' W]	8455	12,440	11000°	1000	[not known]	12879	13950–11046 15387–9965
11. Alice Boer, Bed III, Brazil	[22°24' S, 47°33' W]	8702	12,880	10950	1000	[TL date]	10920	11920–9920
12. Abrigo de Santana, Brazil	[19°0' S, 43°53' W]	8744	12,440	11960[‡]	250	GIF-5089, charcoal	13895	14231–13589 14607–13309
13. Monte Verde II, Chile	41°30' S, 73°15' W	8840	12,900	**MV-5:** 11990[‡] 12230[†] *13565*[‡] 12000[†] 11790[‡] 11920[‡] <u>12450[†]</u> 12095 **SCH-4:** 12650[‡] <u>12740[‡]</u> 12621 **Average** 12271	200 140 *250* 250 200 700 <u>150</u> 91 130 <u>440</u> 156 109	TX-3760, mastodon bone Beta-6755, wood *TX-3208, charcoal* OAX-105, collagen TX-5374, charcoal TX-5376, charcoal OAX-381, wood TX-4437, wood TX-5375, wood	14332	14540–14146 14760–13972
14. Cerro La China II, Argentina	37°57' S, 58°37' W	9213	13,480	10610[†]	180	AA-1328, charcoal	12497	12689–12270 12867–11939
15. Cerro La China I, Argentina	37°57' S, 58°37' W	9213	13,480	10720[†]	150	I-12741, charcoal	12611	12767–12440 12916–12234
16. Piedra Museo, Argentina	47°54' S, 67°52' W	9669	[N/A]	10400[†]	80	AA-8428, burned bone.	12243	12376–12079 12489–11862
17. Fell's Cave, Argentina	52°4' S, 70°0' W	9987	14,320	10080° *10720°* *11000°*	160 *300* *170*	I-5146 *W-915, ash* *I-3988, charcoal*	11321	11999–11001 12291–10954
18. Tres Arroyos, Argentina	53°21' S, 68°15' W	10170	14,420	10280° 10420° <u>Average</u> 10395 *11880°*	110 100 <u>90</u> *250*	Dicarb Radio Isotope Co., both bone *Beta Analytic, burnt bone*	12291	12425–12128 12541–11910